GENDER
MADNESS

GENDER MADNESS

ONE MAN'S DEVASTATING STRUGGLE WITH WOKE IDEOLOGY AND HIS BATTLE TO PROTECT CHILDREN

OLI LONDON

Skyhorse Publishing

Skyhorse Publishing books may be purchased in bulk at special discounts for sales promotion, corporate gifts, fund-raising, or educational purposes. Special editions can also be created to specifications. For details, contact the Special Sales Department, Skyhorse Publishing, 307 West 36th Street, 11th Floor, New York, NY 10018 or info@skyhorsepublishing.com.

Skyhorse® and Skyhorse Publishing® are registered trademarks of Skyhorse Publishing, Inc.®, a Delaware corporation.

Visit our website at www.skyhorsepublishing.com.

Please follow our publisher Tony Lyons on Instagram @tonylyonsisuncertain

10 9 8 7 6 5 4 3 2 1

Library of Congress Cataloging-in-Publication Data is available on file.

Cover design by Brian Peterson
Cover photo by Jamie Baker

Print ISBN: 978-1-5107-7806-1
Ebook ISBN: 978-1-5107-7815-3

Printed in the United States of America

Contents

PART 2

Preface

We live in an era in which change is constant, technology and social media are shaping our very thought processes, molding the minds of Generation Z, and the paradigm of normal behavior is shifting ever further from reality. Common sense is no longer common. In his dystopian novel *1984*, acclaimed English novelist George Orwell said that "the heresy of heresies was common sense," something that we can all agree seems an accurate prediction for where modern society was headed. We now live in that very society that Orwell warned us about: a dystopian world where the very notion of truth is rejected, much like the Ministry of Truth in Orwell's novel, a propaganda ministry responsible for the total opposition of truth in order to mold the minds of the masses to persuade them to reject it. This is the unfortunate reality of the world we live in. Our minds are fed ideas from the day we are born, through films, television, news broadcasts, music, celebrities, pop culture, schools, textbooks, and of course the modern phenomenon of social media. We are indoctrinated into believing notions that at one point in time would have seemed absurd to us, yet now have become "normalized" and "rationalized," as an accepted part of our belief system.

The Overton Window concept refers to a technique that changes public perception of certain extreme ideas that are far from being publicly and socially acceptable. Over time, these ideas are slowly pushed into the "window" until they become acceptable and mainstream. This is exactly what we are seeing now in the trend of self-identifying, the sharp rise in young people changing their genders, the erosion of women's spaces and rights, the removal of parental rights, and children being subjected to science experiments under the guise of "kindness" and "care." Twenty years ago, the very notion of society heading in this direction would have been rejected, dismissed as a conspiracy theory, and completely unimaginable. We have been conditioned to believe that what is going on right now with the thousands of children being medically transitioned is perfectly normal and all who oppose this are heretics—"the heresy of heresies was common sense." We have reached a point in society where those who question the current gender ideologies are labeled as extremists, hateful, phobic, right-wing, and bigots. Those with common sense are now the ones being shunned, cast out, and silenced and forced to accept the status quo. The "Ministry of Truth"—the gender clinics, the LGBTQ organizations, the influencers, the trans activists, and the government officials pushing this massive science experiment on the masses reject any opposition and want to outlaw common sense and freedom of expression. We are seeing parental rights being rapidly eroded and children taken away by social services in the name of affirming the child's gender identity. Women are being forced into submission in the name of trans rights, and children are being pushed to change genders instead of simply navigating through their difficult teenage years as teenagers have always had to, without outside influences.

We know that trans people have existed throughout history (Chapter 31 in this book covers this in more depth), and we know that there are people who generally do feel that they have been trapped in the wrong body their whole lives and must traverse the difficult journey to find happiness on their terms.

But what has become the real issue concerning many today is the startling "trend" of gender ideology, spurred on by social media apps like TikTok, which is causing significant and irreparable harm to the mental and physical well-being of Generation Z. While we have seen examples of trans people for years, what we have seen over the last decade has been alarming to say the least. Within a fifteen-year period, over sixty pediatric gender clinics have appeared across the United States, transitioning record numbers of young vulnerable teens by way of hormone replacement therapy, puberty blockers, and gender reassignment surgeries. A mere decade ago the numbers of those seeking medical transitions were extremely low, and back then, in order to change gender, many checks and balances had to be in place to ensure the person was in the right frame of mind and generally felt changing gender was the only solution. Now clinics are all too eager to prescribe hormones, even for eleven-year-olds, and are pushing for medical interventions on increasingly younger ages. Unless we speak up now, reveal what is driving this phenomenon, and warn others of what is going on before our very eyes, then we are going to see millions of young people go on to struggle for the rest of their lives. We will see millions struggle with the scars of surgery, struggle with the long-term health effects of hormones and puberty blockers, and struggle to ever truly feel like themselves again. We owe it to every vulnerable person out there who is being coerced into making life-altering decisions that no child can truly make to protect them from harm. I know firsthand how it feels to feel trapped in the wrong body, to want to change my identity so that I was beyond recognition, to struggle for decades with mental health, and to be easily influenced by modern societal trends. I have fought many identity battles myself, wanting to look like a completely different person: undergoing thirty-two surgeries to erase the way I looked; risking my life time and time again during dangerous operations, including have my chest cut up; wanting to adopt the identity and way of life of a culture—Korea—that I admired; and eventually becoming a transgender woman. My struggle was long and arduous, but now I have finally seen the light, found internal happiness, found faith, and have come out on the other side—and the other side is filled with so much light, love, and happiness. We are now at a pivotal moment in history: the Overton Window has been opened wide, and it's our job to close it shut. If we don't take a stand now and become aware of the dangerous direction toward which society is heading, then it will be too late. It's now or never.

Part 1 of this book details my own journey and battle with self-identification and which factors drove me to want to change myself so drastically. Part 2 lifts the lid on gender ideology and the harm of self-identification while examining research, data, and studies on the issue; state laws; and new legislative bills being introduced to outlaw medical transitioning of children. I'll walk you through my own years-long grapple with identity and show you how I eventually overcame these struggles, so I could be here today to warn of the irrevocable destruction of common sense and the damage being inflicted on millions of young people in the name of self-identity.

Introduction

Faux Façade

What if you were given one chance in life to be reborn, to reinvent and mold yourself into an image of your choosing? Would you do it? Would you alter your entire image and identity and change the essence of who you are if it gave you the chance to achieve lasting happiness? Some of you may jump at the chance if it meant you could be eternally happy, while others may say that we are all created in God's image and should be happy with the way He made us. Before I found faith, turned my life around, and underwent my subsequent detransition, I had been convinced that it was possible to reinvent and alter oneself beyond recognition in a relentless and reckless quest for fulfillment and lasting happiness.

I didn't see it at the time; I didn't see that everything I had done to myself in the name of changing my identity was only part of a self-destructive route I had been venturing down at a dangerous speed. I tried to conceal my unhappiness by creating a faux façade, a man-made mask, courtesy of plastic surgeons, to try and veil my own insecurities, to hide my struggles and disguise the traumas that had been purposely repressed inside of me. I created a persona to match my new look and new identity, but it was not enough—it was never, ever enough. The more I would change myself and struggle with acceptance, the more I would question my identity and become convinced that I had been born in the wrong body. Eventually, after battling with self-identity for a decade, I made the decision to transition. I moved to South Korea and embarked on an obsessive quest for perfection, altering my image and identity in such an extreme way that I ended up erasing every single part of me, to detrimental effect. That still wasn't enough, and I was never satisfied. It became a snowball effect that resulted in my undergoing thirty-two operations and ultimately believing I was transgender. This led to my decision to transition, after undergoing a staggering eleven facial feminization surgeries in one day.

Less than a year after publicly announcing my transition, I realized I had made a tremendous mistake and that all my identity struggles, self-esteem issues, and traumas had been completely misplaced. I had an epiphany moment along with a spiritual awakening and came to a realization that I should have dealt with my mental health struggles head on, instead of pursuing a damaging path of self-destruction in my attempt to create a faux façade. Deep behind the façade, I was broken, lost, confused, and helpless, yet I alone had the power to change that, the power to pick up the fragmented pieces and slowly begin the process of piecing them back together. A journey of rediscovering that long-lost boy who had been trapped inside of me all those years crying out for help and crying out for freedom from self-imprisonment.

PART 1

Chapter 1

Hospital of Horrors

It was a cold spring day in April 2018. My eyes were fixed on the clouds surrounding me as I stared endlessly out of the plane window, en route to Yerevan, Armenia. My mind was filled with conflict, darkness, and anxiety, yet I was dead set on the mission I was about to embark on. Nothing could have convinced me to turn back now, even if there was a chance I may never return, and this would be my final journey. My mind was consumed with graphic images, imagining myself lying on a cold table in a dark room hearing the sound of sharp chisels being bashed into my bones and saws cutting up my flesh. It sent shivers down my spine, but I knew deep down that I had no other choice; I was compelled to do this if I ever wanted to have an ounce of happiness return to my life. I had to prove the bullies wrong, I had to remove parts of me that for years had been the target of their cruel taunts—only after removing them could I finally find solace and start to move on with my life.

After the seemingly endless hours passed by, the plane began its descent, passing through the clouds and the mist and unveiling an ancient stone city below that had stood the test of time since its founding in the eighth century BC by King Argishti I or Uratu in 782 BC.

Reflecting on the historic significance of the city as I glanced out the window, I realized just how short life was. I imagined the millions of people throughout Yerevan's near three-thousand-year history that called this place their home and the millions whose spirits had passed on into the afterlife, into another realm of eternal peace. I wondered whether I would be joining them soon and if Yerevan would be my final resting place if what I was about to embark on did not go according to plan. Suddenly, my mind was jolted by the loud thud of the wheels landing on the tarmac and screeching down along the runway until finally the plane that had been traveling as fast as the countless thoughts running through my mind came to an abrupt stop. I stood up and collected my bag from the overhead locker. I had finally made it to the city that would either be the answer to all my problems and give me everlasting happiness or be the city where I risked having my life cut short. It wasn't like UK or US hospitals and medical facilities that had the highest standards and a scrupulous duty of care. Hospitals in Yerevan did not have the same strict rules and guidelines and didn't even have the latest up-to-date equipment and technology. But I had been told by countless doctors in London that they would not operate on me, so I knew I had no other choice but to go far away to a place where doctors would say yes to my every demand and would not even question my motives or my dire state of mental health. I needed somewhere without the prying questions from psychologists, who were employed by plastic surgery clinics in London to assess whether a patient was suitable for surgery. I needed a "yes man" who would cut off my chest and nose without questioning me. I knew this was one of the few countries where I could mutilate myself without anyone trying to stop me. I was away from family and away from friends, in a country that was cut off from anyone who knew me, so I finally felt I could be free of the self-loathing that had been weighing me down since my teenage years.

I checked into my apartment, four kilometers away from the clinic, and prepared myself for my first meeting with the plastic surgeon I had found while searching through Instagram. Two months prior to arriving in Armenia, I had grown desperate in my search for a doctor who would perform multiple procedures on me in one day: gynecomastia surgery (male breast reduction), areola (nipple) correction, and a revision rhinoplasty with septoplasty (nose). I had stumbled across this Armenian doctor's account on Instagram, though it had just a few thousand followers and there was extremely limited information about the doctor on Google search. I liked what I saw in the before-and-after photos on his page, and, hoping that he would be the one to solve all my problems, I took a deep, hopeful breath and reached out to him. He immediately got back to me, all too eager to have a customer from a foreign land, and within an hour I had booked my surgery with him, no questions asked. I could not find any accreditation for the doctor or the clinic during my searches across the Internet and barely found any reviews from former patients. But I didn't care. I didn't care if he was qualified or not, I didn't care who he was so long as he would perform the surgeries on me to make me happy. I could not even find information of the existence of the hospital itself where I would undergo the drastic procedures. I searched all over the Internet but failed to find any photos, videos, websites, or news articles about the hospital. For all I knew the doctor, if he even was an accredited real doctor, could have been performing surgeries in a back alley, but I would have still gone along with it—that's how desperate and hopeless I felt about the way I looked. I was willing to risk anything, including my life, to change the way I looked and remove parts of me that reminded me of traumas from severe bullying inflicted on me during my school years. I knew I was about to undergo the most painful procedures of my life, but little could I imagine just how severe and unbearable that pain would turn out to be.

After falling asleep that evening in my Yerevan apartment and dreaming of a better tomorrow, I woke up feeling ready to meet the man who would either restore my happiness or potentially kill me through a botched back-alley procedure. It was a risk I was all too willing to take. When I arrived at the hospital—if it could even have been classified as one—I instantly felt a sinking feeling in my stomach. It didn't look like a hospital at all; instead it seemed more like an old Soviet-era mental asylum or an abandoned warehouse. Even the nurses' and doctors' uniforms looked like they had been taken out of a 1960s Soviet museum, dusted off and repurposed in this so-called hospital. I was ushered in to meet the doctor for a ten-minute consultation where he examined my chest and nose and told me he could easily "fix" me. I didn't ask any questions about the procedure other than asking how soon he could do it. I had been patient enough waiting for this moment my entire life and wanted it over and done with at the earliest available opportunity. He scheduled me for the operation three days down the line and sent me to a nurse for an ECG (electrocardiogram) test to check my heart rate and a blood test to check my blood pressure. The room was poorly lit and almost unfurnished except for a few cupboards, a chair, and a table. There was no flooring, just a cold stone floor like I had visualized in my thoughts and vivid dreams prior to arriving in Armenia. I was starting to have a dangerous sense of foreboding that everything I had imagined about this hospital was true. My heart filled with dread and questions swirled around inside my head, *What if my dreams are actually a vision of my future? What if I actually die on the operating table? Maybe it will all come true.* In that moment I was filled with so much fear and a sheer sense of desperation, yet I still told myself I had no other alternative but to risk my life for that chance I would get through it and come out on the other side a different person. I had convinced myself over years of self-loathing, identity struggles, and traumas that doing this was the only way I would ever have a true chance at feeling good about myself. I had spent hours each day staring in the mirror, being critical of my own reflection and longing for the day when I could finally remove all my imperfections and sculpt myself into a redesigned and reimagined version of Oli. I wanted to erase any trace of my father and his features so that I could finally forget what he put me through. This was a terrifying experience, but I felt like I deserved to suffer, that I was worthless, and putting myself through agony was something I felt I deserved due to years of torment. I deserved to be mutilated, and I deserved to be in pain.

The doctor warned me during the short consultation that I would not be able to walk for days due to the gynecomastia surgery, which would remove all of the excess fatty tissue from my chest, and he informed me that this was a very intense and risky procedure. At the same time as having this painful procedure, I was also getting nose surgery to try and fix the mistakes of previous rhinoplasties that had gone terribly wrong. It was a lot to put my body through, but I felt I had no other option. I remembered those long hours throughout my teenage years of staring in the mirror, hating what I saw after being told every single day at school I had "breasts," being teased for being "like a girl," and being mercilessly mocked during swimming class for my chest that looked more like a woman's than a man's. But now I finally had a chance to change that reflection and alter my own mirror image.

• • •

I was wheeled into the operating theater through the seemingly endless, dimly lit corridors of this old, worn-down circa 1960s building, with a bright light shining above the uninviting stone floor in a room that looked like a concrete prison cell. The medical equipment and operating tools looked old and worn, the table where I would lie for the next four hours looked cold and grim. An outside observer would be forgiven for thinking this room was a scene from the horror movie *Hostel*, where kidnapped hostages are operated on and tortured with an array of sharp penetrating tools by masked men. I closed my eyes and kept telling myself everything would be okay, and that if I did die, it was worth the risk to try to improve the way I looked. I was scared, this time more than any other time I feared I would never wake up again. This could be the end for me, but I had to do it. I had to take that risk or I would never be happy and never be able to achieve anything with my life. I closed my eyes, and a nurse placed the anesthesia mask over my mouth. I started to count to ten. 1, 2, 3, 4, 5, 6 . . . and suddenly lost consciousness.

When I woke from the procedure, I panicked. I was confused, I didn't know where I was, and I couldn't speak. I was wheeled down the corridor into a recovery room, where I was placed for several hours while the anesthetic wore off, then wheeled into another room where I would recover over the next few days. I was nauseated and threw up multiple times and my whole body felt like I had been possessed by a demonic spirit. I was starting to regret and question my decision to do this to myself, to mutilate my body and my face and put myself through such trauma and unbearable feelings. I was in agony and unable to move even an inch for three endless days in the hospital bed. Those three days were, without a doubt, the hardest of my life; the amount of physical pain and discomfort I was in was staggering, I couldn't even move an inch in my bed or even reach for a glass of water. The nurses barely checked on me over those three long, never-ending days. Each passing hour seemed like twenty-four hours. When I peeked under the tight bandages wrapped around my chest, thinking I look like an ancient Egyptian mummy, I saw plastic tubes with a bag filled with blood hanging off me. What was this tube connected to? I dreaded to know the answer. But then my heart filled with fear realizing to my horror that the plastic tubes were inside my nipples draining the blood from my internal bleeding. The thought of this was too much to comprehend, and my heart started racing in panic, my breathing became heavier, and my mind became overwhelmed with emotion. I felt like a modern-day Frankenstein. I could have died, all for the sake of vanity and trying to feel more confident. Yet in a peculiar way I felt like I deserved to be in pain, I deserved to suffer, I was worthless, ugly, and after all I wasn't a real man if I had "man boobs."

After my three days of extreme discomfort, pain, and being practically paralyzed, the doctor called me into his office and removed my chest binder. He inspected my nipples; I glanced down quickly and saw dried blood and those dreaded plastic tubes inside my body. Without any warning, the doctor ripped them out. I screamed in pain, and tears flooded down my eyes. Why didn't he warn me? Was it because it would have made my heart race and I may have resisted him doing it so aggressively? I shook uncontrollably, and my whole body reacted in shock. He then picked up what looked like a cattle branding iron and put the hot metal rod on each nipple, burning my skin and fusing it back together. It was like being in a horror movie and I was the victim of Victor Frankenstein, like I was his science experiment. I was traumatized, shaken, and begging for morphine. I couldn't believe what had just happened. Then he removed the dried cotton from inside my nose and cut the stitches; more pain, and by this point I didn't think I could take any more, but I had no choice. I was traumatized after sitting for an hour to recover from the shock.

During the two weeks I was staying in Yerevan, major anti-government protests erupted involving the roads being blocked each day by thousands of cars and people that took over the streets. The protests were completely peaceful; however, it meant that after

I was discharged from the hospital I could not get a taxi to get back to my apartment. Instead, I had to walk four kilometers (2.5 miles) from the clinic after having the tubes ripped out of my nipples, while covered in bandages and in significant pain and discomfort. It felt like running a marathon; every step was painful and agonizing. But I kept telling myself I chose to be in this situation after all, the pain was my burden and my burden alone. I should embrace it; I should suffer. After all, I was used to suffering.

• • •

Several days later, I had to make the long arduous journey back to the clinic. Meandering through the protesters, trundling past the roadblocks in severe pain, and worrying with each step I took whether I was damaging my nose and chest, as I was supposed to be keeping big movements to a minimum. After several hours of walking, I made it back to the clinic for a checkup. I was frightened about what would happen at this visit, given how excruciatingly painful the last one was. I was relieved when it was over after the doctor examined the bruising and told me I was good to go. I then had to walk the four kilometers back to my apartment for the final time.

I lay in bed that night unable to sleep, reliving the traumas of the past few days over and over again, asking myself why I put myself through that. But I rationalized and told myself at least no one could tease and taunt me again saying I had women's breasts. Those bullies from my school years would never again be able to use that insult. I could finally go to the beach, finally go for a swim without the paranoia of people laughing at me, a man, for having female breasts. I never thought that one day I would seriously consider getting female breasts during the period I was living as a trans woman and that I would have wished that I never removed my man boobs back in 2018 in Yerevan, Armenia. On that day, I promised myself as I lay in bed that night pondering my existence that I would never have surgery again and I would never put myself through a near-death experience again. My promise, however, was to be short-lived.

Chapter 2
Childhood Traumas

I was born on January 14, 1990, in the English countryside, in the small town of Sawbridgeworth in Hertfordshire, ninety minutes north of London. It's an idyllic, peaceful little town steeped in history, old stone cottages, streams trickling through meadows filled with buttercups, and a history dating back to the Norman conquest of England in 1066. The town is filled with old Tudor, Elizabethan, Stuart, and Georgian townhouses, built through various reigns of some of England's most notable royal families. Throughout history, the town was populated by English nobles and aristocrats including Anne Boleyn, the famed wife of King Henry VIII who later met a gruesome fate at the hands of her tyrannical husband. The town features various medieval churches including a thirteenth-century church, Great St Mary's Church, which, although built in the 1200s, actually sat on the top of an Anglo-Saxon church dating back to the eleventh century, prior to the French Norman conquest of England. Surrounding the town, endless fields stretch as far as the eye can see with rich soil that had been cultivated for millennia by local farmers. Sitting on these lands are marvelous manor houses, built for noble families centuries ago who ruled the lands and the people who farmed them. It was an idyllic place to be brought into the world, surrounded by beauty, clean air, nature, and a rich history. It was the perfect place for a child to grow up and have a perfect childhood, until it wasn't.

It was a cold winter's evening when my mother was taken to the hospital to give birth to me. My father, who had acted cold and withdrawn with my mother during pregnancy, reluctantly came with her to the hospital. Prior to my conception nine months earlier, he had insisted he was ready to have a child and had assured my mother he was excited about the prospect. After giving birth that cold winter's night, my mother was abandoned almost immediately after my father had held me in his arms for a brief moment for the very first time. He clutched me in his arms, displaying an abnormal lack of any kind of emotional response. After holding me for a moment, he handed me back to my mother and left the hospital, abandoning her in a moment that should have been a joyous and momentous occasion. Days went by and there was still no sign of him, and even though my mother tried desperately to get hold of him, she was unable to reach him or gain any kind of contact with him. This was a time before cell phones, computers, and emails. If someone went off-grid back then, it was extremely hard to locate them. She had no success finding him that week. After seven long days had passed, he finally turned up. He claimed to have run off after struggling to come to terms with the fact he had now become a father and now had a responsibility and duty to care for a child he had brought into the world. It was childish behavior on his part and heartless, to say the very least, to leave my mother in the hospital clutching me in her arms while he went to "rediscover" himself. After a so-called period of "soul searching," he came back, much to my mother's relief—although she felt terribly betrayed. This perhaps was one of the single most hurtful things my father had ever done to my mother and indeed to me. I only found out about it as an eleven-year-old boy, when my mother bravely told me about my

11

father's abusive and hurtful behavior after I questioned her on his behavior and how it made her feel. It was a terrible act of treachery that I know put a heavy weight on her heart all those years while she nurtured me and watched me grow up.

I was less than a day old, and already I had been abandoned by my father. What chance would I have in life if this was the regard my father had for me? I was worthless, unimportant, and unwanted, and as I grew up I was reminded each day of his coldness and always felt a need to try and prove myself to him, to try to win his praise and respect. I tried to do everything he asked, but the more I saw his cruelty and disregard for his family, the closer I grew to my mother and wanting to become like her. This angered my father, as he was always trying to teach me to pursue the same interests as his, the "manly" pursuits. I tried my best to appease him time and time again, but I was never good enough and never lived up to his expectations. I was too feminine, too "weak," and too timid to be a real man, and he resented this. I felt like I had been set up for failure, and my mind was always filled with anxiety and self-doubt.

Children are like sponges, absorbing everything around them and soaking up every single thing they are taught by an adult. I was trying to absorb everything he tried to teach me; each time he would shout at me to "do better" and be more of a man, I would try to absorb it. But it felt like the sponge was being squeezed so hard because I didn't want to be like him, and eventually I would reject everything he taught me, squeezing all the water out of the sponge, trying to form my own identity and pursue my own interests, rebelling against everything he had been trying so hard to push on me.

• • •

My earliest memory was sitting by a fireplace with my mother watching the crackling flames of the wood burning and feeling an

intense warmth in my heart. I was five years old and I was innocent, naïve, and seemingly happy. I was a *tabula rasa*, as the Latin
term aptly describes a blank slate—my mind and thoughts on the
world were pure and innocent. When any child is brought into the
world, they too are blank slates, and how they grow as a person
depends on a variety of factors from social interactions and their
surrounding environment to parents and nurturing factors. Many
psychological studies on children's cognitive development have
been done over the years, exploring the various factors that can
lead a child to develop in different ways and shape the person they
become. Nature vs Nurture studies examine whether genetics can
have an impact on a person's identity and shape their personality,
or whether it is the way they are nurtured, the home environments
they are raised in, that has the ultimate effect on who they become.
Studies of twins separated from their birth parents and raised in
completely different environments show that while genetics play a
part in a person's psychology and identity, being raised in an environment that encourages certain behaviors can completely and
sometimes detrimentally impact a child's cognitive development.

If a child's home environment is toxic, abusive, destructive, and
unhappy, then the likelihood of that child growing up to become
an adult who finds these behaviors normal and even replicates the
behaviors in their own life is dramatically increased. If a child is
shown love, acceptance, and given positive reinforcement from
early on, they are more likely to become a well-rounded and empathetic individual. There are examples, however, of those whose
childhood was filled with seeing their father being abusive to their
mother and that behavior being "the norm," yet that child grows
up to become the total opposite of their father and shuns these
harmful behaviors. There are also other cases where a child may
have had a perfect fairytale-like childhood with all of the nurturing from their parents, with school life and environment being the

perfect recipe for their cognitive development, yet they still grow up to develop completely different behaviors to what they were taught. In many cases, my childhood was a contrasting mix between elements of a fairytale; beautiful surroundings, a nice home, fond memories of elementary school and opportunities, yet at the same time it was marred by abusive behaviors from my father, watching him treat my mother with disrespect and put her down each day with insults, and with me as the daily target of his strict, cruel, and tough approach to parenting.

My mother cherished me and filled me with love and positive reinforcement, always reassuring me that I was a good kid and had a special purpose in life. Meanwhile, my father criticized me, lectured me daily, punished me if I questioned his authority, and put tremendous pressure on me to be just like him. I was his shadow and instructed to follow his every move. He wanted to mold me into his own image so I would grow up to become a miniversion of him. He trained me every day to mimic his behaviors and instilled in me the notion that being a dominant, aggressive male who looked down on women, like my mother, was normal behavior that was to be encouraged. If ever I was brave enough to challenge my father's authority or to question his behavior or even call him out on his words, I was immediately shut down and punished, often being told to stay in my room and not come out until he said I could. I knew deep down he must have loved me, but it was a tough love approach meant to force me to grow up just like him.

My father came from a broken family, where his father, my grandfather, had a severe lack of respect for women, going through wife after wife, cheating on them, abusing them, and neglecting his son, my father, in the process. My grandfather was a very cold man devoid of any emotion and who lacked any compassion for the suffering or emotions of others. A narcissist, obsessed with himself and lacking in empathy. He had fathered children with numerous women and yet abandoned each child when his relationship with the woman would sour. Despite his considerable wealth, he would offer no financial support toward the upbringing of these children, including my father. He treated my father so badly, showing no love or attention to him throughout his childhood, and at sixteen my father was thrown out onto the streets, forced to fend for himself with no financial or emotional support. However, he was eventually taken in by one of his father's ex-girlfriends and lived with her family until he could get back on his feet and find work. He was taught by his own father that there was no such thing as love, only cruelty, and that the only way to succeed in life was to be heartless, to develop a thick skin and be tough. This toughness helped my father work from the ground up slowly, building a career in interior design before meeting my mother when they were both 28. Two years later, I came into the world. He promised my mother that he would never be like his father and that he would be a loving husband and devoted father. But the promise would be short-lived. The damage was done, and he had developed all the same traits of the man he claimed to "despise" and "detest." Lack of empathy, narcissistic personality disorder, aggressive behavior, outbursts, disrespecting women, and looking down on others—these were all the traits he picked up from his own father. This was a classic case of "like father, like son." He was a clone, and after I was born and started to grow up he tried to pass on these same traits to me, hoping that I would be his protégé. It perplexed me that someone who hated someone so much, like he hated his own father, whom he vowed to never be like, would become an exact carbon copy of this object of his detestation and then want me, his son, to become another carbon copy of him. He didn't even realize he was replicating these behaviors, and more and more each day he became a monster. These characteristics in my father only seemed to worsen and become more visible as I grew older and as I started to see things more clearly with my own eyes. He had left me with traumas that had ultimately contributed to my struggle for self-acceptance in later life, which led me to self-harm and self-mutilation in the hope of erasing any trace of my father. His ultra–alpha male aggressive energy was what also led me to want to rebel, to reject everything my father had pushed on me and to instead become more feminine, more timid, and more like my mother. What we experience in childhood is often what shapes the person we become in later life: it molds our character, our beliefs, and our behaviors.

I have many other unpleasant memories of my father that have stayed with me to this very day, especially in regard to the way he treated my mother. My father always mistreated her, on a daily basis, from the way he would speak to her, lose his temper, belittle her, and make her feel inferior. He thought he was an intellectual superior, and he would call her names, saying things like, "you're a stupid woman," or "you have achieved nothing in your life," or "there is a reason why you are just a housewife, that's your job." He would make her feel worthless, and I would bear witness to this on many occasions and place my ear against the door, worried for my mother and her well-being and anxious to hear what was happening.

While he was never physically abusive, the emotional abuse he inflicted on her scarred her for life. Due to daily psychological abuse over twenty-five years, she was made to feel no self-worth, her self-esteem was knocked, and it was instilled in her that she was never good enough. I was a silent witness to this day in and day out, and I was conditioned to think this was a normal relationship. This would later go on to affect the man I became, through these suppressed and subconscious memories of seeing the person I worshiped and adored, my mother, having her confidence knocked on a daily basis and being made to feel of no value. As I grew up, I also suffered with low self-esteem and started to question my value and my place in the world.

While my father would not level the same type of insults on me, he was extremely strict and tough with me and would go out of his way to try to raise me as his masculine son, taking me out on outdoor adventures, hill walking, river visits, camping, and various other masculine pursuits, while my mother was left at home taking care of the housework. These strong gender roles were drilled into me from a young age: A man had to be strong, aggressive, self-assured, and dominant. A woman had to be at home, like a quiet mouse diligently taking care of the home and raising the children. But I didn't want to mimic my father's traits; I wanted to be like my mother, and I developed an especially close bond with her, offering her love and support through the difficulties she was forced to endure each day. I wanted to grow up one day and be just like her and have absolutely no resemblance to my father. My mother was a housewife, a homemaker, and a devoted parent who made sure I always had everything I needed in life, filling my heart with love and teaching me how to be empathetic to others and how to be kind. She was my role model, I looked up to her, and wished I could be just like her when I grew up.

Though my father pushed me to do outdoor activities like hiking, rock climbing, karate, and sports, I rejected all of this and expressed an intense lack of interest. Instead, I was far more interested in doing "girly" things, so when I received pocket money each week, I would spend it on buying "girls'" toys. I would play endlessly with my Barbie dolls, toy babies, My Little Ponies, Polly Pockets, and Disney princess dolls. I found an intense happiness while playing with girls' toys; it felt right and gave me a sense of escapism, helping me to develop a strong connection to anything considered "girly." As a child I also had a big dress-up box, filled with various costumes from different periods of history. There was an explorer's hat, a Sherlock Holmes suit and cap, a doctor's uniform, a fireman's costume, and even a male army officer's costume.

But I took no interest in them at all; instead I was transfixed with the women's costumes: a Victorian lady's dress, a Marilyn Monroe-esque wig, and sparkly dresses and heels and handbags. I was fascinated by the way I looked while wearing these pieces, the feel on my skin and the confidence in my step as I strutted around the house feeling like I was some kind of old-fashioned glamorous lady. I felt empowered, I felt confident, and I felt like this was the real me. I was only around five when I first started experimenting with wearing the costumes in this dress-up box. I was curious, like many kids' minds are filled with curiosity and wonderment when trying something new. I felt more like my mother being dressed like this, and thus began the start of my early gender dysphoria which reappeared at various points in my teenage years and later in my adult life.

While I was playing with girls' toys and dressing in girls' costumes, my father would counter this and buy me Action Man, Lego, racing cars, remote-controlled trucks, basketballs, footballs, and other typical boy toys. He wanted me to be just like him, and I wanted to be just like my mother. He would tell me, "Oli, you're not a girl, act like a boy!" and discourage me from playing with girls' toys and dressing up. It was a conflict of interests, and I was just a young, naïve boy trapped in the middle, longing to be accepted and longing for my father to treat my mother right. I often wonder if I would have ever questioned my gender in later life, had it not been for my father's behavior, his treatment of my mother and his treatment of me. I believe that his behavior significantly contributed to me wanting to change the way I looked, my characteristics, behavior, and my very own identity.

As a child I didn't think too deeply about these things, as this was all I knew. All of this behavior, this family dynamic, seemed normal to me, and I still viewed my childhood as idyllic until later into my adult years. It was only with age that I realized this was not a healthy environment for my own cognitive development and that what I bore witness to day in and day out had a drastic impact on the person I became, my lack of confidence, my desperate need to fit in, and my insecurities. Yet, I still had a great childhood in many other ways: a beautiful home, a beautiful garden to play in, friends to hang out with, and a wonderful elementary school where I developed a great passion for learning art and history. Indeed, it was hard to picture a more perfect environment in which to grow up, in the English countryside surrounded by hills, forests, sheep, and fields filled with buttercup flowers.

• • •

Looking back on my childhood in retrospect, on the surface it was a happy one filled with many joyous memories yet without realizing it at the time, from a psychological perspective, which I was only able to process in later life, my mind was being shifted by the behaviors of my father and his treatment of my mother. I witnessed daily abuse, I witnessed the callous nature of my father, who had become just like his own father and who wanted me, in turn, to become just like him. I rejected this, pushed back against his dominant masculinity, and instead opted to grow closer to my mother and adopt more feminine traits and feminine interests. This is where my journey of transformation and struggle with identity began, and I believe this was one of the root causes, combined in later life with traumatic bullying experiences and societal influences around me, that would ultimately compel me to change my gender identity and transition.

Observing and bearing witness to these constant daily arguments would have led me down one of two roads. One road could have steered me to emulate my father's behavior, as I did look up to him as a child, and see him as an intelligent, powerful authority figure, and as an adult I could have easily adopted these behaviors and become a clone of my father, which is what he would have wanted. However, instead I adopted the kind and compassionate behaviors of my mother, and due to my father's treatment, I had low confidence, low self-esteem, and never felt good enough. I emulated her behaviors that had unfortunately, through no fault of her own, become a part of her identity at the time, due to years of abuse and being made to feel worthless. Emulating these behaviors shaped my future path of self-destruction, struggles with self, identity, and ultimately put me on the path to alter myself beyond recognition to try and find the confidence and self-assurance my father had knocked out of my mother and me.

Chapter 3

Never Good Enough

The way my father behaved and the dynamic between my parents, the dominant, abusive male vs the timid, abused female, led me to question my identity from a very young age. I would always question who I was, through suffering from low self-esteem and wondering if coming into the world was a mistake and always struggling to come to terms with the fact that I felt like my father never really wanted me. I was more of an inconvenience to him, and he tried to change me and mold me into his own image. I tried for a period of my childhood to emulate him, but nothing was ever enough. My only sense of escape was getting closer to my mother and finding an outlet to reject all of this, through doing "girly" things, playing with girls' toys, and trying to craft out a new me.

As I went through elementary school, I remember being different from all the other kids. I wasn't like the boys playing soccer, basketball, cricket, or running around the school field for athletic practice. I also didn't take part in the popular games that boys in England loved at the time, such as conkers, where two seeds from horse chestnut trees, known as conkers, are tied on to a piece of string with the aim of the game to strike the opponent's conker to break it—a game that is now banned in schools due to supposed "health and safety risks." I also didn't like to play British Bulldog, a game where two opposing teams had to charge at each other across a field and try to "tag" the other team, the winning team being the one who had tagged all members of the other team. This, like conkers, has also been banned at schools thanks to woke policies deeming it a "health risk." Every single boy's pursuit and game at school just didn't appeal to me, and I preferred to spend time with girls, feeling that I had much more in common with them. I would play with my girlfriends' Tamagotchi, a Japanese keychain virtual pet simulation, as well as playing Disney princess dress-up games on Nintendo Gameboys, the predecessor to Nintendo Switches. The game involved choosing a Disney princess and getting her ready to attend a ball to meet her prince. I would sit with girls over the lunch hour playing this game endlessly, dressing the princesses in beautiful pearl necklaces, doing their makeup, and finding the most lavish and elegant dresses for them to wear. I was so fascinated by female beauty and the glamorous side of being a woman and wished that I could become a real-life princess one day, beautiful like Belle from *Beauty and the Beast*. All my school friends were girls; I identified with them, just like I identified more with my mother. It felt right to me, and while I had no concept back then of gender identity or transgenderism, I started to develop questions that had no answers. Why did I feel like this? Why did I feel more like a girl, but I had the body of a boy? These were confusing thoughts for a young child, and I always felt like I was different from everyone else, that something set me apart from other boys.

When it came to school classes, I generally enjoyed them, especially history, where I would learn about the Ancient Romans and Egyptians and have to do fun art projects on the topics. I also enjoyed school church trips, as my school was a Church of England school, meaning that religious education and church trips were included as part of the curriculum. Even though my family was not religious, some of my fondest memories at elementary school were activities organized by the church. Easter egg and spoon races were among my favorite activities with the local church each year. We would boil eggs and paint them with various colors, then all of the children would line up on the road outside the church, which had a steep incline as it was situated on a hill, and run down while carefully trying to balance the egg without letting it fall off. It was hilarious: so many eggs were smashed, and barely anyone made it to the finish line. But it didn't matter who won or whose eggs were smashed; it was a day where everyone laughed, smiled, and had not a single care in the world. Another fond memory from attending the church with the school was Christingle, where we would decorate oranges with patterns and draw faces on them, then place four small candles inside and wrap the orange in a red ribbon. The orange is meant to represent the Earth while the ribbon represents Jesus wrapping his love around the world, and the four candles represent the four seasons: winter, spring, summer, and fall. I loved this activity and loved all the other fun and exciting things organized by the church that still to this day evokes many fond and cherished memories. During weekly church sermons, we would have two-hour-long Bible readings and sermons by the vicar, Reverend Jameson, who always tried to make it as engaging and fun as possible. He would encourage all of us to sing along, to dance, and to interact with one another by asking us rhetorical questions and asking us to recite what he had just read. I was never good at reciting anything, as I always had a bad memory and terrible attention span. But I still fondly remember these moments and cherish the memories of this happy time. A time when I was free to feel a connection to Jesus and a time when I could escape my father's ever-watchful gaze.

But when the school day or church service came to an end, it was time to take the route home in my father's car, where I would never know which mood he would be in or whether he would scold me and shout me down. I was always on edge. Some days he would simply ask about my school day, my classes and what I learned, which I was always happy to talk about because I loved my school and always had so much fun. But on other days, the journeys were not so easy-going. I vividly remember sitting with my father on the way home from school one day, talking about the school church service and questioning his judgment on the topic of Christianity (as he was an atheist and always believed his judgment and authority was superior). He started screaming at me and slammed the brakes on the vehicle, almost crashing into a truck while he threatened to throw me out on the freeway if I did not stop questioning him about why he didn't believe in God and Jesus. This happened regularly and continued when I was a teenager. I was never allowed to question his judgment, and if I ever dared to, I was met with the same angry response, shutting me down and making me feel inferior. Just like the way he would speak to my mother on a daily basis, making her feel lesser than he and forcing her to never dare to question him on any matter. No one was allowed to question his authority, an authority he had learned from his own abusive and ruthless father. He was intimidating and unnerving, and going to school was a chance to escape his authority and dominance. I actually enjoyed being at school and escaping my father and had many happy memories from age five to eleven of attending classes, playing with my girlfriends during lunch hour, and learning about the vastness of the world that seemed so big and alien to a small-town boy like me. But alas, these happy school memories came to an abrupt end once I began the next step in my life, going to high school and puberty at the same time. Everything was about to change, and my life would never be the same again.

Chapter 4

Mirror, Mirror on the Wall

My fond and enjoyable elementary school days where I eagerly participated in classes and enjoyed spending lunch hours playing girl games with girl friends were over in a flash the moment I began high school (secondary school in the UK, ages eleven through sixteen). That happy boy who was top of his class in art and history and enjoyed school activities like the church Easter egg race was about to have the smile wiped off his face. I was eleven years old, and my body and face started to rapidly change as I hit puberty, and I started to grapple with my emotions going up and down each day as I experienced these new and unexplainable feelings. It was a confusing time, like for any teen, and I struggled to comprehend why my body and the way I looked was starting to alter at such exponential speed. Going through these feelings was hard enough without having the added anxiety of starting a new school and beginning high school. It was time for a complete change—new friends, new teachers, new classes—all while experiencing the drastic onset of puberty. The school was not even in my hometown, so I didn't know any of the other children attending it. I would have to start all over again, making friends and trying to fit in as a boy who felt more like a girl.

The first week at my new school was almost unbearable because I didn't know anyone, and there were no familiar faces. Whereas most of the other kids came from the same elementary school and already had their set friend groups, I was an outcast, a nervous loner eager to try to fit in and blend with everyone else. But no one wanted to be my friend, no one was interested in me, and I started to blame the way I looked, due to my recent changes with hitting puberty, for this lack of interest from other students in wanting to be my friend. It was a hard adjustment to make, going from somewhere I was happy and had friends to an unfamiliar place where I had no one. As the weeks went by, I still struggled to fit in and find people who would accept me, and over time, I became more and more self-critical, blaming the way I looked for all of my problems. I had begun to develop an obsession with looking in the mirror, analyzing the changes to my face, the development of rosacea and acne on my face, and being overly disparaging of the way I looked. The mirror became a complete fixation that started to consume me as I went through puberty and as the months went by at my new school. Every day I was consumed with looking at my own reflection and wondering why I had been cursed with these changes that were taking place in the way I looked. The mirror beckoned me each time I walked by, calling me to stare at my reflection, to judge myself, and to tear myself apart. I became my own worst enemy and my own worst critic each time I looked at my ever-changing reflection in the mirror.

A mirror, as we know, can have many different meanings and interpretations. In the literal sense, it is a reflection of oneself. In a figurative or metaphorical sense, it takes on a wide range of connotations: holding up a mirror image to the world, a different perspective, seeing something that is usually hidden from plain sight, and seeing a reflection with flaws and faults.

The Greek god Narcissus, from which the terms narcissist and narcissism derive, was famed in Greek mythology for his outstanding beauty and his perfect looks, yet because he was so obsessed with his own image he rejected all romantic advances and eventually fell in love with his own reflection in a pool of water. As the legend goes, because of his obsession with looking perfect he stared at his own reflection for the rest of his life until the day he died. Thus, the term *narcissist* is used in the modern English language to describe someone who is fixated upon oneself. A mirror is a metaphor for fixation, a view of one's own self-image often distorted to evoke emotion either positive or negative.

From a young age, I had an obsession with mirrors and reflections. I recall as a six-year-old sitting in front of my mother's washing machine, watching the clothes spin round and round while looking inquisitively at my own reflection in the glass door. I would sit there for hours staring in wonderment and fascination and never tire of the seemingly endless cycle. I would become fixated by my own reflection for hours at a time, studying myself as if I were some kind of science experiment to be dissected. Just like the mythological Greek god Narcissus, I never tired of my own reflection, and it became a fixation, an unhealthy obsession to continuously look at my mirror image.

It wasn't until I became a teenager that this "mirror, mirror on the wall, who's the fairest of them all?" type of mentality became a source of darkness and internal struggle. After I hit puberty at age eleven, I started to break out all over my face with spots, boils, and acne. My entire face became covered in these hideous red lumps, and it only got worse and worse as I progressed through my teenage years.

Suddenly the reflection I long admired as a child was gone and was replaced with what was, in my eyes, a hideous unattractive monster. I was no longer like the Greek god Narcissus and now more like the son of Zeus and Hera, Hephaestus, the only Greek god who was deemed ugly and unsightly. Hephaestus too had a terrible skin condition, a skin cancer said to be caused by arsenic exposure from metalworking, and he was mocked and cast out by the other Greek gods. His romantic advances were rejected by Aphrodite, the goddess of love, all because of his appearance—no one wanted to be near him.

In psychology, the term *Mirror Effect* has been coined to describe individuals who change their opinions, emotions, and notions of self-worth based on what they see when they look in the mirror. Additionally, the "Self-Awareness Theory" stipulates that when an individual is in a heightened state of self-awareness, such as looking at themselves in the mirror, they are more likely to experience negative feelings and thought processes and develop a self-critical opinion of themselves.[1] I certainly felt this way, the more and more I stared at myself. The more I tried to cut or pick my spots and acne and remove them from my skin, the more time I spent in the mirror hating myself, lowering my self-esteem by ten-fold each time and even developing suicidal thoughts and feelings. I couldn't live a life on this Earth for eighty years looking like this. How could I ever succeed in life if I looked like a monster? No one would want to date me, no one would love me, no one would employ me. I would be like a leper in a leper colony, like in the biblical times, living far away from society, tending to my own wounds and hiding my skin from the world. This was my thought process each day, ideas swirling around my head about how my life was destroyed, and that my life was over all because of my skin condition and hormonal imbalance at the beginning of puberty. I wasn't of sound mind; I thought

---

1   Selimbegović, Leila, and Armand Chatard. "The mirror effect: Self-awareness alone increases suicide thought accessibility." *Science Direct*, Consciousness and Cognition Volume 22, Issue 3, 14th April 2013, https://www.sciencedirect.com /science/article/abs/pii/S1053810013000573?via%3Dihub. Accessed 8 March 2023.

the whole world revolved around my skin breakout and that everyone would be judging me for the rest of my life.

According to a 2013 study by researchers from the Department of Psychology at the University of Poitiers and National Center for Scientific Research in France, participants in a study on the Mirror Effect and the effects of prolonged exposure to one's reflection in a mirror found that mirror exposure during a period of heightened self-awareness, such as going through puberty, can temporarily increase depression, suicidal thoughts, and negative feelings.[2] Something with which I had definitely grappled during my years going through puberty and being fixated with my own reflection.

While it may seem far-fetched that I or anyone would have such extreme feelings and emotions on something so seemingly trivial, as a teenager we all go through puberty, and we all experience self-esteem and self-confidence issues and don't fully comprehend the changes we are going through at the time. Many of you reading this may have experienced similar feelings about your looks or identities during your teenage years, a normal process while going through hormonal changes.

Of course, my experience is a lot more extreme than most, since in later life I developed a very unhealthy and dangerous obsession with self-mutilating and self-harming through endless plastic surgery. I cut up my entire face and parts of my body as a coping mechanism for these traumas, beginning my first surgery at twenty-three and finally stopping when I reached the age of thirty-two. A decade of extreme struggles in response to my experiences at school paired with wanting to erase every trace of my father. However, the difference between other people and me is that many people who have gone through similar feelings of disliking their appearance

---

2   Ibid.

as teens are normally able to recover, grow out of it, and become well-rounded and happy adults. I wish that had been the case with me, but sadly the issues I developed during these years stayed on to haunt me throughout much of my adult life, leaving me with scars that will never truly heal.

• • •

Looking back through the period of my life aged eleven to sixteen, I had no concept of what was happening to me or my body, and I resented it. I stared endlessly into the mirror, pondering and wondering why I had been so cursed to suddenly look like this. This self-loathing and hatred was only reinforced more deeply each and every day when I went to school. Each time I sat in class, kids would call me cruel names and taunt me for my acne outbreak and appearance. I became a loner. I was isolated with no support system at school and barely any friends.

The few acquaintances I did have at school were also like me, outcasts bullied for the way they looked, and they, like me, tried to keep to themselves and appear as loners for fear of drawing the bullies' attention. "Shrek," "ogre," "ugly," "gross"—I grew accustomed to daily insults. As my skin condition worsened, the insults only increased. This greatly knocked my confidence and sense of self-worth and in retrospect was comparable to how my father would knock my mother's sense of self-worth through insults and name calling. After having to endure my mother being the target of these insults and diatribes, I too was now being subjected to what she had to cruelly endure. It got to a point where it was so bad that I would make myself physically sick in an attempt to have time off from school. Yet I was still made to attend each day without my parents realizing the pain I was truly going through. My father would dismiss my feelings as "ridiculous," "unbecoming of a boy," "trivial," and "stupid" and send me each day to school despite my protests and attempts to stay home.

Attending school each day, and in response to my skin getting progressively worse, I started to isolate myself more and more. During lunch break, I would stay in the classroom studying hard for exams and reading textbook after textbook to try and keep my mind off things. This was also my way of trying to be invisible, not wanting to be seen by other kids with the hope that they would forget I was there and eventually stop bullying me. I wanted to blend into the background of each class and be invisible, and I would always sit at the back, away from the other students, never raising my hand, never making eye contact with others, and never speaking unless spoken to. I was like a mouse, huddled in the corner: timid, shy, and afraid.

Kids can be cruel because they don't know better, they can hurl insults without knowing the lifelong ramifications they can have on someone's life. Many victims of childhood bullying like myself can be left psychologically scarred for years to come, and this can lead to insecurities, anxieties, depression, low self-assurance, and questions about self-identity. Indeed, even adults can be traumatized from bullying and cruel words whether in the workplace, domestically in the family unit, or through the modern-day phenomena of social media. Bullying is never justified, yet it is so commonplace and widespread across society. The bullying I experienced in the classroom was unbearable and is what ultimately led me to want to change myself so drastically that I would no longer recognize who I was and instead adopt an entirely new persona and identity, so people would only praise and love me and call me "beautiful" and "perfect." This is what I craved in my teenage years leading into adulthood, and this is the same thing social media users and influencers seek these days to make them feel value. It is deeply traumatic to want to change ourselves so drastically whether through surgery, changing our gender, wanting to look a certain way, or trying to become a person we are not. Yet because of being bullied relentlessly, people can be driven to do extreme things in order to escape that. Granted, my story may be more extreme than most, but it demonstrates that cruel words can have devastating consequences.

To this day, that mirror, mirror on the wall still beckons me. A dark magic spell that tries to lure me in, like Narcissus and his own reflection in the lake that he stared at for eternity until his day of reckoning.

Chapter 5
Bullied & Broken

When I was at high school, before social media became a thing, I had very little exposure to the outside world, outside of my own small bubble. The small high school I attended in the English countryside was like something off a postcard, surrounded by fields and hills and endless green grass and blue skies. It was an idyllic and picturesque setting to be surrounded by such natural beauty, the calmness of the wind brushing against the trees, the butterflies fluttering by, and the bright blue skies stretching endlessly as far as the eye could see. The school would organize cross-country races through the forests where we would have to run for an hour through mud, dirt roads, and across streams. Teachers also organized sponsored walks where we would have to hike up a mountain for 10km to raise money for the local community. Additionally, the boys, including myself, took part in the Duke of Edinburgh Awards scheme, where we would take part in outdoor challenges, camping trips where we would be taught how to light fires, how to pick berries from bushes, kayaking, horse riding, and team-building exercises. While it sounded fun and adventurous, it was the complete opposite of what I was interested in. I was much happier playing with dolls at home, but my father urged me to "man up" and participate in these tough outdoor pursuits. I also had to join the Scouts to learn how to be more of a man, again at my father's behest, where I learned how to tie ropes, set up tents, bicycle, and plant trees. All the other boys were tough, masculine, and having fun participating, but I was always the loner at the back, afraid to get involved in activities and especially reluctant to participate in group exercises where I was always called out for being the weak member of the group who always let the team down because I was like a "girl." While this may have sounded like a perfect school life, surrounded by nature, participating in exhilarating outdoor pursuits, I felt far from perfect inside.

I vividly remember one of the sponsored walks at my school, where we trekked all day long and I was purposely tripped by one of the boys who always picked on me in class. He stuck out his foot while I was walking up the stone path on the hill and I fell to the ground, grazing my knees and drawing blood. He and the other boys next to him laughed and called me a "pussy," and after I burst into tears they all sneered and called me a "wimpy girl." It was humiliating, but just another day being the feminine kid whom everyone liked to pick on.

In classes, as I sat at the back trying to blend in, some of the boys around me would throw pieces of paper, pencil sharpeners, and other objects at me to try to provoke a reaction from me, and called me "gay," "ugly girl," and other words they knew had a deep impact on me. I would try my best to ignore them, but sometimes I would start crying, which made them gloat with glee and throw even more things at me. Sometimes the teacher would notice and shout at them, which would give me brief respite before they would continue once the teacher's back was turned again. It was endless, and I felt truly miserable inside, wishing one day I could escape all of this and defeat the bullies.

Another school experience I used to dread was swimming. I had a condition called gynecomastia, referred to colloquially as "man boobs," which led me to develop excess fatty tissue around my chest, making my body look more female. I still remember the feeling of profound fear I had each time I would have to get undressed in the locker room and walk into the pool area with my "man boobs" exposed. I felt vulnerable and on edge that people would notice me, and all of my fears were realized when they did notice. I tried to cross my arms over my chest while standing waiting to enter the pool, but it was ineffective and drew more attention to my chest. Kids would laugh at me saying I had "breasts" and I was a "girl," mocking my gender and emasculating me by saying I was not a real boy. Each week for swimming class I would conveniently "forget" my bathing suit and try to avoid being seen. I just wanted to be invisible. Yet each time I would leave my shorts at home, the swim instructor would find a spare pair and I would be forced to participate, much to my despair. It was degrading and it was humiliating and that's exactly what the bullies enjoyed—making me feel humiliated. They would make a point of doing it in front of all the other children, so they could all point and laugh at me. *Ha ha ha ha ha ha*—their laughs echoed throughout the pool, their goal to shame me and make me feel worthless. And it worked, every single time. I hated my body, I hated having "breasts," and I told myself I would do anything it took to get rid of them.

At age twelve, I vividly remember when a boy came up to me during swimming class and said I looked so fat and like a pregnant woman with big breasts and laughed in my face. His cruel taunts and harsh words still stay with me to this very day. I was haunted by being constantly taunted over my "breasts," so later in life as an adult I underwent the most painful surgery of my life, gynecomastia reduction, to remove all my chest fat and rearrange my nipples to look more masculine—a procedure that almost killed me.

At the same time I was going through all of this on a daily basis, I started to struggle with my sexuality. I developed confusing feelings that I tried to resist for as long as I could. I was from a small town that had a small-town mentality; being gay was not commonplace or something anyone in my bubble was really familiar with. I struggled to come to terms with the feelings I was experiencing inside; it was confusing, and it made me feel more isolated than ever before. I didn't even know what it meant to be gay. It felt wrong and unnatural to me, and I tried to force these thoughts and feelings out of my mind. There was no one at my school who was openly gay, lesbian, or bisexual. If there had been, I am sure they would have been mercilessly mocked for it and made to feel like a complete outcast. Although there was one boy in science class named Michael, whom the teacher would sometimes pair me up with for study practice and class activities like dissection, which I hated. He hated it too, and he preferred doing girly things like me. We never became friends, as we rarely had a chance to interact except in science class, but it felt comforting to know that there was another person, who was also a boy, who had similar feminine traits to me and seemed to also be like me, struggling with sexuality and identity. Although we never spoke about this, for fear of the bullies overhearing, and although we would only get the chance to interact and talk once a week, I knew he was also struggling with similar feelings. Even though I often felt alone in my struggle, it made me think for a moment that perhaps there were others like me. But I was scared for anyone to know about my feelings for fear of the bullies using it against me. After a while, as my feminine traits started to become more obvious and as I continued to be different from all the boys in my class, the bullies realized I was gay, even though I had not accepted it myself—in fact, I did not accept it until I was twenty-three. This was also one of the reasons they would taunt me and call me a "sissy boy" and a "femboy." They could sense that I was different from the other boys; I was feminine, I was unusual, and I did not express romantic interest in other girls in my class. They would zone in on this, and it became another reason for them to target me. This led me to want to hide my sexuality until later in life, when I was finally able to come to terms with it after struggling for many years to accept myself.

During lunch hour, instead of going outside to play sports, run around in the field playing tag, or hanging out with other kids, I became a geek and would instead spend the hour sitting in the classroom. I would even eat my lunch there, which consisted of vegetarian sandwiches (my parents were both vegetarian), a bag of chips, fruit, carrots with hummus dip, and a box of raisins. While eating my lunch in the quiet, empty classroom, I would read books, research for assignments on the class computer, learn about nature, science, and history, and find out about the world outside my bubble. I studied books on the history of England from the Norman Conquest to Henry VIII and his six wives to the Renaissance, Victorian era, and the two World Wars. I became a complete nerd, dedicated to study, dedicated to furthering my education and developing my mind. It was the perfect distraction, to detract from the way I was feeling inside, and it also kept me out of the sight of bullies during lunch hour who I knew would be lurking around the field looking for their next victim. I felt protected in this bubble, the classroom, where teachers would come in and out and I would be the only student—knowing that the bullies couldn't touch and taunt me for one hour of the day. This work ethic and thirst to study helped me greatly throughout my life and helped me develop the skills I needed for future jobs and careers. I realized that hard work and dedication could pay off and could act as a way to keep my mind from my dark and normally all-consuming thoughts. However, despite my best efforts to study and immerse myself in my assignments, I could never truly erase the thoughts of the bullies and the impact they had on me. I was merely providing myself with a distraction, like I would always do in later life—it was my go-to response to deal with any traumas. I was never truly able to correctly process the way these kids had treated me and the impact their words had on my mental health.

Another instance at school, in the boy's locker rooms during sports class, was when I would be repeatedly verbally abused each time I had to take my clothes off to dress into my sports kit. I would try my best to hide my body, changing my clothes as quickly as possible while trying to keep my body pressed against the wall, but it was no use. They knew their bullying tactics got to me and they would jeer at me every time calling me fat, ugly, girly, pregnant, pointing out my "man boobs" and a variety of other insults. Some of them would even rip my shirt away as I was changing so everyone could see my chest and laugh. *Ha Ha Ha Ha.* Again, their cruel laughter echoed throughout the room, and to this day, when I walk into a room and hear everyone laughing, it takes me back to those school days and reminds me of when everyone would always be laughing at me. Some traumas and anxieties sadly never disappear, no matter how much you work on yourself.

While an outsider observing my school and the surrounding natural beauty would think it was a picture-perfect setting, surrounded by boundless beauty, they only saw what was going on at surface level. Like a huge iceberg, they would only see the tip and not see the vastness of the iceberg deep under the water. The adults couldn't see what I was going through; indeed, I never confided in any of them for fear of the bullies finding out and making my school life a whole lot worse. It was as if I were living in a bubble, where I felt I was trapped inside looking out, longing to be freed, a small-town boy trapped inside a prison I felt like I would never escape. Yet as an adult, when I was finally able to break free from this bubble, I became a completely different person—determined to change everything and undo all of the years of bullying traumas and reinvent myself. I suffered an identity crisis that lasted over a decade, and I fell victim to the influences of the outside world. Was it simply down to being bullied and broken, being a loner and never feeling like I fit in, or were there other forces at work?

• • •

As we have seen so far in my personal experiences with bullying, it can cause lifelong ramifications to a person's psyche and self-image and shapes how a person values themselves. My teenage years were filled with constant reminders of how I was "not good enough," "feminine," and "worthless," which were reinforced in my mind every day. As children, we are susceptible to the words and influences of others and tend to believe what those around us say. In today's modern society, children are equally impressionable, and if a classmate or even a teacher tells a boy he is too feminine or too like a girl, that child can be actively made to believe they were born in the wrong body, encouraged to develop gender dysphoria, or influenced to change their gender. My own teenage years taught me that if someone tells you something too many times, you generally believe it. I was told each day I was worthless, ugly, too feminine, and a girl, so I started to believe their every word and eventually acted upon it later in my life. Indeed, many of us often tend to focus on the negative words of others and let these words weigh us down. Even in modern times with social media apps people tend to hone in on the negative comments, try to interpret the meaning and tend to believe what these people tell us—even though in many cases we don't even know who these people are. We believe what others tell us about ourselves and try to change ourselves accordingly in order to stop the negativity and bullying and to try and prove these people wrong.

Looking back on my school memories, I have come to realize that I was broken down, my character was destroyed, and my own identity brought into question because of the daily insults about my appearance. I often wonder, if I had never been subjected to any of this bullying and if I had never been told repeatedly that I was feminine, would I ever have wanted to change myself? Given the fact I grew up with a bubble around me, protecting me from the outside world, I didn't have a clue about plastic surgery, and I didn't have any knowledge of people changing their gender or wanting to become a different person. I was protected from these ideas that now all too often many children are being exposed to. Yet the bullying led me to hate myself so much that the moment I left my bubble, the moment I entered the outside world and finally had my first taste of freedom when I moved to South Korea in 2013 (where, for the first time, I finally had independence), I immediately gained access to new ideas and the chance to physically alter my appearance and become someone else entirely. Little did I know as this shy, insecure teen boy that I would one day grow up to erase every single aspect of who I was in reaction to these traumas.

We know that bullying in our teenage years has a detrimental effect on our development. It causes increased stress levels, depression, severe anxiety, and can lead to a person feeling angry, insecure, isolated, and withdrawn. Victims of bullying always wonder how they can become different to escape their bullies' notice, or how they can somehow put an end to being a target of bullies. Around 20 percent of students in the United States report being bullied each year at school with the main reasons often being physical appearance, gender, ethnicity, disability, and sexual orientation. When it comes to cyberbullying, one in five nine- to twelve-year-olds have said they have been bullied online, and a staggering 49.8 percent of kids in this age group have reported being bullied at school.[1] Yet

---

1   U.S. Department of Education. "Student Reports of Bullying." *Results from the 2017 School Crime Supplement*, 2019, p. 61. *NCES*, https://nces.ed.gov/pubs 2019/2019054.pdf. Accessed 04 01 2023.

these statistics are just what are reported, based on students telling either a teacher or an adult. When you are a victim of bullying, like I was, you often don't report it for fear of the bullies reacting and bullying you even more because you reported them to an adult. It can often make that child's life worse if they complain about it to an adult or a teacher, so they tend to keep it to themselves. We also know that many teens who now experience gender dysphoria and those who want to change their identity are victims of bullying, and the bullying itself may have led them to want to change their gender identity, as was the case with my experience. In two of the leading studies into the factors leading to a gender dysphoria diagnosis, in Finland [2] and in the UK, half of adolescents with gender dysphoria reported significant bullying and periods of social isolation during childhood prior to questioning their gender.[3] The Finnish study found 45 percent of children had experienced a history of extreme bullying, low self-esteem, and, as a result, depression. In a separate Canadian study, children who had been bullied were also far more likely to develop gender identity issues than children who had not reported any bullying in childhood and as adolescents.[4] I, too, like the participants in this study, had been bullied severely and experienced gender dysphoria, which, as these studies suggest, go

---

2   Kaltiala-Heino, Riittakerttu, et al. "Two years of gender identity service for minors: overrepresentation of natal girls with severe problems in adolescent development." *National Library of Medicine*, PubMed, 9 April 2015, https://www.ncbi.nlm.nih.gov/pmc/articles/PMC4396787/. Accessed 8 March 2023.
3   Holt, Vicky, et al. "Young people with features of gender dysphoria: Demographics and associated difficulties." *National Library of Medicine*, PubMed, 26th November 2014, https://pubmed.ncbi.nlm.nih.gov/25431051/. Accessed 8 March 2023.
4   Steensma, Thomas D., et al. "Behavioral and emotional problems on the Teacher's Report Form: a cross-national, cross-clinic comparative analysis of gender dysphoric children and adolescents." *National Library of Medicine*, PubMed, 4th May 2014, https://pubmed.ncbi.nlm.nih.gov/24114528/. Accessed 8 March 2023.

hand in hand. I was also made to feel isolated, suffered from low self-esteem due to the way my father behaved, and experienced many symptoms of depression—all leading me to struggle with my gender identity.

The bullying I had experienced as a teen from being teased about my bad facial acne to having my gender mocked due to my "man boobs" while being constantly emasculated and made to feel like I was a girl—and an "ugly" one at that—left me with deep scars both mentally and physically that followed me into adulthood. This, paired with the unhealthy obsession with my mirror image where I had been severely critical of my own reflection, led me down a path of obsessive extremities. Just like the Greek god Narcissus, I was under a deep and dark spell, and the only way I ever felt I would lift that spell was if I made the person in the reflection perfect so that I could no longer criticize what I saw. That way, I hoped, I would be less focused on staring in the mirror and instead be able to go out into the real world, explore new things, and succeed after finding newfound confidence within myself. But alas, it was not as straight-forward as that. All of this led me to develop a dangerous addiction to plastic surgery from the age of twenty-three through thirty-two, where each year I would undergo more and more extreme plas-tic surgeries in an attempt to "fix" the imperfections I had been reminded about each day. I would stare longingly in the mirror, each time reminded of the cruel taunts of the bullies and their wicked laughter echoing throughout my mind as an ever-present reminder of my worthlessness and lack of value as a human being.

My mind was filled with these hurtful memories coupled with the reminders of my father's cruelty toward my mother and the way he would speak to me. I was reminded of his harsh tone as he scolded me for being different from the masculine boy he had tried so hard to make me become. I recalled him screaming at me in the car for ques-tioning his authority and his push to mold me to develop his cruel traits. A lot of difficult traumas overlapped for me to process and I was never able to fully process them, so I ended up down a dark and destructive path resulting in thirty-two plastic surgeries consisting of six nose surgeries, chest reduction, facial feminization, three eye surgeries, three face lifts, and having my bones shaved down and completely restructured. Over a nine-year period, I destroyed myself in an effort to escape the bullies, escape my father's image, and also escape my own reflection which I had grown to despise. It wasn't until I was thirty-two, until my eventual detransition, that I was finally strong enough to deal with my issues head on and try to come to terms with them. I have now been left with permanent scarring, my face and body mutilated, and I have been left with facial muscle paralysis with muscles that no longer function. The scars of my teen years ran deep; they had become not just mental scars, but physical ones. Each facial and body scar was a reminder to myself of the pain and trauma I had suffered throughout growing up. Each scar was a reminder of what the bullies had forced me to do, and each scar was a reminder that I was never good enough. Even to this day I look at my own mirror reflection and see these scars, yet I cannot change them and go back in time. Instead, I must learn to live with them and allow them to teach me lessons, lessons that I hope to never repeat, and lessons that I hope to use to be able to warn others and prevent them from undertaking such harmful courses in life.

Bullying is a catalyst and leading cause in many other developmental problems and can completely alter a person's view of themselves enough to want to change themselves so that they can fit into peer groups, become socially accepted, destigmatized, and draw away a bully's attention. Certainly in my case, I wanted to change myself completely, eradicate every single inch of my identity, and transform myself into a different person—someone who would never again be the target of bullies and someone who could fight the bullies with success and inner confidence.

If there was a lesson others could learn from my deeply personal experience, it's to be kind to others. Words can have a profound impact. It costs nothing to be kind, to give a person reassurance and to elevate them to feel good about themselves. If we turn a blind eye to others being bullied whether in schools, sports classes, workplaces, or other environments, we will be complicit in allowing victims of bullying to suffer, to have their lives destroyed, and to want to completely change their identity whether that be gender, the way they look, or how they present themselves in public. We owe it to every single child, every single person, to protect them and to face bullies head on and encourage kindness and compassion. Because kindness costs nothing and it can make a huge difference in uplifting a person and putting them on the right path to happiness and success while giving them the ability to love themselves for the way they are.

If we tackle bullying in schools and pay closer attention to signs of bullying, we can also tackle many of the issues that lead to gender dysphoria, depression, and other psychopathological issues that often stem from our experiences as children. By promoting kindness while stopping bullies in their tracks before they have the opportunity to cause real permanent damage to a child's cognitive development, we can help save many lives and help many children grow up into happy, healthy adults with fewer traumas weighing them down and more chances to grow and succeed. We must always choose kindness and always stick up for the underdog.

Chapter 6

Big Dreamer

At age sixteen, I was relieved to finally graduate high school; finally, I had some level of freedom and an escape from my tormentors, those who had bullied me relentlessly for the previous five years. I had finally escaped the cage where I felt like a canary, trapped and unable to spread its wings. I was now well on my path to becoming an adult—soon I could start working toward my future career and plan my future, whatever that would entail. I started college feeling apprehensive about how others would treat me. I wondered if I would be treated the same way or would finally be accepted into social circles and be seen as a human being, someone with thoughts and feelings. I had grown tired of being looked at and treated like the Greek god Hephaestus, rejected and cast out for his unsightly appearance. I was longing for a change, and I just wanted to be accepted.

It was 2006 and time for a new chapter as I began life as a college student. I had been apprehensive about starting college, due to everything I had been through at high school. I was incredibly reluctant and wary of going through the entire process again, of being bullied and broken for another two years of my life but hoped that perhaps this would finally be different. I had no room for doubt or any other option but to attend, as my father was very insistent on the importance of higher education and I didn't have any other alternative. How would I ever escape my deep unhappiness and find a career if I didn't have a college degree? Thus started my search for a college, looking endlessly into all the colleges in Hertfordshire and beyond. I even looked at colleges in the great big city of London, though I found the prospect of being in a city with 7.5 million people (the population at the time in 2006) very intimidating. If I went to college in London, where my father was from, I felt like it would mean I would have thousands more eyes on me than before, whereas my school had just six hundred students. That would mean thousands of people to judge me, laugh at me, mock me, and bully me. Of course, in reality, most people are not bullies and most people are kind. But due to my years of horrific bullying I had come to believe that everyone was like the bullies I'd known and that kind people didn't even exist. Eventually, I settled on and was accepted into a college thirty minutes away from my hometown. I felt on edge and nervous about starting my first week, when the summer holidays were over, but it was a step I had to take if I was ever to have a fighting chance at making anything of my life. I selected the courses I would study based on my interests, Theatre Studies, Geography, English Literature, and Psychology. The latter subject appealed to me, because I had so many thoughts constantly trundling through my mind, questions about my identity, my struggles with repressed memories, and my desire to be loved. I felt that if I could somehow understand my thoughts and feelings, it would help me improve my mental health and come to accept who I was, for all my flaws and imperfections.

My first week at college was a nerve-wracking one, as it is for many teens. Trying to find new friends when you are not even used to having friends and trying to form social groups where you can "fit in" and feel welcomed. There were the cool kids, the emos, the goths, the library-loving intelligentsia, and of course the geeks who devoted their days to studying, reading books, computers, talking about sci-fi movies, and obsessing over the latest Pokémon trading cards. I looked at each group, wondering who I would connect with and wondering who indeed would connect with me—the shy, reclusive, acne-covered feminine boy that seemed like a mouse in the corner, avoiding eye contact, only speaking when spoken to, and trying to avoid being seen during lunch hour. I knew I would never in a million years be with the cool kids; I wasn't cool, I certainly didn't *look* cool, and I was the sort of person this clique would want to bully, so I had to avoid them at all costs. Instead, I joined the geeks group, as they were the only ones I knew would really accept me for who I was, and they embraced me and made me feel human again. This warmed my heart, knowing that I would finally have real friends. I was a geek at heart anyway, and I loved studying and learning about the world and computers and all the other things geeks were passionate about.

Every teen goes through this process while at school or college. Most aspire to be accepted into the cool kids clique, the "populars," or the jocks. Few aspire to be labeled a geek, or as some cruel kids would call it "the freaks." But it didn't matter to me; I was just relieved to finally have found people who would talk to me and accept me for being me. I was also happy to be in a group, so I wasn't a loner like in school, which makes anyone a far easier target for bullies. I finally had a protective shield and safety net. I was consumed with what other people thought about me throughout my teenage years, how I was judged and treated by others, but thought that finally I would be able to blend in at college and hopefully deter the bullies by not being an easy lone target.

If only I had thought the way I do now about not taking notice of what other people think. The older you get in life, the more you become immune to people's opinions and less obsessed with fitting in. I wished I could have been carefree, as almost every teenager also wishes, but instead my mind was consumed with trying to be seen as cool, trying to attract attention from girls, in order to disguise my true sexuality and be seen as a cool guy—as every cool guy had a girlfriend. I wished I could have had better skin, better looks, and be celebrated as the popular good-looking boy. Alas, I was far from that ideal. I could never be a handsome guy; it was impossible, and I convinced myself that my whole life would be filled with despair and unhappiness. My own fate had been sealed for me, but at least I finally had some friends.

This was also a moment in my life when, besides going through the big change of leaving high school and starting college, I also started to question my identity more and more. At sixteen, I again started to question my gender and began to experience symptoms of gender dysphoria. I had always felt more feminine and remembered that I always used to like playing with Barbie dolls and girls' toys and even dressing up in girls' costumes as a young child. Now these feelings and questions were coming back to me again. And this time it was different. I wanted answers to the confusing questions that had plagued my mind for many years. I was fast becoming an adult and began developing a new understanding of the feelings I had felt for so many years. While at college no girls were interested in dating me—they all thought I was either terrible looking, too feminine, or they could see I was gay—they did start to befriend me and wanted to "hang out" with me. This was a sudden change from the way I was treated at high school, where not a single person wanted to know me. So most of my friends at college were girls, girls who were part of the "geeks" clique—they weren't the trendy, cool girls or the mean girls that everyone wanted to be like. These girls were different and unique and, like me, were rejected by the majority of their peers. Perhaps it would have been more fitting for our friendship group to be called "the outcasts" or "the rejects," as no one else seemed to want us. But it didn't matter, I was just relieved to have friends and people to stick up for me. We would do girly things together, painting each other's nails, doing makeup, reading celebrity fashion magazines, and dissecting each famous person's outfit, rom-com movie nights watching *Devil Wears Prada* and *The Notebook,* and anything considered stereotypical girls' activity. This reinforced my belief that I was meant to be a girl since I identified with girls and every one of their interests throughout my life and even more so now. I started to grow my hair, dress more feminine, and even speak more like a girl. It felt good, and all of my geek friends would say how much they loved me and that I was just like them. I was finally starting to feel better about myself until Geography class would come around, where the "jocks" would see how many times they could call me gay or lesbian before I would snap and either tell them to stop or appear visibly upset. That was their ultimate goal, to upset me because I was different. Just like in high school, they homed in on me because of my feminine traits and clear struggle with my sexuality and identity. I was an easy target and each time I gave them what they wanted, unwittingly of course, because I became visibly upset, sometimes trying hard to hold back tears, and they would only increase their taunts until I finally broke. Other classes weren't as bad—nobody bullied me in Psychology or English, a few people did in Theatre Studies class— but I began to dread Geography class, reminding me of my difficult teen years that I could seemingly never escape. All I ever wanted was to escape from reality, to escape from the bullies, and to become someone completely different and unrecognizable so I would no longer be their prime target.

During my two years attending college from the age of sixteen to eighteen, my father told me it was important for me to get some real-life experience, saying it would improve my confidence, help me earn my own money, and set me up with skills for later life. I was reluctant to do any job that involved dealing with people; I wanted to be hidden away in the shadows where no one could see me and laugh in my face. I took on a part-time job as a dishwasher in a local restaurant. While the job didn't sound appealing or very fun for that matter, I was happy that at least I would be hidden away in some dark corner of a kitchen where customers could not see me. The hours were long and the task of cleaning dishes was an arduous one, yet at least I was learning some skills. Although I wasn't sure how washing plates would help me in later life, I continued to convince myself it was a good thing. Until one day, due to a staff shortage, I had to become a waiter for the day, serving customers, using the cash register, and taking orders. My stomach sank upon being told I had to do this and the thought of hundreds of people seeing my face all day. But I had no choice, I had to do what my manager said, so I plucked up the courage and did it. I was probably the most nervous waiter in the world. I remember spilling gravy across a customer's lap, forgetting most of the coffee orders, not being able to distinguish between a latte and cappuccino—a mortal sin for any coffee barista—and being as slow as a snail at making drinks.

After my first disastrous day, I felt humiliated, stupid, and convinced myself that I never wanted to be a waiter again. Yet at my next shift at work, I had to be the waiter again despite telling my manager that I wanted to remain in the kitchen. It happened again the following day and then yet again until suddenly my main job was to be this customer-facing person, to have to make eye contact and speak with actual people. It was daunting, and I thought it soul destroying. Until it wasn't. After a while of doing this, I started to build up my confidence, develop my communication skills, and learned how to interact with people. No one taunted me, no one commented on my looks . . . sure, they may have commented on my slowness or forgetfulness with my job, but at least they weren't fixated on calling me names or commenting on my appearance.

Maybe grown-ups didn't care about my appearance, how feminine I seemed, and maybe for once I was just a normal boy that people didn't judge. I felt an enormous sense of relief, and this certainly helped boost my confidence.

Yet college was a different story. While I was treated much better by classmates in most of my classes, except Geography, I was still judged for being too feminine, rejected by girls to go on dates because I "wasn't their type" or "not manly enough," and I wasn't even acknowledged as existing by the cool kids. I still had the terrible skin and acne condition that I had suffered with for the past four years and it hadn't really improved, despite the fact I tried every possible remedy from antibiotics, laser treatment, microdermabrasion, fractional laser resurfacing, to every single acne product on the market, even putting toothpaste on my spots before I went to sleep each night. I prayed to the universe, prayed to whoever was listening, God, anyone who would answer my one prayer—make me beautiful. Was anyone listening? It didn't feel like anyone was out there looking out for me, and after diving headfirst back into my unhealthy obsession with looking in the mirror, being self-critical, and struggling with the way I looked, I eventually began to withdraw again, climbing back into my shell that kept me safe and alone with my own thoughts and my own company. I continued with this mindset throughout the rest of my time at college, continuing to pray that I would one day be the cool kid that everyone wanted to know and be inundated with people wanting to be my friend. Some may call me delusional, others crazy, but every single day I told myself one day I would be celebrated, cherished, and popular like Narcissus and everyone would want to know me. It was a far-fetched dream, and it all stemmed from just wanting to be accepted and validated, like many teens these days.

Back when I was at college, social media had only begun to emerge, and it was before the days of Instagram and long before

TikTok. Back then it was Myspace, one of the first social media networks that allowed users to create a webpage with photos, their favorite music, videos, status updates, and the ability to connect with people all over the world. It was a way for teens like me, who had little confidence and little self-esteem in the real world, to create an online persona and to reinvent themselves completely. I instantly jumped on this, seeing it as a way to escape the problems of my real life and find some sort of validation online, and it worked by giving me a sense of escapism from reality. Using filters, lighting tricks, and edits, I was able to make myself look different from how I really appeared in real life. I started to spend hours each night after college on Myspace, building a following and trying to be cool. My look wasn't complete without a head-to-toe Ed Hardy by Christian Audigier tracksuit, all the rage in the Myspace era, and oversize sunglasses to disguise how big my nose was. I looked cool, I acted like a trendy kid, and this carefully curated image worked. It actually worked. I became popular on the site, had hundreds of thousands of profile views, thousands of followers, and high engagement rates. This was the first time in my life I actually started to feel good about myself. Even though it was in an online virtual world, and it wasn't reality, it gave me the confidence boost and validation I needed my entire life. I didn't have to be Oli the ugly spot-covered feminine boy, I could be a filtered and improved version of me or a different person completely. Oli the cool Ed Hardy–wearing Myspace guy.

Young people flock to social media in order to feel better about themselves, to escape the real world, and to reinvent themselves as whoever they want to be. In the modern day, 92 percent of teens use social media on a daily basis. Many teens spend hours upon hours each day scrolling through content and uploading their own in the hope of getting likes and engagement and a dopamine rush. In a study by UCLA, researchers found teenagers get the same dopamine rush getting likes on Instagram as they do when winning a prize or a competition. Using brain-mapping techniques on teenagers thirteen to eighteen, UCLA researchers found that the teenagers who received the highest number of likes had a flurry of activities triggered across different regions of the brain.[1] The high number of likes was associated with the reward processing, social cognition, and attention regions of the brain and highlighted the power of peer influence during adolescence. It also highlighted how social media, for teens, has become a source young people rely on for their happiness and escape from reality, something which I certainly identified with in my teenage Myspace years. Just like the study found, the validation, likes, and attention I received on Myspace gave me a temporary rush to the brain and short-lived positive reinforcement each time I got views and praise. However, when I was not online and instead at college, I did not have any of these positive feelings of validation, so each night I would instead go back time and time again to my Myspace page to try and get that sense of fulfillment and validity that I had been missing throughout the day. Like an addiction, I craved it more and more, and the only way I ever felt any sense of self-worth was being online with my filtered cool kid persona.

In between college weeks and Myspace sessions, back at my part-time job, my role became more and more difficult. On weekends, I would sometimes have to serve forty tables of customers alone. I was run off my feet, made to make and remake more cappuccinos than I could imagine, and spent hours upon hours each day washing pots and pans, rubbing grease off deep fat fryers, and mopping floors. It was a tough job, but my father kept telling me that hard

---

1   Sherman, Lauren E., et al. "The Power of the Like in Adolescence: Effects of Peer Influence on Neural and Behavioral Responses to Social Media." *Sage Journals*, UCLA, 31st May 2016, https://journals.sagepub.com/doi/abs /10.1177/0956797616645673. Accessed 9th March 2023.

work was good for me and that I must keep it up because he wasn't going to support me financially now that I was sixteen—just like his own father had cut him off financially at the same age. So I had no choice; I kept washing dishes, making coffees, serving food, and cleaning floors. Week after week, month after month. Yet the whole time I never gave up hope that one day my life would be radically different, one day I would be loved and validated, and one day the world would celebrate me for who I was and I could be like the beloved Myspace persona I had so carefully curated. I was a big dreamer like many of us are at a young age, and I never stopped believing that one day everything would change, that one day, in the not-too-distant future, these dreams and aspirations eventually would become true.

I always wanted more, I always dreamt bigger and hoped that my prayers and wishes could be answered so I could fight these bullies. I prayed that I could make them envy me and want to be me so that I could finally take the power away from them. I firmly believe in the power of perseverance, as those who keep on going no matter what and those who work tirelessly toward their dreams can achieve anything if they just believe in themselves and never give up hope. Proving the bullies wrong, outshining them, and making them envy your every move is the best revenge.

• • •

If I could share a lesson with the world from my life as a teenager and from my struggles to be accepted, it would be that no matter what someone's circumstances, no matter which obstacles you may face, anyone can achieve their wildest dreams if they have the sheer determination and willpower to do so. Never giving up can seem impossible sometimes as we all face hurdles that set us back and make us lose faith in our very existence, yet if we remain firm and committed to our goals each of us can achieve anything. As soon as the bullies see you becoming successful, they suddenly switch up and fawn over you, admire you, and envy you.

Chapter 7

University of Life

After two years of battling through college and navigating the waters of working in a fast-paced environment, I finally spread my wings and it was time for university. I wanted to study Theatre Studies, because I had always had an interest in performing arts. However, again, my father told me to study English Literature, because I was good at it at college and performed well in exams, and because it would give me a broader range of career opportunities for the future. While drama and acting was my main passion and, indeed, one day I wanted to become a professional actor, I knew this was a tall order, so English it was. Like many other times throughout my life, he was again exercising his control and dominance. I had to do what he wanted. As a teenager being thrown out of his own father's home, he never had the opportunity to pursue higher education, so he was going to live the life he had wanted, through me, though on many occasions I had been a full disappointment to him and he was always sure to remind me of that. I didn't become the strong, aggressive masculine man he had trained me to become. I became a timid, emotional, self-conscious, and shy feminine boy. So it was decided I would study English Literature at the University of Reading, just outside London.

During this period of time, as I got ready to start university, I was feeling more optimistic than ever before. My skin condition had finally improved, though far from perfect, and I felt much happier looking in the mirror and had more confidence and more vigor about this next journey in my life. In 2009, I moved into the dorm at my new university, one hour's drive from London. It was a big step and a big change, but I felt like I was ready for it. I met the other students in my dorm; they all seemed extremely welcoming and friendly and a diverse group of people from across the world. I hadn't really had much experience with people from different countries, after growing up in the English countryside and rarely leaving the vicinity of my county. It was an exciting prospect; there were students from Nigeria, South Africa, and even Japan and Korea. It was fascinating for a small-town boy to finally be exposed to the outside world and venture outside my bubble. I was all too eager and keen to learn about their cultures and find out about the world. The first week at university was known as Orientation Week, but most students called it "Freshers Week"—a week of partying, drinking, and getting to know one another followed by yet more drinking and partying. This was my first time ever drinking alcohol, and it wasn't something that appealed to me before then. I went to a dance club organized by the university during Freshers Week and probably drank the weakest alcohol there was, Smirnoff Ice™—it just tasted like sugar diluted with water but after a few bottles of this I felt confident and ended up having my first ever kiss with a woman; in fact, many of the boys had a competition that night who could kiss the most women, and I managed to kiss seven. I had never kissed anyone before and of course wished I could have accepted my sexuality and had my first kiss with a guy, but this was still a crazy experience and made me feel more confident, giving me hope for the future, that maybe I was finally becoming more attractive and finally people were starting to see me as cool. There were a lot of parties organized by the student committee: bar crawls where we had to dress up in themed costumes and drink ourselves into a standstill; club nights where we had to see who could drink the most vodka from a beer bong; silent discos; and even roller skate parties. The partying was intense and constant, and even though I didn't like the taste of alcohol, I did whatever it took to be seen as "cool" and try to make people like me, so I drank copious amounts until I passed out or vomited. It was a crazy first week, but I saw it as an opportunity to try and get to know others and make friends quickly. It wasn't that I even enjoyed drinking; I didn't, and in fact, I hated the taste (even to this day I don't drink alcohol) and most of the days I was throwing up endlessly at the end of each night. But none of that mattered. I was just trying to fit in, and drinking was a great way for everyone to let their guard down and be more open-minded. I had finally found a place where people actually liked me. I wasn't seen as a geek or outcast like I was at college—I was finally just Oli, the nice guy who liked to party.

After the first week ended, I immediately felt more comfortable being there and felt like I had finally started to become popular. Classes and lectures had started, and I was enjoying each class so far, especially the literature side of things. Reading and discussing classics like *Moby-Dick*, *Huckleberry Finn*, the poetry of Walt Whitman and Robert Frost, and of course no literature class was complete without reading a few Shakespeare greats: *Hamlet*, *Macbeth*, *Taming of the Shrew*—these were just some of the titles I enjoyed reading. I was really starting to enjoy being somewhere I could learn and feel like I belonged.

I also felt happy to have started to make friends. Two of the people I became closest to were from Asia, a continent and place I had always been curious about but that seemed so far away and foreign. One of the people I became friends with over the course of the first few months at university was a man named Joon from Daegu in

South Korea. He was the first person I had ever met from South Korea and introduced me to Korean culture and K-pop, something I had been completely unfamiliar with. I was instantly intrigued by everything he told me and became inquisitive, asking him questions about Korean history, food, the people, Korean technology, and about the music style. Little did I know everything he taught me about Korea would eventually lead me to moving there—something that would change my life forever.

Another friend I made during the Orientation Week was Monica, who was originally from Guangzhou, China, and who studied business and management. She introduced me to Chinese history and culture and other things I had previously had no knowledge of. She also talked to me about women's fashion and her family's major luxury goods business in China, which she told me she would join after graduating. I was fascinated to learn about women's clothes, dresses, trends, and style, having been so curious about it as a little kid dressing up in women's fashion in my home and as a teen reading my mother's fashion magazines like *Vogue* and *Vanity Fair*. She taught me a lot over my two years at the university and over the course of our friendship, and eventually she would give me the opportunity of a lifetime when our paths would cross again a few years later. It felt good to form such strong friendships and bonds, and it distracted me from my own issues, which I had managed to push back into my mind only to emerge on days when I felt down.

Back when I studied in 2009, it was a time of free speech and the ability to speak with people with different opinions without fear of retaliation. Before the advent of wokeism and cancel culture, universities were a place of open dialogue, healthy debate, and an emphasis on discussing both sides of an argument to encourage students to form their own opinions. In English literature class we would debate each book, trying to decide what the author's intentions were and dissect what message they were trying to convey.

From the thought-provoking and brave *Narrative of the Life of Frederick Douglass*, which told the story of the American abolitionist who, after escaping slavery, went on to become a vocal activist, powerful orator, and leading voice in the movement to abolish the slave trade, to the poems of American feminist Emily Dickinson, which detailed her struggle as a woman living in Victorian society and how, through a series of tragic illnesses, she helped overcome the social stigmas that women of her day faced. I felt a connection to the author and the struggles she faced in society and how she tried to navigate through these difficulties and find her own internal voice that had been suppressed by society. In fact, I tended to identify more with female characters and authors in the books we read in class; I felt like I was just like them and had many of the same struggles.

In classes and study groups, I remember gaining my voice and learning to speak up and offer my opinion without fear of judgment. Finally, the years of being silenced by bullies and feeling inferior were starting to evaporate. No one called me names anymore, or said I was too feminine or not a real man. I felt good for once, but my need to feel consistently validated led me to drink alcohol and party on an increasingly regular basis. Soon I was drinking daily, going out to bars and clubs almost every night, partying and dancing until the early morning, then going to after-parties in the shared kitchen or dormitories. The partying never stopped. As these bad habits developed, I started to miss more and more lectures due to the hangovers and lack of sleep. My priorities were wrong; when I should have been attending class, I wanted to party. My priority was to be validated and loved. It was the first time in my life, and I wasn't going to let this new and exciting feeling stop. My grades were going down, and the quality of my assignments were also on a sharp decline. Not that I cared at the time—as long as I was becoming popular, that was all I needed from university. I had been seeking these feelings of acceptance my whole life. Perhaps, if I had faced these challenges earlier on through therapy, I may have been able to tackle them and would have been able accept myself without the need to seek approval from others.

In my year-two final exams, I failed my grammar test and phonetics, two of the subjects I had struggled with the most. Despite having a private tutor for the three months before the exams and despite pulling my weight and putting in extra effort for these last few months, I had failed. My chance of achieving a bachelor's degree was gone, unless of course I went though year two again and went through the exact same classes and exactly the same curriculum, which I didn't want to put myself through again.

My father reacted with intense anger at the news and was furious that I had not fulfilled his exceedingly high expectations for me. He couldn't understand how I had let him down repeatedly throughout my life and acted as if this were the biggest blow I had ever inflicted on him. He told me I would never amount to anything and that I would always be a failure. I was his biggest disappointment, and my mind immediately went back to the story my mother told me of him abandoning me when I was born. I felt terrible about myself and fell into a deep and severe depression and eventually sought medication to treat the way I was feeling. Doctors prescribed citalopram, an antidepressant, but it did little to mitigate my feelings of self-hatred.

I had always tried so hard to make something of myself and to succeed but had failed again. Time and time again, I had proven that I could never amount to anything. I was a failure, just like I had always been. I had failed with my looks, failed in life, and now failed my university degree. Was this a reflection of who I was? Or was I ignoring the simple reality that I was reckless during my time at university, partying too hard, missing classes, putting little effort into my assignments all because I wanted to be accepted by others? Had I been accepted as a teen, had I not been bullied and cast out,

I am sure the outcome would have been far different. If I had not been so desperate for the validation, love, and praise that had been missing, then maybe I wouldn't have become such a heavy drinker at university and so irresponsible and reckless when it came to my study. I had failed.

Yet, at the same time, there was one thing I finally felt some semblance of happiness about—that I was popular. In my mind, it was a worthwhile trade. Who cares about good grades if you are popular? Surely that would be more helpful to my adult life than a degree in English. This was my reckless attitude at the time. I had finally experienced validation, and my only wish in life was to continue that feeling, the serotonin rush and confidence boost that I had always craved. But after failing university, I went back to live with my parents for the next year, struggling to come to terms with my life. I felt completely worthless, and my father would remind me of it every day.

During this period, when I constantly criticized myself for my shortcomings, I started to convince myself that the real reason for all my failings was my identity and the way I looked. I convinced myself that all the thoughts that had been going through my mind throughout my life had been ultimately responsible for my failure, and the only way I could remedy my situation and turn my life around was to change myself completely. Maybe then my father could look at me with some semblance of pride, and maybe then I would finally prove him and others who had doubted me my whole life wrong.

Chapter 8
Ethiopian Enlightenment

My failure to pass my university exams ultimately sent me into depression and even more feelings of low self-esteem and self-loathing. A year had passed since I received the news that I had failed. The time seemed to drift by so slowly as I wallowed in self-pity, feeling a complete sense of hopelessness for my future. Until one day, tired of lying in bed all day with these dark and depressing thoughts, I was finally able to snap out of it. I told myself that I needed a drastic change, a new challenge to help me turn my life around and help me gain some perspective. I was sick of feeling the way I did, sick of hating myself for my looks and failings, and decided I needed to try something completely new. I wanted some sense of purpose to help me put my life into perspective, something to lessen my unhealthy obsession with being self-critical and hating the way I looked. I needed to do something drastic that would distract me from my own problems and help me focus on doing something positive. I also wanted to delay starting a job and a career for as long as possible, so I started researching places where I could volunteer abroad.

A lot of ideas came to my mind: helping turtles in Costa Rica, helping to build houses for an indigenous village in Peru, volunteering with orangutans in Borneo, or teaching English to underprivileged children in Tanzania. There were so many worthwhile causes to volunteer with and so many countries I wanted to explore. As a child I had always read a lot of books about the world, nature, oceans, rainforests, and the importance of protecting the planet and all of its inhabitants. I searched and searched over several weeks for the right opportunity to volunteer and came across a site for volunteering in Ethiopia. From my knowledge of watching news channels, I knew Ethiopia had a lot of problems with poverty, a lack of educational facilities, and had suffered through droughts and famines, and I knew it was one of the poorest countries in the world. So, when I saw an opportunity to help in some way, I immediately jumped at the chance. It was a selfless act to want to help others, but I was also doing it for myself, because I knew that this would make me feel like a better person, it would help me have perspective and realize my issues were completely irrelevant in the grand scheme of things. It would also help me try to prove my father wrong and show him that I could amount to something in life, and I wasn't the true failure he had painted me to be. I settled on the project, reached out to the organizers, and offered my time to help in their mission to alleviate poverty. When they responded to my email, they invited me to London for a meeting to explain to me the various work of their organization and see if I would be up for the task of helping local communities. I was elated and jumped at the opportunity. They then invited me to a three-day training session where I met some of the other volunteers who would be joining me. They were all friendly and kindhearted. It was comforting to meet people who were kind and not of the same character as those I had been bullied by throughout my teenage life. Of course they were kind; if they were willing to give up their time to help others, they had to be good people.

After training, I felt emboldened and ready to make a difference. I began preparing for the upcoming trip by getting vaccinated against various diseases, including malaria, diphtheria, and measles, and packing lots and lots of mosquito spray. I was finally ready to be lifted out of my depression and ready to set out on an adventure that would enlighten me and change me forever.

• • •

Upon arrival in the ancient capital of Addis Ababa, in the place often referred to as the "cradle of civilization," I was mesmerized by the greenery, the forested hills, and the tropical plants. It was not what I had been expecting, based on everything I had seen on news channels. I was expecting dry, arid landscapes as far as the eye could see, but it was green and luscious.

As we were driven to a charity compound on the outskirts of the capital, I saw endless rows of houses stacked tightly together like sardine cans with their corrugated iron roofs and crumbling concrete walls. I saw people sitting on the side of the streets, holding cups, begging for someone's spare change. I saw stray dogs and cats, malnourished and frail in appearance. I saw many things that night that made me reevaluate my own life and realize just how lucky I was. That night I slept uneasily, tossing and turning, not knowing what tomorrow would bring. I knew that the next day I would be sent out into the field to help the local people who needed help the most.

As the sun shone brightly through the window, I woke up and checked the clock. It was 5:00 a.m., time to get up and ready for the bus ride to the charity I would be working with. The ride was bumpy, traversing down dirt roads lined with donkeys pulling carts in hard, backbreaking conditions, with tuk-tuk vehicles whizzing by, some stuffed with goats. After a three-hour journey, we arrived in the southern city of Awassa. The city was in the tropical part of the country, toward the far south and closer to the equator. It was tropical, filled with palm trees, banana trees, sugar cane trees, fields of maize, and various other luscious vegetation. The rain started to pour down from the skies, and I was driven to the place I would be staying for the next three months.

I was dropped off at the home of a local family who would be letting me stay with them; the charity would be providing them with compensation for housing and feeding me. It was a chance to immerse myself in the local culture fully and see what it was like to live as a local. As I pulled up at the end of a rocky dirt road, the rain pouring overhead, I started to feel a tremendous uneasiness inside—what had I gotten myself into and how would I ever survive this tough living? I was used to my comforts in England, which I took for granted: a warm bed, a television, air conditioning, furniture in my room, all the things we grow accustomed to having and don't even take the time to appreciate. I was about to be stripped of all these luxuries. I knocked on the gate and a tall, six-foot-three man with a beard emerged. He greeted me with a handshake and welcomed me through the corrugated iron gate into a courtyard. A banana tree dripping with rainwater stood in the middle, and I was led into a tiny room through a wooden door that was hanging off its hinges, into a room with nothing more than a bed covered in a mosquito net. My heart sank. What had I gotten myself into? A cold, hard, and uninviting concrete floor greeted me, four concrete walls, and, to my horror—cockroaches. Cockroaches everywhere: small ones scuttling through the cracks in the wall and big, huge, monster ones scurrying, to my shock, under the bed. I couldn't imagine a more nightmarish place to sleep, but then I remembered my own father and his tough approach—"Man up, Oli. You need to be a man."—and so I reluctantly took a deep breath and stepped into the room, tiptoeing carefully for fear of being touched by a cockroach. The man, who said his name was Tewodros, told me it was late and that I should get some sleep and tomorrow I would meet the family. *Sleep?* I thought that was the last thing I would be getting that night. I was terrified of bugs, especially cockroaches, and jumped into bed as quickly as I could without even taking any of my clothes off. I wrapped the mosquito net under the mattress and around the bed board, ensuring that there was no possible way any bug or insect could reach me. I put my head against the pillow and looked around the room nervously. This was a whole new experience, and it would either make or break me, but deep down I knew I had no other alternative. The only choice I knew I had was to continue being unhappy and obsess over my identity and image in England, or put myself through a tough new experience to help me forget about all my own problems and focus my energy on helping to make the world a better place.

The daylight started to shine though, hours had passed by, and I still was unable to sleep. My mind was abuzz with fear of the unknown and wondering what struggles and challenges the next three months would bring. An hour passed and my eyes were beginning to close when I heard a loud bang on the door. "Time to get up, Oli, breakfast." I lifted myself off the pillow, still in my clothes from the day before, and slowly peered over the bed, checking if any bugs lay in hiding, waiting to pounce on me. It was all clear, except for a cockroach I could see in the corner of the room. I jumped out of bed, into my shoes, and raced out the door. The sun was shining, the rain had stopped, and the man who had greeted me from the night before was waiting. He took me into another room in the house where I was greeted by his wife, Dinah, and three children. Their smiles were from ear-to-ear. This was their first chance to ever meet a person from a foreign land, and they were all too eager to welcome me. The table was filled with food they must have been preparing for hours to welcome their guest from a faraway land. One plate was filled with a pancake type of flatbread, which they told me was called injera, which was made from a type of long grass called teff, grown in the Ethiopian highlands. Another plate of boiled potatoes, one with yellow lentils, another with chopped greens, and some goat's cheese in a bowl on the side. I had never seen food like this before and wished I could have had a full English breakfast instead (baked beans, toast, hash browns, and mushrooms). But I was in Ethiopia, far from home, and I had to get used to immersing myself into this unfamiliar culture. They gave me a plate and piled it so high with food that I knew I would never be able to finish. I took a bite, and it was surprisingly delicious, then took another bite and another until I was so full I could barely move. "You must eat more, you are our guest," Dinah said, before proceeding to pile my plate high again. I told her how thankful I was for such a lovely welcome meal and that I was so full I couldn't possibly eat anymore. However, she persisted, and not wanting to come across as unappreciative, I reluctantly took a few more bites. I didn't realize it that day, but in Ethiopian culture it is rude for a guest to stop eating, even when full. It's a sign of love and kindness for Ethiopians to offer what they can to guests and feed them until they are ready to explode. I found it very endearing, because I knew these people didn't have much, yet they wanted to make sure I had a full stomach. When I could no longer take a single additional bite, Dinah said she would take me for a shower. I slowly got up, holding my full stomach, while Dinah led me into another room, the kitchen. I wondered for a moment where the bathroom would be and guessed they wouldn't have a bathtub, as they didn't even have electricity. However, I was shocked to realize there was no shower. Instead, the mother had a bucket in her hand. A bucket of cold water and a large plastic bowl. I trembled at the thought of being doused with cold water, but I had no other choice. I undressed down to my underwear, and she proceeded to fill the plastic bowl with water and cover me with it. I flinched at the icy cold temperature until I couldn't take any more. It was only my first day, and already I wished I was back in my own house with all the luxuries that had become so familiar. She quickly grabbed a towel and wrapped me in it while I shivered. She was the mother of three children and a real motherly figure. Now I was her fourth child and she would care for me the same, showering me with kindness and fussing over how much I ate and making sure I was okay.

I went back to my room, again keeping a close eye out for cockroaches, and quickly opened my bag to put on some clothes as quickly as I could to then head to my first day volunteering at the charity.

I was placed working at a local nongovernmental organization (NGO) for orphaned teens and those living in extreme poverty who were unable to get an education, health care, or even the basic supplies like rice, potatoes, toilet paper, sanitary products, and soap. I met with the NGO's founder, Getachew, whose name I struggled to pronounce, and was informed about the work I would be doing at the charity. My role was to raise awareness of the charity's work, help contact potential donors, and help create documents to be used in outreach work in order to expand the charity's reach. I was also tasked with helping to get some of the vulnerable teens accommodation, school access, school materials such as books and stationery, and medical supplies. I also went on home visits to meet the parents and the children to assess their living conditions and see what necessities they required and which ones were the most in need of urgent accommodation. I probably visited about ninety homes over the space of a week, along with several local workers from the charity. We had the difficult task of selecting the two hundred most vulnerable children from these homes out of a total of three hundred who needed support the most urgently. Sadly, it wasn't possible to help every single one of them because the charity was only available to provide school and board for two hundred of them due to capacity and budget limitations.

It was truly heartrending to not be able to help every one of them—they all needed urgent help—but we could only assist the ones who had the worst living conditions. Some of the houses were just one room with up to ten family members living in that tiny space: the grandparents, the parents, the uncles and aunties, and the children. Walls were decorated with old newspapers instead of wallpaper, mattresses were without bed frames, and all the cooking was done in a pot on a hot stove in the middle of the room. This was their life, twenty-four hours a day, seven days a week, 365 days a year. I couldn't imagine how they must have felt inside, the hopelessness and despair of knowing that their future was bleak and opportunities to escape this life were almost impossible. They were stuck in the poverty cycle, generation after generation trapped inside a never-ending loop of suffering. After bearing witness to their terrible living conditions, I knew in my heart I had a duty to help them in any way I could. It also put my life into perspective at the time and made me realize just how lucky so many of us are, having homes, food on our tables, education, and opportunities. No matter how difficult our own lives and struggles may seem, when we compare it to the lives of those that have nothing and are trapped, it should make us grateful and appreciative of what we have because we are lucky to have even the little things that we take for granted in our lives.

One house I visited during my time at the charity had cows living inside the room along with the family. They were so poor they didn't even have a barn to keep their cows in, so they simply kept them on some straw in the one room they also slept in. It was truly tragic to bear witness to this, but this was all they knew. Their whole lives had been in this one room from the day they were born. After visiting all the homes and having meetings back at the charity, we selected the two hundred children that needed help the most, and the charitable organization was able to get them school and boarding for the next two years on the charity's property. I felt like for once in my life I had made a difference. The kids would not only be taught on-site at the school each day, but they would also be taught vocational skills that could help them get a job in the future: carpentry classes to help them learn to build furniture they could sell and use the profits to feed their families; sewing classes to help kids learn how to make clothing to sell; and farming skills to help them learn how to be self-sufficient. There was an on-site vegetable field filled with cabbages, potatoes, lettuce, and more for them to practice. These skills would help give these kids the training they needed to then support their families after graduating and give them a more hopeful prospect for the future. Seeing the smiles on their faces when they started this two-year skill-learning process and knowing that I had played a part in getting them there really melted my heart and made me realize the power that one person can have and the effect one person's actions can have on an entire community. Every single one of us can make a difference, big or small, and we all have the power to effect changes in the world. As famed Indian lawyer and political activist Gandhi once said, "Be the change you want to see in the world."

Each day I would return from my hard day's work feeling grateful and lucky that I had the life I did and realizing that my struggle with my looks was completely irrelevant and unimportant when there are people in the real world who have nothing. It was a chance to give myself an entirely new perspective. Every day, I went get back to the family home and was greeted by another huge meal that I would be expected to finish, and Dinah would be smiling to welcome me back and make sure I was okay. Tewodros, however, reminded me of my own father. He was very strict and stern each time he spoke while acting commanding over his family. He also, like Dinah, treated me like his own son, and I was expected to behave in a way that he thought appropriate. I had to follow his strict rules, speak only when spoken to, and was never allowed to express my feminine side—that was a big no-no. He was a deeply religious man, expecting his children to recite passages from the Bible each day and expecting me to learn it, too. If anyone got a word wrong during recital, they were punished or made to do manual work around the house. I had always had a bad memory so I would fail at this recital each time; I would then have to clean the outside toilet, which I dreaded, because it was filled with a menagerie of insects. Massive centipedes, my biggest fear on Earth, crawling with their hundred legs across the toilet floor, a toad that would always stand in the entrance to the toilet, cockroaches everywhere, and mosquitoes, hundreds of them. It was my very idea of hell on Earth. Yet no matter how much I tried to practice for Bible recitals, I was never able to retain more than a few sentences.

Besides doing nightly Bible recitals, the family and I would also go to church every Sunday. As a child, I had gone to church with my school and had many fond memories. However, throughout my teenage years and adult life I had lost touch with faith and lost all sense of belief, feeling abandoned and hopeless because I had been cursed with my terrible looks and identity struggles. I couldn't imagine that there could be an all-powerful God if I had been made so ugly and so unsightly that people would bully me relentlessly. My mind just could not grasp why I would be punished so much during my teenage years and why I would feel trapped in the wrong body. I had always believed in a higher power, but I had felt completely abandoned by it and therefore lost touch with my beliefs during the years I struggled the most.

In Ethiopia, however, going to church rekindled many fond memories of my childhood when I went to church with my school and everyone sang hymns and did fun community-building activities. While the church service in Awassa, Ethiopia, was far different from those in the UK, it still had some similarities: people coming together to support one another, giving praise and thanks for what they were grateful for, and feeling part of a community that was loving and accepting. It was mandatory to attend with the family I was staying with, who were deeply religious and went to the local church every Sunday for a three-hour service conducted in Amharic (the Ethiopian language). While I didn't understand what was being said for much of the sermon, what I did like was the gospel songs, sense of community, and uplifting spirit of everyone in attendance who were all happy being in God's house. Many of them had very little in their lives, barely had a roof over their heads, and some could not afford to eat and buy basic essentials. Yet I was struck by their strong spirit and how, in the face of all these problems, they seemed content and happy. This perplexed me, as I knew how difficult living conditions must have been for them and I had witnessed firsthand how locals were living on my home visits with the charity. I wondered, if I had to live like this could I ever be happy? Was the bullying I received in my teenage years and my struggles with identity and the way I looked even of any importance compared to this? Why should I obsess over something so trivial when others have very little but are generally happy? Part of me wished I could get rid of my material possessions and live like this, if it meant I could be happy and content. I admired the strength of these people greatly, and seeing how God and Jesus brought them all together for a common purpose was truly inspiring. It made me question my own belief system and wonder if this was what I was missing from my life, but I still could not comprehend if God was really there guiding me and giving love. If so, why was I punished so much, why was I made into such an unattractive and unfortunate soul, and why did I always have all these bad feelings and thoughts in my mind? It would take me another eleven years to manage to break free of these all-consuming thoughts and realize the answers to my own questions lay in rekindling my long-lost relationship with God.

While the church services were empowering and thought-provoking, I was taken to one service over an entire weekend that truly terrified me and has scarred me for life. It started on a Saturday morning and Tewodros told me to wear something smart, as this would be an extremely important service. I had a million questions in my mind: "How long is the service? Is it a new church? Could I be excused after a few hours to go and see some of my work colleagues?" I dared not ask these questions out loud, for he, like my own father, would shout at me or punish me for questioning his authority. So, I put on a shirt and blazer and some smart black pants and shoes, ready for this "special" service. Tewodros led the way out of the house, with his family and I following behind. After a twenty-minute walk, we arrived at a large outdoor church. It had a roof but no walls, and I can only describe it as a large tent-like structure, large enough to fit three thousand people under its roof. There was a large wooden stage with several priests and pastors standing by ready to give the sermon. Although this was no ordinary sermon . . . it was an exorcism. I had watched the Hollywood horror film *The Exorcist* a few years prior and had been unable to watch it in its entirety due to being petrified and filled with fear. Now I was about to witness real-life exorcisms.

The service began, and I held my breath nervously for what I was about to experience. As the priests spoke in Amharic, Tewodros would translate to me what they were saying. "Be our protection against the wickedness and snares of the devil; May God rebuke him, we humbly pray; And do thou, O Prince of the Heavenly Host, by the power of God, thrust into hell Satan and all evil spirits who wander through the world for the ruin of souls. Amen." The priests would repeat the same prayers again, and again the audience would start chanting, "In Jesus's name," in perfect unison, as if possessed. Again and again, they repeated the chant until their voices became deafening. Then it began. A disabled woman with special needs and no limbs was dragged through the audience, pulled off her wheel-chair, and marched through the crowd by a group of strong burly men, screaming and crying against her will. It was horrifying to watch—how could these people do this and be so cruel? I had tears streaming down my eyes, and Tewodros gave me a sharp, stern look as if to intimidate me. He told me, "You are behaving like a girl. You need to see this. It will help you become a man." I tried not to look, but the woman's screams were deafening. It was so cruel, a woman with severe disabilities being dragged through the mud and thrown onto stage where everyone chanted, trying to supposedly "cure her" of her ailments. The priest chanted and shouted at her while she wept uncontrollably, while the thousands continued to chant, "In Jesus's name, in Jesus's name, in Jesus's name." Then the crowd began to search for the next victims they believed needed an exorcism. A screaming boy was pulled out of the crowd; he fought back, protesting against the men violently manhandling him, but to no avail. He wept as the crowd became more fervent in their chants and was thrown onto the stage. His possession? He was supposedly "too feminine" and "gay," according to Tewodros, who translated what was going on. The boy's parents had selected him as a sacrifice to be brutally dragged onto the stage to "cast the demons" out of him. Again and again, the crowd dragged people out of the crowd, a young girl whose screams were echoing throughout the room was pulled, she resisted and fell to the ground into a puddle of mud and water while trying in vain to escape. She continued to resist but the men pulled her as hard as they could, striking her across the face when she resisted, then pulled her by her arms and legs and brought her to the stage for the exorcism. Now there were multiple children and adults with disabilities on the stage. They were screamed at and hurled with abuse while the priests placed their hands on their heads pushing them down onto the hard wooden floor while they exorcised the "demons."

I couldn't take it. It was beyond traumatic, and the most horrific thing I had ever seen in my life. I didn't want to be there anymore. I could not believe humans could be so cruel and callous. But I was forced to stay by Tewodros, who tightly gripped my hand. I had no choice; I had to live with them for another six weeks until the three months would finally come to an end. My heart was broken for those poor children who were pulled onto the stage that day, who will undoubtedly have the most horrific traumas and scars that will stay with them forever and affect their everyday lives. I promised myself after that moment that one day I would give a voice to children and the vulnerable who were abused, traumatized, and mistreated, and one day I would fight for laws to be in place to protect them from evil.

• • •

Ethiopia was a life-changing experience in many ways. I learned many skills working at the charity, I learned the importance of helping others and had put my own problems into perspective. Even though I experienced some truly tough moments, including the shocking church exorcisms, everything I experienced helped me to become stronger, tougher, and have a better and more comprehensive understanding of the world. I had undertaken three months of grueling work, living in extremely tough living conditions, and under the control of a dominant man just like my father, who tried to mold me in his image. I had seen firsthand the suffering of others and the cruelty of the world, and I had come out of the experience with a new outlook on life. I promised myself I would change, I promised myself I would make something of myself and one day be a voice to help others and elevate their problems onto the world stage. That promise would, however, only be fulfilled after a decade of struggles during which traumas and repressed memories from my teenage years would come back to haunt me.

Chapter 9

Repressed Memories

Trauma that occurs during the teen years is detrimental, causing permanent damage to mental health and leaving a person with psychological scars that never quite heal. Trauma never truly disappears and tends to wind itself in and out of a person's life like a snake winding around its prey, suffocating its victim. While my university years were much more bearable than high school and college, and while I had a transformative experience in Ethiopia and gained some perspective into the real-world struggles of others, the trauma of my past would soon come back to haunt me.

For several months after volunteering in Ethiopia, I felt a renewed sense of purpose and meaning in my life. But the feeling dissipated quickly when I once again started to struggle with severe depression, body dysmorphia, and gender dysphoria stemming from teen traumas that I had tried to hide in the back of my mind for so long. I was living back home, and as these traumas resurfaced, I also witnessed my father treating my mother even worse than before. He left her for long periods of time with no explanation as to where he was going, and when he returned and my mother questioned his whereabouts, he would lash out and tell her she was controlling and that she was the reason he hated being at home. He was victim blaming as he always did, making the person he bullied feel like they were in the wrong. I hated being around him and tried to avoid him as best I could but found that I could no longer be a silent witness to his abusive behavior. I would confront him and argue with him in an attempt to defend my mother, and he would scream at me and shout me down, as he always used to do when I was a child. He would punish me by locking me in my room and cutting off any financial support he had been giving me while I struggled with my depression. Each time he would shout at me and my mother, it would trigger my old, repressed memories and take me back to my younger years, when his behavior had destroyed me internally.

I had suppressed a lot of my memories from my teen years as a coping mechanism, and even thinking about my past was difficult, leaving many gaps in my memories. I had dissociative amnesia, a disorder characterized by memory gaps, the inability to recall certain information due to a response to trauma.[1] Deliberate thought suppression as a reaction to PTSD (Post Traumatic Stress Disorder) led me to lose my sense of who I really was. In those teen years, the Oli I knew had died. I became a shell of a person and my only coping mechanism in later adult life was to self-harm through having extreme plastic surgery.

Young people have different ways of dealing with repressed memories; some turn to alcohol, some turn to drugs, and some lucky ones even turn to religion to seek a new way of thinking. At age thirty-two, after wandering around my whole life like a lost sheep in a flock, I turned to the church for help. Just like the Parable of the Lost Sheep in the Gospels of Matthew 18: 12–14 and Luke

---

1   Leong, MD, Stephanie, et al. "Dissociative Amnesia and DSM-IV-TR Cluster C Personality Traits." *NCBI*, National Library of Medicine, January 2006, https: //www.ncbi.nlm.nih.gov/pmc/articles/PMC2990548/. Accessed 16 January 2023.

15: 3–7, where a lone sheep separates from a flock and becomes lost in the wilderness. The shepherd leaves his flock of ninety-nine sheep in search of his beloved lost one, leaving behind the group in order to help the one that needed it most. Jesus retells the story to demonstrate that the Kingdom of God is accessible to all, no matter how far you go astray. I had gone far astray, yet I was brought back into the light, offered a second chance in life and a chance to rejoin society. Other young people who have struggled with traumas and have wandered astray in many cases seek coping mechanisms to suppress these memories further instead of finding the help they need to deal with these repressed memories head on. As human beings we often let pride and our own internal struggles get the best of us instead of reaching out for help. Yet learning to deal with our issues, speaking with others, and remembering that life doesn't always have to be this way can help you get out of the rut you feel trapped in. If we choose to open up these hidden memories and deal with them head on, it can help to finally overcome things that were holding us back an allow us to find the real person trapped inside and to set them free.

Whether we choose to find religion or find some other way to cope, it is important for everyone struggling to always know there is light at the end of the tunnel. I was about to undergo a nine-year battle with plastic surgery addiction and identity struggles, stripping away my very soul and trying to become a clone of another human being, all as a way to deal with my trauma and repressed memories. It wasn't a healthy approach, and it wasn't the right approach. I am glad that I am now able to look back and learn from these mistakes and share my story to help others who reach rock bottom and help those who seek to self-identify while changing the very essence of who they are as a coping mechanism to their past traumatic memories.

I generally believe that while there are a variety of factors that influence a young person to want to change their gender, to change the way they look and change the way they identify, in most cases this is in response to suppressed childhood traumas. I believe many of those with gender dysphoria who have had childhood traumas are trying to reinvent themselves so that they are accepted and embraced by society and so that they can feel validated while trying to erase their past experiences. Of course, everyone's case is different, and we have to take into account the environment they grew up in, what they have been exposed to online and in school, how much access they have to harmful Internet content, how their parents raised them, and other factors. But we must not overlook the fact that many of these kids, like me, just want to fit in and be accepted, and they crave change because they want validation, to be celebrated and to be loved. As we see with today's society, anyone who comes out as nonbinary, gender-fluid, or trans is immediately held on a high pedestal, celebrated as "stunning and brave," and given positive reinforcement on a daily basis helping them to feel validated. If these kids had a tough upbringing, whether from bullying or from their home environment, then suddenly they would feel valid, get the attention they craved, and be seen as popular and trendy.

Dealing with these repressed and traumatic memories head on is also fundamental in unlocking a person's subconscious emotions and coming up with a solution to tackle them directly to ensure the person does not partake in a self-destructive lifestyle as a coping mechanism for their repressed thoughts and feelings. Dealing with these through somatic modalities, a body-oriented therapy that includes breathwork, meditation, yoga, group therapy, and using art to express repressed memories, and even Cognitive Processing Therapy (CPT), can be an effective approach to tackling these memories directly and avoiding future struggles. These approaches can help significantly reduce the risk of a person having an identity crisis, like the one I underwent during my adult life.

If I had dealt with these repressed memories head on and learned to process them in a healthy way, the next chapter I was about to embark on could have been preventable and I may never have undertaken such a drastic and damaging approach to trying to make myself feel valid and better about myself.

Chapter 10

Seoul Searching

At twenty-three, I embarked on a journey that changed my life forever. I was tired of my lonely life in England. While university had built my confidence, I still felt I was missing something in my heart and had not overcome my internal conflict with my identity. A Google search one fateful day for "Working Abroad" generated a result for teaching in Korea. It was the first thing that came up in the search results and little did I know this fateful search would be life-altering. I recalled all the things my university friend Joon had told me about his home country and its rich cultural history, and how he had introduced me to K-pop music. This Google search immediately sparked my interest when I saw I could potentially have a chance to visit this country that I was so intrigued by. For better or worse, this could be the start of a brand-new chapter in my life. I clicked on the search result and took a risk and applied. Weeks went by and I heard nothing, then suddenly I received an email saying I had been rejected due to all the jobs being filled. I felt a deep, sinking feeling in my stomach; just another disappointment to add to the long list of disappointments that made up my life. I was used to rejection anyway, so I would just soldier on and try to find another working abroad experience. Africa again maybe, or even further afield, Australia. However, weeks later I received a wholly unexpected call saying a teacher had dropped out of the program and there was a place reserved for me. I couldn't believe it—my luck was finally changing. It felt like I was dreaming, and for the first time in my life I felt like I was lucky and that fate was finally on my side. This would change my life forever. Immediately after the call ended, I went to my local bookstore to search for a "Korea guide," or *Basic Korean for Beginners*—any book I could get my hands on that had the word "Korea" on the cover. I frantically started reading these as I got home and then watched back-to-back Korean language lessons on YouTube.

Finally, I had been given a chance to move to a brand-new place, a whole new country on the other side of the world, where no one knew who I was and I could start afresh. Although I had been to Ethiopia a year prior, this felt different because Korea was bursting with opportunities, and it wouldn't be a challenging experience like Ethiopia, where I had little chance to reinvent myself due to Tewodros, the controlling father figure I'd lived with. Korea would be a perfect opportunity to find myself.

As the weeks and months went by leading up to my flight to Seoul, my excitement only grew until finally the day arrived and it was time for me to head to my new home, South Korea.

• • •

It was February, one of the coldest months in Korea. As I landed at Incheon International Airport, I was greeted with blankets of thick snow, frosted windows, and a blistering breeze as I stepped off the aircraft. It was at least 14°F (-10°C), yet this icy cold felt like being hit by a wave of excitement and anticipation. I couldn't wait to begin my journey. I boarded a bus destined for the small town of Jochiwon, a town of just 46,000 people and home to Hongik

University and Korea University Sejong Campus. The bus journey took around two hours and thirty minutes, and I remember it feeling like a lifetime as I gazed longingly out the frosted windows at endless snow-peaked mountains, rice fields, fields littered with cabbages, and small rural villages along the way. It was enchanting, as if I had been magically transported through a wormhole into a fairytale, and I pondered if I would be the fairytale prince, the handsome and charming Englishman that I wished I could be perceived as. We arrived at the campus of Hongik University, where I would be staying along with the other teachers for our training course over the next three weeks. We were shown our rooms for the duration of our stay, and each paired up with another teacher whom we would share our room with. I was paired with a Californian teacher called Logan; he was very friendly and welcoming, and we had a lot in common with our music tastes and interest in Korean culture. After a brief introduction, we headed to the food hall where I was introduced to Korean food for the first time.

When people talk about culture shock, one of the things that can be hardest to get used to in a far-off land is the food and traditional dishes. And boy, was Korean cuisine a culture shock for me! As a vegetarian, I had never eaten fish in my life, yet the first dish I was served I mistook for bean sprouts and started eating with my chopsticks. Then I suddenly felt nauseated and looked down at the food. To my horror and dismay, they were tiny little fish with eyes. I spat it out in shock. I had never eaten fish before, and the thought of it made me feel so sick. One of the Korean members of staff came over and told me it was Myeolchi bokkeum, stir-fried anchovies. I was so jetlagged at this point and so put off by this first dish that I tried to wish my appetite away, yet I couldn't because I was so hungry. So I reluctantly forced myself to eat a bowl of rice with some Korean Sigeumchi-namul (seasoned spinach), a little bit of pickled cucumber salad, and kimchi—the national dish. Everything tasted peculiar. It was my first time trying Korean cuisine and I hoped my last, for it was far different from the English food I was used to. But I thought to myself afterward that I was in this new country and I needed to get used to it. Appreciating the food would be an important part of immersing myself into Korean culture—though I wished I could have had a baked potato with cheese and beans and a salad instead. Or even a peanut butter sandwich!

I hit the pillow feeling overwhelmed at the sensory overload of my first day. It was exciting and magical, but after the culture shock hit me over dinner I started to feel somewhat homesick. Over the course of the next few days, I attended seminars and training courses with the teachers from around the world, mostly from America, Canada, the UK, Australia, New Zealand, and South Africa. Half the teachers were also Korean natives, who would be eventually paired up with each of the foreign teachers to help with translations in class.

Classes ranged from language classes, introducing basic Korean greetings and common phrases we would need in the classroom with our students, to how to order a meal and ask for directions. I raised my hand and asked for the word "vegetarian," thinking that if I at least knew that one it would help me with my next meal so I could avoid accidentally eating fish again. "Chaesigiuuiia," the class teacher uttered. I tried to repeat it but failed miserably. How on Earth would I remember such an unusual-sounding word? Besides, I had a terrible memory, so I knew it would be a struggle. Still, I wrote it down and tried to practice every day in anticipation of mealtime. Other classes involved coming up with fun game ideas to help teach the alphabet, numbers, verbs, and adjectives. The more fun we could make a class and the more engaging the class was, the quicker the students would pick up the English language.

We also had to practice giving a mock class in front of the several hundred other teachers. I tried my best not to be selected, sitting at the back of the lecture. I still had deep insecurities about my looks and the way people perceived me, and always wanted to hide away in the shadows. Yet in this instance, I couldn't blend into the background because everyone had to come up and deliver a five-minute class. I reluctantly went to the front of the class and was paired with a Korean coteacher. That five minutes seemed like a lifetime, and I am sure my nerves were clearly visible; my voice broke and my eyes averted the gazes of everyone watching. I finished as quickly as I could and scuttled back to my seat, getting compliments along the way. "Well done, Oli, you did a great job," 'Fantastic class, Oli! You are a natural teacher." This lifted my spirits somewhat, and I thought that it was probably helpful for me to be speaking and practicing in front of hundreds of people if I was going to be a teacher in three weeks' time.

The weeks flew by, and in between classes I would venture out to the town in Jochiwon, visiting Korean bakeries (though they were mostly French-themed bakeries). Paris Baguette was my favorite for French bread and pastries, but with a Korean twist. I had started to make friends, too; everyone was so nice, and we were all in the same boat, far away from our homelands, our families, and our friends, and in an exciting new place filled with wonderful opportunities.

Toward the end of the final week of training, we were told that we would each be assigned to a school in different parts of the country and that each school would be in a rural village, not a large sprawling metropolis like I had hoped for. A village that had little exposure to the outside world and had rarely seen a foreigner. It was part of the South Korean government's drive to help bring the English language to all Koreans from elementary schools upward to help modernize the country and make it a global leader.

Korea had come a very long way in this modernization process and its drive to excel, since the end of the Korean War on July 27, 1953, which decimated much of the country, leaving millions in poverty and homes, factories, and entire towns destroyed. The Korean people, who are famed for their incredible resilience, never gave up on their country and over the course of the next six decades worked tirelessly to help Korea become the global superpower that it is today. This drive and determination to succeed against all odds and become a dominant global powerhouse could not succeed without younger generations of Koreans speaking English, to give Korea the chance to become a truly global economy. My job as a small cog in this machine was to help dozens of kids learn English and set them up for success in their future. Even though my role was a small one, when you considered the fact that there were hundreds of other teachers in my program, just for that semester alone, all of us combined could help bring the English language to tens of thousands more kids, thus becoming a larger cog in the machine and making a real difference.

After realizing the other teachers and I had an important role in the education system and helping Korea grow, I felt that I finally had a purpose. I could help others, help to sow the seeds of future generations to succeed. This was probably the first time in my life where I felt I was doing something of value and that I could actually make a difference. I could finally obsess less about my appearance and what others had thought about me throughout my life and instead focus on doing good while at the same time building my confidence and self-worth and feeling good about it.

The day came when we were finally assigned our schools. I was hoping to at least be near a big city like Seoul or Busan, as I had never lived in a huge city before. I wanted something different and exciting. When the class instructor called my name, they said I was assigned to Jeju. *Jeju*, I thought, *where is that? A small village in the middle of nowhere?* I searched on my phone after class and was pleasantly surprised to see luck was on my side yet again. I was going to be on a tropical island. Jeju was an island, not a village like I had originally thought. It was a beautiful island south of the Korean peninsula with warm temperatures in the summer, white sand beaches, blue skies, palm trees lining the roads, swimming pools galore, and so much more. I had struck the jackpot for sure. How on Earth did I get so lucky? My first taste of luck was that fateful day not too long ago when I received the call saying a teacher had dropped out and I had a place in the Korean teaching program. Now luck had struck again and sent me to an island paradise, the "Korean Hawaii," as many had coined the island. I was told the village I would teach in was around one hour's journey from the main city on the island Jeju-si and I could choose to live either in the village itself or commute from the main city. Intrigued by Korean city life—the skyscrapers, the twenty-four-hour convenience stores, the nightlife, restaurants, and museums—I instinctively I chose the city.

When the day came for me to head to Jeju, I packed my bags and bade farewell to the other teachers, after three weeks of intense yet enjoyable training and an unforgettable experience living in the snow-covered town of Jochiwon. Now it was on to the warmer climate of the island paradise awaiting me. I couldn't believe how my life had changed. Less than a decade earlier, I had been deeply depressed, bullied, and had struggled to get through each day. Now, years later, I was about to live on a tropical island in this new and exciting world of Korea. How had my luck changed, and could I make this exciting feeling of elation and happiness last a lifetime?

Landing in Jeju was far different than landing in Incheon when I first arrived in Korea. There was no snow or ice, but the blistering heat I had expected was not there. Having never been to a tropical island before, I had assumed that it would be sunny all year round and thought I would only need to wear a t-shirt each day. I was surprised to learn that Jeju too was experiencing a cold winter, though there was no snow. So it was lucky I still had my winter coats and sweaters that I wore day-in and day-out in Jochiwon.

After arriving at the airport, I was shuttled to another training center for a week of crash-course Korean language lessons and to meet my Korean coteacher and find out details of where I would be teaching, how often, and how to prepare my lesson plans. Staying in a dormitory this time, we had around a week to find accommodation in the city and move in before starting at our new jobs. I made friends quickly with a Canadian woman as well as a lady from Thailand named Jintara, who I realized after some time was trans, though she never mentioned it or made a point of telling anyone. I thought, *Why should she have to tell me or anyone?* It didn't change how we would treat her. She was friendly and sweet, and I was excited to have a new friend. It didn't matter to me how she was born; as long as she was happy, that's all that counted.

This was my first real-world interaction with someone who had transitioned, and although she never talked about it or mentioned it, I always felt curious about what she must have gone through and how good and convincing she looked. She also exuded confidence, spent the majority of the day happily laughing and smiling, and was the life and soul of the teacher group. I looked at her with admiration, wishing I could be as happy and content, wishing I could have just a single ounce of her confidence. I hoped one day I could be like her, be the center of the social group and walk down the street with swagger, my head held high.

But how would I ever achieve the same confidence as Jintara? She was living her best life as a woman, she'd had surgery on her body and face, and she looked incredible, so I thought to myself for a long while that maybe plastic surgery and making some drastic changes would give me happiness, too. This was a pivotal moment, when I started to question my identity, reminding me of my difficult teenage years, when I was told I was a girl each and every day and criticized for my appearance. Maybe I could be happy like Jintara. Or maybe I could be more beautiful, like the Korean pop stars and models I continuously saw plastered on billboards, in store windows, and on Korean TV. I was living in a new world, where anything seemed possible and where dreams could become reality.

As the first week drew to a close, I had managed to find a beautiful newly built apartment for a great deal in Jeju-si city center. In my excitement, I let all the other teachers I had made friends with know, and at least five of us took an apartment there. My new trans friend found an apartment in the building opposite. This was my first time ever having my own apartment, and I was so excited to finally have my freedom and a beautifully furnished apartment with a talking washing machine included, although it only spoke Korean. This immediately took me back to my childhood and my unusual fascination with watching the washing machine spin round and round while I looked at myself in the glass reflection.

I quickly settled in and felt right at home in my new apartment. I even had a brand-new smart TV with channels filled with K-pop music shows and Korean dramas and instantly became infatuated with it. I started to watch the K-pop countdown shows as well as the only English channel, Arirang TV, which featured the *Simply K-pop* show where English-speaking K-pop idols presented the show and introduced the hottest new bands and their addictive new singles.

I was inspired and allured by this newfound world. I felt like Christopher Columbus—prior to his cancellation by woke culture—on his first voyage to America and all the amazing discoveries he made, a new world filled with promise and hope, with wonderment and treasures beyond imagination. *Wow*, I thought, *I really got lucky again*. My luck did not seem to be running out, so maybe more of my dreams would come true in this new world of Korea and K-pop.

Spellbound by my new life on Jeju Island and discovering the fast-paced world of K-pop, I set out on my first day of work. It was a thirty-minute walk through the city center to the bus station, where I would meet my coteacher, Chaeyeon. I was happy to be working with her and to have a friendly face to greet me each day; she was kind with a warm smile and a sparkle in her eyes. We boarded the bus, which was filled with pensioners, elderly ladies known as *ajummas*, a term used for elderly Korean ladies with flair, attitude, and sass. As the one-hour bus journey commenced, we passed fields upon fields of cabbages being harvested by these *ajummas*. Some of the women looked about eighty years old under their straw hats and visors, yet they were doing back-breaking work, plucking these cabbages out of the soil to be later chopped up and fermented in jars for six months to become kimchi. It also struck me that these rural areas were a far cry from the pristine modern cities, with the latest technology, new shiny cars, and luxuries of Jeju-Si or the other Korean towns and cities I had seen on television. Many of the houses were dilapidated, some with their bright blue roofs collapsed and small. How different from what I had seen on television, how radically different from what I had believed. I had grown up in a bubble where all I knew was what I was told on television and through the media. I didn't know about the true realities of the world other than what I had been fed my whole life. Was everything now an illusion? Was what I saw presented on television and through film all a warped view of reality? This certainly looked nothing like what I had been presented with on Korean TV.

While I knew the history of Korea after the Korean war and that there had been widespread poverty, I had no idea people still lived like this and people still suffered from low incomes and a lack of access to basic needs and modern conveniences. Yet, looking at their faces as they raked the soil and toiled away, they seemed content and satisfied with life. Indeed, they were clearly in excellent health at age eighty, to be able to still work the fields.

As the bus pulled up to the village where I was assigned to work, I got out with my eyes wide open in wonderment at this little village, which felt like it was some kind of Korean movie set. There was a little shop with a poster advertising Soju, the popular and tasty Korean alcohol that everyone from young adults to grandparents would enjoy with their meals each day, despite it being a strong 15 percent alcohol. I popped into the shop with my coteacher to buy some Korean corn chips and a few Lotte-branded chocolate bars. Both proved to be exceedingly tasty, and much more enjoyable than the foods I experienced on my first day in Korea when I was in complete culture shock. I was getting used to this new world and new life and starting to feel at home.

After purchasing the snacks, we headed to the school, which was adjacent to the shop, to meet the teachers and students. The school playground was pristine, surrounded by vegetation and a football field. It all looked so well kept, like a scene from a postcard, with the endless fields on either side filled with crops of vegetables, cabbages, tea leaves, and even orange trees. The school building was huge compared to the size of the village, and it was hard to believe that I was only an hour away from the big city and my modern apartment. I met the teachers, and many were shy about speaking English, as I later grew to discover is common with adults in Korea. They were afraid to make a mistake with their pronunciation or say the wrong word and worried they might lose face or embarrass themselves. I met the main teacher, Bora, who would be my superior and who I was to present my lesson plans to. She would guide me through the English proficiency levels of the students in my new class, what they had been taught before, and what kinds of things I could teach them to help them improve. She was very sweet and spoke English well, although she was very shy about speaking it and kept apologizing each time she spoke, "Sorry for my English," and I would say each time, "Your English is excellent, don't worry," and we would repeat this same process back and forth, again and again, each time we saw each other.

I walked into the class and was greeted by twenty or so smiling faces all welcoming me and happy to have a new teacher, "Seonsaengnim," as they would call me in Korean. They were happy and eager to learn English, especially from a foreigner. Many may never have experienced meeting anyone from the outside world, especially given that they lived in such a small rural village, far away from the mainland. It was an exciting prospect for them, and also exciting for me to be able to share my language, teach my culture, and help these students improve their speaking, grammar, pronunciation, and writing in order to help give them more opportunities with their future careers. A win-win for all.

After the introduction was over, I was urged to start the very first class with my Korean coteacher Chaeyeon right away, which would be a simple basic English greetings class so I could assess the proficiency of each student. They all responded with excellent English, and I was greatly impressed by their proficiency. My coteacher was there to help with any translations and any questions from the kids that they had about the class. After the class was over, I said my good-byes and expressed my gratitude to the students and teachers and headed back to the old rickety bus, and back to the big city.

On the return journey I reflected on how smoothly my first day on the job had gone and how happy I felt that everyone was so nice to me, and that I was welcomed with such kindness. I was really starting to love being there, in Korea, a place where everyone showed me kindness and warmth—something I lacked and craved my whole life and had finally found in this place where I felt like I belonged, and I was one of them.

We all spend much of our lives searching for a sense of belonging, wanting to be included and validated. Some of us may never find that place, others with luck and the right circumstances can find it at an earlier age. When we finally find this sense of belonging, we feel content and happy inside and assimilate ourselves more and more into that particular society. I was starting to assimilate myself into Korean culture; I felt at home and wanted this new happy place to be my forever home. I wanted to be one of them—I wanted to be Korean.

Chapter 11

Hallyu Wave

The Hallyu wave is the term for the global K-pop and K-culture phenomenon that has swept the world over the last decade. Not only did the Korean wave reach millions of people across the world and infect them with the delightful addictive music style, but it also hit me like a tsunami. I felt like the wave had hit me so hard within just months of living in Korea that I actually thought I could be Korean, or at least look Korean. I was about to undergo my very first surgery after a plastic surgery billboard had convinced me that I could look as good as they did. I was living in a world where anything was possible and looking beautiful was the only way to succeed. After all, every single K-pop star and every Korean person I saw on television looked perfect, and that must have been the reason they had become successful, happy, and celebrated—because of the way they looked.

I started to visualize how my life could change for the better and how I could be worshiped and adored by others, and as far-fetched as it may have been at the time, years later I would achieve many of the dreams I visualized back in those memorable days living in Korea. The power of affirmations, telling yourself daily that one day your life will change, one day your most far-flung fantasy can become a reality.

I would look at each billboard, watch every music video, and stare at every K-pop idol on television, telling myself every day that one day I would be like them, one day the Hallyu Wave would come to claim me and wash away the old, mundane, and unattractive Oli, and give rise to a new Korean version, a feminine-faced, perfectly symmetrical, and aesthetically pleasing Hallyu-upgraded version of me. The male K-pop idols often presented as feminine, with soft facial features and feminine mannerisms, something I strongly identified with. In the world of K-pop and K-drama, while the men are effeminate—soft-spoken, elegant, and in touch with their feminine side—they are still considered men, and not like we see in predominantly western countries, nonbinary, or trans people. They didn't have pronouns like they/them, and they didn't call themselves women like we see so frequently now in the United States and European countries. Korea, like many other Asian countries, had clear gender definitions for men and women and as a collective society were perfectly okay with some men being more feminine and some women being more masculine. Yet they did not encourage or promote the idea that these effeminate men or masculine women should transition. They simply accepted them, and they remained in their clear gender roles. This resonated with me completely and helped me as I tried to reckon with the fact that all my life I had felt more feminine and acted more like a girl. Perhaps I was just like these Korean pop-star men: effeminate, soft-featured, gentle-natured, but still clearly men. I wanted to be like the K-pop stars and thought it could be the answer to all my problems. I had always been called feminine or girly, and at this stage of my life I thought maybe I should *look* more feminine by undergoing surgery and transforming my image, while I still identified as a man. Although I had met a trans person in Korea, I was still unfamiliar with the idea of transitioning and swapping genders. It was only in my later years, when being trans or gender nonconforming became so mainstream on social media and across pop culture, that I felt pressured to change in order to conform while also convinced to believe I was born in the wrong body.

But to achieve my initial dreams of changing the way I looked and altering my identity, I had to immerse myself more and more each day into this culture, into the mindset of K-pop idols, the driving force behind their success, and how they achieved such perfect aesthetics. Was it all a natural phenomenon? Was looking so perfect thanks to the great genes of the Korean people, or was it part of a manufactured process, a plastic surgery factory that each idol had to pass through before their debut, to ensure they were the best possible version of themselves? Was looking good the key to success? These were questions I sought answers to during my time in Korea, the plastic surgery capital of the world.

When I appeared on *Dr. Phil* in 2021, one of the comments he made to me about wanting to look like a K-pop idol, like Jimin of BTS, was that I needed to realize that K-pop idols have a "manufactured image," that what I was trying to achieve wasn't real; it was a man-made, carefully curated image, and that almost every K-pop star has their image altered in order to give them a higher chance of success in such a tough and competitive industry. Nothing was real; these boy bands and girl bands were not natural phenomena, and these stars didn't just get plucked out of obscurity. They had to go through years and years of grueling training, their looks were completely changed, many had to undergo surgery at the request of their agency—knowing that if they dare refuse their contracts could be terminated and they would never make it in the industry. This was the harsh reality of K-pop, which few people were willing to admit. At this point in time, I was still under the illusion that these idols had such great, wonderful lives. They were rich, they were famous, and most importantly they were beautiful. I looked up to them, as do millions of young people around the world who worship them as demigods. The term idol is literally defined as the image or representation of a god or goddess used as an object of worship. These idols were presented as immortal, god-like, to be worshiped and obsessed over. With their incredible dance moves, impressive fashion, perfect symmetrical faces, and fame, who could disagree with calling them idols and worshiping them as such? I was under the K-Pop spell and illusion that they were the pinnacle of success, and as my time in Korea went on, the spell only strengthened its grip on my mind and my heart.

From an outsider's perspective, as we have seen with pop music since the 1990s with the advent of pop boy bands and girl bands, a model the Korean entertainment industry has successfully emulated, everything is manufactured down to the finest detail. Nothing happens by chance, and the way many of these celebrities look and act is part of a carefully curated image designed to influence the minds of millions to worship them and ultimately buy their music, concert tickets, and merchandise. A genius marketing technique to lure young fans in and sell them the dream. The Hallyu wave is one of the most successful marketing techniques of the modern day and is attributed to the enormous determination of the South Korean government and its people for packaging up their culture into movies, music, and entertainment and selling it to the world while creating a wave of adoration and generating billions in revenue. The K-pop industry and its export also bring millions of tourists to Korea each year, resulting in a win-win for businesses of all types and helping make K-pop a national treasure. In 2018 it was estimated that Korea's most successful boyband, BTS, alone helped to generate $3.8 billion for the Korean economy.[1] In addition to this, the

---

1   Hyundai Research Institute. "K-pop's BTS 'worth $3.6 billion a year' to South Korea." The Korea Herald, Hyundai Research Institute, 18 December 2018, https://www.koreaherald.com/view.php?ud=20181218000811. Accessed 23 January 2023.

combined revenue generated from the K-pop and Hallyu industry as a whole each year is over $10 billion.[2] This is a sharp increase on the much lower $1.8 billion the industry generated just under two decades ago in 2004. The Korean film and television industry has also stormed onto the world stage with *Squid Games* becoming the most viewed TV series in Netflix history, and Korean film *Parasite* winning an Academy Award, a first for any Korean film.

Much of the country's success stems from the sheer will and determination of the people whose drive to succeed has been relentless since the end of the Korean War back in 1953. In the 1990s, K-pop was born and continued to grow through the 2000s, copying the successful template of bands like the Backstreet Boys, NSYNC, and The Spice Girls. The very first K-pop group, Seo Taiji and Boys, revolutionized the Korean music industry by blending Korean pop with American pop and creating the mega fandoms and cult following K-pop idols have today. Groups that followed this success story started mixing English words into the lyrics of their songs, particularly in the catchy chorus hooks, which helped K-pop appeal to a wider English-speaking audience who identified more with the music due to the few recognizable English words that appeared in between the Korean lyrics. From the first K-pop groups making waves across the world, the ensuing four decades (from 1990 to present) would be divided into four categories; First Generation K-pop (1990s–2000s), Second Generation (2000s–2010s), Third Generation (2010s–2019), and finally Fourth Generation (2019–present).[3] Each generation saw huge exponential market growth,

2   Gaikwad, Sumeet. "K-Pop is making billions for South Korea." AsiaFund Managers.com, 28 May 2022, https://www.asiafundmanagers.com/us/kpop" -and-economic-impact-on-south-korea/. Accessed 23 January 2023.

3   Fury, Rick. "A Brief History of K-pop—The Los Angeles Film School." The Los Angeles Film School, 6 April 2021, https://www.lafilm.edu/blog/a-brief-history -of-kpop/. Accessed 23 January 2023.

millions more across the world from Brazil and Chile all the way to Senegal and Nigeria listening to K-pop, singing along to the catchy music, sticking posters of their favorite bands in their bedrooms, and learning the dance choreography for the popular songs of the time.

Before I moved to Korea, I had learned about K-pop for the first time at university when my Korean friend Joon introduced me to the genre. I found it interesting and unique but only truly developed a passion while living in Korea. I moved to Korea during the first few years of the Third Generation of K-pop, my personal favorite, when some of the biggest bands of the time were 2NE1, Big Bang, and Girls Generation—names that are still very much fixed in popular culture today with K-pop fans and non-fans alike. The first time the Hallyu Wave truly hit me was on a day trip with the teachers from the English teaching program as we rode on a ninety-minute coach journey to visit a traditional Korean cultural village. I heard songs by Girls Generation, "Gee Gee" and "Oh" on the radio, and everyone on the coach started singing along to the catchy and easy-to-remember lyrics. The coach also had a small TV at the front, above the driver's head, and we all enjoyed the colorful, fun-filled, and happy dance routine and beautiful aesthetics of Girls Generation. I was instantly hooked, mesmerized and addicted to the songs and band, and then started to become addicted to every other song that played afterward. It was like I had been cast under a magical spell and my mind had been overwhelmed with K-pop music, and it was all I wanted to listen to from then on. It's easy to see the appeal of Hallyu and Korean culture when everything looks and sounds so perfect, everything is fresh and new and exciting. Millions across the world have watched K-dramas, *Squid Games*, K-pop music videos, or Korean film, and they too get easily reeled in like a fish on a hook, never wanting to let go of this new world that gives many a real sense of escapism from reality and the illusion of an alternate universe in our very own world.

This sense of escapism that many of us seek helps us get away from our problems and temporarily escape reality while being in a happy place where we can dream of becoming a part of this new world. Having this sense of a new world where I could create a new me and new identity led me down a unique path in life. The Hallyu Wave had lured me in, filled my head with fantasy, and made me want to become a part of that, a small cog in the world of K-pop. A new identity, an upgraded version of me. Anything to escape the realities of my life, where for years I had put myself down and struggled with identity and body dysmorphia. This was my chance to finally change.

Chapter 12
Silicone Seoul

I was fast adjusting to my new life in Korea and fast becoming immersed in the unique culture, including the K-pop phenomenon. Each day after finishing my teaching work and traveling back to the city, I would switch on the TV and put on a K-pop music show while cooking myself dinner, normally something English like a potato with corn and cheese and a salad garnish. I still wasn't used to the unusual tastes of pickled radish, spicy kimchi, avocado kimbap (Korean sushi), and bibimbap—a vegetable dish with grated carrot, shredded spinach, spiralized cucumber, rice, and an egg on top. While I had certainly tried these dishes, especially each day in the school canteen, I still couldn't accustom my taste palate to the intense flavors.

As I watched the TV each day, I daydreamed about being as beautiful and perfect as the K-pop idols. Their beautiful slick blonde hair, luscious lips, sharp jawlines, and smooth skin. I would watch for hours at a time, dreaming and wishing. I knew it was a far-fetched dream, too far from reality, but I prayed each time for a miracle. I prayed for anything that would make me like them. Very soon my prayers would be answered.

By summer of 2013, I had been in Korea for around six months and had renewed my teaching contract and visa to stay another six months. I was loving my new life, happier than ever, but still something was missing inside of me. Still, I wanted more. This was also a pivotal time in my life in terms of my sexuality. For years I had been confused about my sexuality and had been interested in guys, but I had fought against it for so long. I felt confused inside: I was attracted to guys, yet I didn't acknowledge that I was gay. I tried to rationalize this by telling myself the reason I am attracted to guys is because I was supposed to be a woman. I was just born in the wrong body and that's the reason I liked guys. That was my only explanation and I struggled with it for years. Then I met someone, a Korean guy named Jong Hak, who looked like a Korean pop idol, and I fell head over heels for him. We were only together for a short time, three months to be precise. Love was a feeling I had never truly experienced before, except the love I had for my mother. I had never been in love with someone romantically until now, and I adored him and wanted to spend the rest of my life with him. When you're young and naïve and longing to be loved after a lifetime of loneliness, you end up doing crazy things. One night when I was visiting Seoul, we went to a tattoo parlor and tattooed each other's initials as a sign of eternal love. We had only been together for three weeks, and one week later I proposed to him. It was a whirlwind romance but destined to be short-lived. We broke up when he cheated on me while I was asleep in the bed and he was in another room with his supposed "friend," who turned out to be his ex-boyfriend, and they had been seeing each other the whole time. Even the day we got tattoos and got engaged, I later discovered, he had been messaging him telling him he loved him. This tore my heart in two and shattered me to the core. For the first time in my life, I had genuinely been feeling truly happy, and it was suddenly and cruelly ripped away from me. How could someone be so cruel and break the heart of someone who gave them nothing but unconditional love? I was destroyed and confused and immediately reverted back to the old me, the unhappy, depressed, self-critical Oli. I descended into a deep depression, a period of self-loathing. Even though he had cheated on me, I still wanted to be with him and blamed my being unattractive as the reason he cheated on me.

The only way to escape the turmoil I felt after the breakup was to find an outlet and a distraction, something to keep me focused and give me a new goal in life. I turned to K-pop, one of my newest passions, and became infatuated with the way these pop stars looked. I hoped that one day I could look as good as them. I promised I would do anything to change myself in order to prove my now-ex-boyfriend wrong and make him want me again, while at the same time proving everyone that had ever bullied me or judged me wrong and showing them that I could be beautiful and happy—or at least I could create a façade to convince them of that.

This was when I first discovered BTS, now the world's biggest boy band but back then just a rookie group, an unknown band trying to make it amongst the thousands of other groups that debuted each year. They made their debut on June 12, 2013, with their smash hit single "No More Dream." I was instantly hooked. Instantly lured in by their incredible vocals, dazzling dance moves, and perfect aesthetics. I had never seen a more perfect-looking group of people in my whole life, and I wished I could look as good as them, have people cheering me on, and be celebrated and admired. All seven of them were incredible, but there was one who instantly stood out to me: Jimin. His effeminate visuals, the symmetry of his facial features, his bone structure, his small nose, and his mesmerizing eyes looked like he had been carved by Michelangelo, a modern-day Statue of David—except he was real.

I had seen numerous K-pop stars perform on TV over the last six months, but none struck me as much as Jimin. In Korea, K-pop is intrinsically linked to every level of society, so when you go to a convenience store you will see a poster of a K-pop star advertising a beverage. When you enter a skincare store, you are greeted by life-sized cardboard cutouts of idols, and when you ride the subway you are surrounded by perfect-looking advertisements with idols advertising products, most notably plastic surgery.

These plastic surgery billboards were part of everyday life in Korea; they were everywhere, literally on every corner. They were on storefronts, plastered on the side of buses, on subways, and of course all over television. You cannot live in Korea and escape them; they presented an idealized image of what a person should look like and showed just how easy it was to look this good, just like a K-pop idol. The more I was exposed to these subliminal messages, or not so subliminal given the fact they were so blatant, the more my mind told me that maybe this is the solution to all my problems. If I just had a few plastic surgeries, I too could look that good, I could look just like one of these perfect-looking human beings. Maybe then people would treat me differently, I could become popular, people would want to date me, and everyone would finally love me.

I started to think about this more and more, every day while I walked to the bus station. I would see the signs outside clinics offering deals on plastic surgeries, advertisements showing how easy it was and how it was so accessible. Then I would get home at night, put on the TV, and again watch K-pop shows and see BTS and Jimin appear. I was almost sucked into a whirlpool where all this exposure to the same messaging, "Plastic Surgery, Plastic Surgery, Plastic Surgery," had been drummed into my head like I was part of an MK Ultra brainwashing experiment or some kind of CIA-funded social experiment. My brain was told every minute of every passing day to get plastic surgery, everything was pointing me in that direction, and eventually my resistance levels were worn down.

We know through advertising that if a consumer sees a product over and over again it captures their mind, and they are more likely to buy it because it is familiar and because they have seen the product everywhere. Subliminally, our mind tells us that because this is something familiar like Coca Cola, which we see on a daily basis, we become conditioned to wanting to make the product part of our daily lives. It is a well-known fact in the marketing world that brand familiarity, brand awareness, and brand choice are highly correlated. In a research study, "Brand Familiarity and Advertising: Effects on the Evoked Set and Brand Preference," researchers found a direct link between how often a consumer saw a product correlated with their increased likeliness to want to buy the product and identify with the brand's messaging.[1] I too had been influenced based on advertising exposure to the same product, in this case cosmetic surgery, pressured into wanting to buy and consume the product. With Korea being the plastic surgery capital of the world, with the highest rate of surgeries per capita than any other country, beating surgery hubs like Brazil and Thailand with over one million procedures performed annually, I had no way of escaping my fate, which had now been sealed.[2]

I was clearly not the only one being lured in by these advertisements and convinced that I needed to change myself to achieve happiness, advance my career prospects, and succeed in life. Everyone else was getting the same messages, and if over one in three Koreans have had plastic surgery and thousands of foreigners flocked to the country annually to undergo the knife, then surely we were all being sold this dream.[3] And what about all the K-pop

1   Baker, William, et al. "Brand Familiarity and Advertising: Effects on the Evoked Set and Brand Preference | ACR." *Association for Consumer Research*, ACR, 1986, https://www.acrwebsite.org/volumes/6570. Accessed 18 January 2023.

2   Jacobs, Harrison, and Annie Zheng. "Biggest Misconception About Plastic Surgery in South Korea." *Business Insider*, Insider, 28 June 2018, https://www.businessinsider.com/south-korea-plastic-surgery-gangnam-biggest-misconception-2018-6?r=US&IR=T. Accessed 18 January 2023.

3   Gallup Korea. "Meet the South Korean women rejecting intense beauty standards." *South China Morning Post*, Gallup Poll Korea, 5 February 2019, https://www.scmp.com/news/asia/east-asia/article/2185037/meet-south-korean-women-rejecting-their-countrys-intense-beauty. Accessed 18 January 2023.

stars, whose faces were almost in perfect symmetry, their eyes wide and beautiful, their noses pointed and straight, and their chins sharp and jaw lines defined? While most of these idols would never confess to having surgery, it's common knowledge inside Korea that the vast majority of them do have surgery and they have a manufactured image. Much of what the K-pop industry wanted to present was merely a façade, a warped reality whereby every image, every face, was carefully curated to help sell the dream. So if these K-pop stars were simply manufactured to look that good, I thought I could manufacture and recreate my image to emulate them. It all sounded so easy and so alluring.

I gave in to the dream, I wanted it bad, and I was prepared to do anything. I walked into a clinic near the waterfront in Jeju-si, above a supermarket where I used to get my groceries. I walked past it every week with avid curiosity but never ventured inside. Today was a different kind of day. I wanted to change myself so badly and achieve perfection, and finally I wasn't afraid to do it. I had been saving up my teacher's salary painstakingly each month in preparation for this moment, knowing that every single dollar I had worked so hard for would lead to a lifetime of happiness. I plucked up the courage to finally go inside and entered through the door, then walked across the marble floor and into the elevator. When I arrived at the clinic several floors up, I was mesmerized by the grandeur and opulence of the clinic: it looked like I had accidentally stumbled into an upscale five-star hotel. The wall was plastered with photos of surgeons with Korean celebrities, both pop stars and actors. The nurses at the front desk were a vision in their all-white uniforms, their sharp pointy noses, perfect symmetrical cheeks, and plumped-up lips. I had entered a different world, a far cry from the rural farmlands outside the city where the old ladies farmed cabbages and cared nothing for their appearance, for they had different priorities and more basic needs to meet to simply survive. This was a utopia, a world where everyone looked like a doll or pop star, and I was entering into this world as an outsider desperately hoping to become an insider and look just like them. "Annyeonghaseyo," the receptionist greeted me with a warm, friendly smile. I replied in broken Korean, but she didn't understand me, and I figured it must have been my pronunciation or something. I greeted her again, but she still gave me a blank confused stare. I tried one more time, but clearly my pronunciation was not up to scratch. She left for a moment and returned with an English-speaking nurse who also looked like a manufactured doll. "Welcome to our Clinic, we are happy to have you. How can I help you today?" I asked her, rather sheepishly, if I could arrange a consultation with one of the doctors to discuss my nose, which had bothered me my whole life. She replied with, "Of course, we can do everything here, you name it we can do it. We can make any changes you need and our doctors have years of experience working with some of Korea's biggest celebrities." I was immediately enthralled by her words, then I realized I was staring so deeply into her eyes in awe that I may have come across as rude. I averted my gaze and she then insisted on giving me a tour of the luxurious clinic and offered me some leaflets about the surgeries offered as well as discount packages for combination surgeries (having multiple surgeries at once would give you a bigger discount, thus an incentive to do more). I sat there reading the leaflets and noticed on the coffee table some weird plastic blobs that looked like some alien being or sea creature. I picked one up and squeezed it, then picked the other up and squeezed it, too. It felt good and squishy, and I remember the feeling of being drawn to these silicone objects. I was so naïve at the time, I just thought they were stress relief balls until I realized they were actually silicone breast implants. I immediately put them back on the table and glanced around to see if anyone had seen, feeling embarrassed that someone may have laughed at me for my naïve curiosity. Thankfully no one had noticed, and I stared at them again wanting another feel, but resisting for fear of being seen and judged. I thought about them while I sat and waited and wondered how they must feel once they are inside a person. Did my trans friend, Jintara, whom I had met upon moving to Jeju, have these too and did they feel real once inside? My thoughts started to drift and think about the scenario of what it would be like if I was a woman. Would I feel happier? Would I feel beautiful? Would I feel confident like the women in the clinic? I reflected on my school years of being told I was a girl, feminine, and not a real man, so maybe I was just born in the wrong body, maybe this chance meeting with the two silicone breast implants was a sign from above for me to be a trans woman.

Suddenly, my thoughts were interrupted by the nurse, who had returned. She asked me to fill out a document explaining my concern with my face, and what I wanted to change before she could move me forward with a surgeon. I filled in everything hurriedly, as if the clinic and this opportunity to change could suddenly vanish in the blink of an eye. I wanted the procedure there and then. I gave the form back, and she returned to me ten minutes later: "The doctor will see you now, Oliver." I entered the room, apprehensive yet excited—a mixed bag of emotions, but readier than ever to commit myself to change. The doctor spoke perfect English. He asked me what parts of my face or body concerned me, and I told him everything. I wanted to change everything. He said, "I cannot do that," and I told him that my chest area had always bothered me due to the excess fat around my nipples and that it looked like I had women's breasts. He laughed politely and then asked to see the problem area, so I lifted up my shirt and he examined them. He paused for a breath and then told me I just needed to work out and exercise and the problem would go away. I knew it wouldn't. I had been stuck with these man boobs for the entirety of my life, and I had tried everything. Dieting, gym, cardio, swimming . . .

you name it, and nothing had shifted the excess fatty tissue. It was clear that the doctor wouldn't budge in his belief that I didn't need surgery on this area, so I reluctantly moved on to discuss my face. I told him my nose was my biggest concern because it took up half of my face, the nose tip was so bulbous and protruding, and the bridge was so wonky and bony. He agreed that my nose could look "much better" and explained to me what he could do. He could break the bone along my bridge and shave it down and perform a closed rhinoplasty through my nostrils, slimming them in the process, reducing the size of the tip and pulling in the alar area to make my nose thinner and more symmetrical. This was all music to my ears, I was glad to finally hear this surgeon could do something for me, after he flat-out rejected performing on my chest area. He then said that he could insert a silicone implant along my nose bridge to make it perfectly straight, adding symmetry to my face. At this point I didn't care what he put in my face, although he did offer an alternative to the silicone: pig skin. He told me they had a process using pigs' bone and cartilage to rebuild people's nose bridges instead of using silicone or a patient's own cartilage. This was certainly not for me, and I instantly told the doctor no, sorry, I am a vegetarian, so I will have to go with the silicone. That very moment sealed my fate, and little did I know choosing to have this silicone implant would lead me down a continuous cycle of surgery after surgery trying to fix myself, eventually becoming an addiction and leading to my future gender identity battle.

My consultation ended, and I left the room with an overwhelming feeling of excitement that this was finally going to happen. I arranged an appointment with the nurse and time for my surgery, and she explained the process beforehand and after. It sounded so simple and easy; they even told me I would be home on the same day of surgery. No need to stay overnight in the hospital, which is standard with most plastic surgeries. I would be free to go home, relax, and recuperate. It was perfect. I was soon to become a new person, and one simple surgery would boost my confidence levels, make me feel beautiful, and fix all my problems in one go. Again my naïveté was shining through, just like when I was squeezing the silicone implants without realizing what they were.

I just had to wait two months, until the summer vacation, when I would have time off from my teaching job to have the surgery. I also had two months to save every dollar I earned to pay for the surgery. It seemed like a long time to wait, and it was; each day got longer and longer until the anticipation became almost unbearable. Sixty days seemed like six hundred days, but I knew it was well worth the wait for a lifetime of happiness and to look like a beautiful K-pop star. During the two months prior to this life-changing procedure, I reflected a lot on the doctor's words about my male breasts and how I didn't need surgery and simple exercise would work. I didn't believe it would work, but I was determined to try whatever I could anyway. I started working out intensely at the gym, two hours every evening after work. I even got a personal trainer; he was Korean, but his name was Terry. It didn't sound very Korean, far more English than Korean. But I had grown accustomed to Koreans having English names: it was very commonplace, and they pretty much all had a Korean name and an English one. Many of them had made pretty unusual choices for names, older names that would typically be associated with the Victorian age such as Arthur, Clyde, Bryce, Ethel, Walter, and Josephine. I found it very endearing that they chose such names, but quite sad at the same time. I would also call them by their Korean name, which I thought was more respectful, because it's the name they were assigned at birth, and a name from their own culture. I thought calling them by a different, English name almost took away their cultural identity, stripped them of their Korean-ness, and made them seem westernized just like everyone else around the world. Yet I grew to realize that Koreans often identified more with westernized societies and cultures than their own. Even many of the surgeries they had were to give them more of a westernized or Caucasian look.

As I pondered these questions, triggered by meeting Terry and other Koreans with English names, I continued on my countdown to my surgery. The days were going by slowly, I was working out to kill time and lose weight, trying to shift my chest fat. It wasn't enough, so I decided to drastically reduce my food and calorie intake. I cut out practically every source of protein, milk, eggs, nuts—absolutely everything. I put myself on a crash diet consisting of heated rice in milk (rice pudding) for breakfast, a bowl of rice for lunch with a few Korean vegetables (spinach, pickled cabbage, and bean sprouts), and a bowl of rice with tomato ketchup on top for dinner. This was all I ate for two months, with the hope that if I lost my man boobs and got a new nose at the same time, everyone would be amazed by my transformation and everyone would love me and give me the attention I had been missing my whole life. I continued with my workouts, and they were getting more intense each time, given that my personal trainer was upping the number of sets and reps and increasing weights each week. I was running on no protein and merely rice to keep me going, so it was tough, but I continued to keep it up with the hope of losing all my fat and looking like a brand new person, just like a K-pop star—manufactured to perfection.

The day had almost arrived. After repeating the same extreme diet and intense workout day in and day out, I had lost so much weight—42 pounds (4 stone), a drastic change and adjustment—yet I was starting to feel beautiful. I loved the new me, and the chest fat, though still visible, had reduced significantly, and my face had much less puppy fat than before. I had failed to realize that other people around me, especially my loved ones back in England and my friends in Korea, thought otherwise. They grew increasingly concerned with my weight loss, thinking I was going through a crisis and suffering from anorexia. And I was—I just didn't realize or admit to it at the time, yet another symptom of my low self-esteem and my identity. I had become a skeleton, literally and figuratively. There was barely any meat left on my bones. My family grew extremely concerned after I posted some pictures of my new look online and were so worried and anxious that they planned to come to Korea to bring me home and save me from myself. I strongly resisted their plans to visit and managed to convince them I was "fine," that I had just been working out a lot and the Korean diet and food didn't have much protein.

My family continued to remain worried but had no idea of what I was about to do and that I was about to alter my face completely. They had never been to Korea, they had never seen or experienced the wonders of plastic surgery, and I thought they wouldn't understand my actions. So better to keep it secret and surprise them with the new me; otherwise, they may have tried to stop me, and that would shatter my dreams.

After a few more days of anxious anticipation, the day was almost upon me. I had one final appointment with the doctor to talk through the procedure again and receive pre- and post-operative instructions. I was instructed to stop drinking all liquids by midnight the night before, have my last meal by 8:00 p.m., and prepare some comfortable clothes for the day of operation. I tried to sleep that night, but it was almost impossible with the range of thoughts pacing through my mind and the dryness of my throat from lack of water. I kept imagining various scenarios in my head of how the operation would go. Would it be painful? Would it go wrong? Would I accidentally wake up during the surgery in agony? Would I die under the knife? My naïveté and lack of experience ever going to a hospital and having any procedure, let alone a major plastic surgery, made my nerves get the better of me. I was naïve, I had many questions, I was unsure. I kept thinking, *What if I die? What if I don't wake up?* But then another part of my brain would tell me, *Take the risk, it doesn't matter what happens, it's worth it for a lifetime of happiness.* I knew I couldn't go on for much longer living with such a heavy burden on my shoulders—that feeling of worthlessness, of being ugly, of being unattractive was what made me go on and still want this procedure more than anything.

Unable to sleep, I got out of bed and started writing a letter to my family and loved ones just in case I didn't make it. Just in case I never woke up again. I had seen statistics that one in a hundred thousand people die under anesthesia, and I convinced myself that my luck, which had continued since I moved to Korea, could finally run out and I would be that one in one hundred thousand.[4] Writing the letter, I felt an enormous sense of worry in my mind, then tears started to run down my eyes. What if I really didn't make it? How would my loved ones feel? I had to write everything I was feeling in the letter just in case I became that frightful statistic. I sealed the letter in an envelope and left it on my kitchen table hoping that no one would ever have to read it, because I was going to be okay, it was just a surgery, after all, and Korean doctors do this all the time. The logical side of me started to break through and convinced me to take a deep breath and stay calm, especially given that I needed to keep my blood pressure down before anesthesia. I went back to bed and managed to get a few hours of sleep.

I woke up at 6:00 a.m., hungry and thirsty but remembering that I could not have food or water, as that was the clear instruction from the doctor. I dressed, brushed my teeth, and packed my backpack, ready for the big day and excited that the day was finally

---

4   St Heles Hospital. "Risks associated with young anesthetic: Death or Brain Damage." *NHS*, NHS, 6 January 2023, https://www.sthk.nhs.uk/media/.leaflets /62e91e40358572.82183176.pdf. Accessed 18 January 2023.

here. As I arrived at the hospital, the same perfect-looking nurses greeted me and ushered me into a small room to change into the surgical gown. Then the anesthesiologist came in and checked my blood pressure and vitals to make sure I was fit enough to operate on. He then explained to me that they would be using a local anesthetic, not a general one. I asked him to explain the difference between the two, and he told me I would be semiconscious throughout the procedure, but I wouldn't feel any pain and would remain in a dream-like state. It was better, he told me, it's easier to wake up, safer, and it was only a nose surgery—they did this all the time, just like someone getting filler or Botox.

Everything happened so fast I didn't have time to really process the fact I would be under local anesthetic for a major surgery. I didn't even want to think about being "semiconscious," or the possibility of hearing or seeing the surgeon and his team operating on me. The surgeon then came in and spoke to me pre-surgery, reassuring me that he does this all the time, not to worry, and I will be happy with the new nose and the new me. I trusted him; he seemed so knowledgeable and honest. Then came the time for the nurses to come in along with the anesthesiologist to administer the anesthetic, ready for my procedure.

Chapter 13

Under the Influence: Body Dysmorphia

Korea is without a doubt the plastic surgery capital of the world. Gangnam district in Seoul has over seventy plastic surgery clinics in just a few square kilometers. Korea as a whole has over 2,500 plastic surgeons, the fifth highest number of any country. Living in Korea, you cannot avoid the constant pressure to have surgery. Every street corner has a clinic, every subway station has dozens of advertisements for quick, easy, and inexpensive makeovers that can leave you looking like a K-pop star. I soon fell for the dream being sold to me, that anyone can be beautiful for a small price. An estimated one in five Koreans have undergone surgery, with the most popular procedures being double eyelid surgeries and rhinoplasties. Most Koreans had surgery to achieve the "Hollywood Look," predominantly Caucasian features, which had been sold to them through Hollywood movies, fashion magazines, and the media. I, on the other hand, didn't want the Hollywood look; I wanted the Korean K-pop aesthetic. Effeminate, symmetrical, and aesthetically pleasing.

The time had come. I was wheeled into the operating room, a small room in the hospital next to the doctor's office where I initially had my first meeting. I was positioned in the middle of the room, under lights that shone brightly above. I was then administered the anesthetic. I didn't know what to expect or how to feel, as I had never had anesthetic before. I started to feel sleepy and relaxed and calm, yet I still had some level of consciousness; it was a surreal feeling. An anesthesia mask was placed over my mouth, ready for the operation to begin. I was still semiconscious; though I couldn't talk or open my eyes, I could still hear everything that was going on, though some of the sounds were muffled. The operation took around ninety minutes, and I remember the whole time hearing the chisel being bashed into my bone, hearing the saw shaving my nose bridge down, and the indistinct chatter of the surgeon speaking Korean. It felt like I was under the knife for hours upon hours, and to this very day I remember the sounds of my bones being broken, the sound of my flesh being cut like slabs of meat in a butcher's shop. It was like a horror movie, being able to hear and experience being butchered and cut up. When I finally came around and regained consciousness, I felt confused and disoriented, feeling as if I had been abducted by aliens.

I couldn't regain my speech right away, but I was wheeled into a waiting room with a bed for me to lie down in and allow the effects of the anesthetic to wear off. I waited for several hours, slowly regaining my speech and coming back to Earth. After around two hours passed, a nurse came in along with the surgeon and told me everything had gone well and according to plan and that I was going to be really happy with the results. I was then told I would be discharged to go home and would be given some ice packs to help reduce the swelling that would appear under my eyes.

I found a taxi back to my apartment and felt exhausted, like I had been beaten up or hit by a car, and I feared what my reflection would look like in the mirror when I eventually got back to my apartment. When I arrived, the old man who worked as concierge/

security, who couldn't speak a word of English but was always smiling and upbeat, looked at me with a shocked expression and said some Korean phrases to me. I guessed that he was trying to ask, "What happened?" but I just tried to reassure him I was fine with a thumbs up and mustered a smile.

I opened the door to my apartment, and my first instinct was to go to the mirror and stare at my reflection. My old obsession with mirrors had never gone away, and I would spend hours a day looking at my reflection and picking out faults with my features. Today was going to be hard, to see myself with bandages and dried blood and the swelling that would appear overnight. I glanced in the microwave glass to get a hint of what I looked like, then went into the bathroom for a long, hard gaze at the new me. I was shocked but mesmerized by what I saw. A hard cast covered my nose, some dried blood in my nostrils and redness around my eyes, but surprisingly, I looked fresh-faced and radiant, and my skin was glowing. While I couldn't see what the nose looked like under the cast, I could already tell it was smaller than my original bulbous nose, much smaller. I smiled slightly and then got into bed feeling an enormous sense of relief.

When I woke up the next day, as the surgeon had predicted, my face was swollen, my eyes were puffy with black and yellow bruising underneath, my cheeks were inflamed, and my eyes felt sore. I thought I looked like Frankenstein, like a science experiment that had gone wrong. But I thought, *At least it's an improvement on what I looked like before. I would rather look like Frankenstein than Oliver, anything had to be better and more attractive than that.*

At the time I didn't realize, but I had severe body dysmorphia, which later led to severe gender dysphoria in my thirties. Body dysmorphic disorder (BDD) is a mental health condition that typically affects teenagers and young adolescents by making them spend unhealthy amounts of time obsessing over the way they look. The condition often gets misdiagnosed and dismissed as a person simply being self-obsessed or a narcissist. People who suffer from this disorder spend an overly obsessive amount of time being self-critical, looking for flaws in their appearance.[1] Many of these flaws are often unnoticeable to others. Those with BDD also go to a lot of effort to try and conceal their flaws in order to hide their perceived imperfections from others. For example, a person who is critical of their own nose may conceal it as much as possible by using makeup contouring techniques, sunglasses to hide the size of their nose, or even wearing hats to conceal their face. They go out of their way to make this concealment part of their everyday life and often spend hours endlessly staring in the mirror, thinking of ways to try and reduce the flaw, including considering plastic surgery to remove the perceived imperfection. However, many people with BDD, like myself, don't realize that concealment and even having surgery on the area to try and remove the problem never actually solves the problem itself because it means the person dedicates even more time to that area they dislike and always have reminders about their perceived flaw. There is no miracle cure for BDD, and plastic surgery can even make the obsession worse, as my story demonstrates. Gender dysphoria goes hand in hand with body dysmorphia because it involves a state of severe distress, despondency, feeling unhappy with your body, and having feelings of low self-esteem based on feeling trapped in the wrong gender identity. There are often many parallels, including spending long periods of time looking in the mirror and trying to conceal areas of the body that remind a person of their biological sex, such as girls who feel they should be boys wearing chest binders to conceal their breasts. Those suffering

1   Mayo Clinic. "Body dysmorphic disorder—Symptoms and causes." *Mayo Clinic*, Mayo Clinic, 13 December 2022, https://www.mayoclinic.org/diseases-conditions /body-dysmorphic-disorder/symptoms-causes/syc-20353938. Accessed 19 January 2023.

from gender dysphoria also have a profound need for society to accept them as another gender, to reinforce in their mind that others around them recognize what they are going through in order to conceal their true identity, which they struggle to come to terms with.

Looking back on this time after I had this first surgery and compared with my time as a teenager, when I became obsessed with my nose, and with the red swelling on it that looked like boils, I remembered that my family and friends would always tell me I never had any redness on my nose, there were no bumps, spots, or boils. It was simply all a figment of my imagination, and my nose suited my face and was not noticeably oversized. Had I listened to those closest to me, perhaps my life would have taken a different path. Perhaps I would never have ended up in the position I am in today, covered in scars across my face and body, titanium screws holding my facial bones in place, and having self-harmed myself through over thirty-two surgeries. If I had realized I was suffering from a general mental health disorder, body dysmorphia, and tried to get treatment for that, maybe I could have found happiness with who I was, without the need to have gone to such an extreme.

The majority of people who suffer from this warped sense of self are teens, and the symptoms include: avoiding social activities, constantly comparing oneself to others, having unnecessary plastic surgeries, feeling severely depressed and crippling anxiety, and trying to hide body parts or facial features from view.[2] I certainly had all these symptoms and more as I grew older, and as my social media continued to grow, these symptoms became more and more severe. As with many young people today, we start to compare ourselves

---

2   John Hopkins Medicine. "Body Dysmorphic Disorder." *Johns Hopkins Medicine*, https://www.hopkinsmedicine.org/health/conditions-and-diseases/body-dysmorphic -disorder. Accessed 19 January 2023.

with people we see on Instagram and TikTok, we see these perfect-looking influencers and then compare ourselves to them, often judging ourselves harshly and developing feelings of anxiety and depression for not looking as good as they.

So many young people are now experiencing body dysmorphia, many of them undiagnosed and having to suffer alone. Many will no doubt go on wanting to change the way they look or even their identity in order to try to feel better about themselves. Whether by resorting to plastic surgery or changing gender, the way we view ourselves in our younger years has a dramatic impact in shaping the person we become. We need to remove the stigma of BDD and gender dysphoria; we need to make social media, magazines, pop culture, and advertisements more realistic and representative of real people with all their flaws being celebrated. We need a world where people can thrive without the constant need for filters and plastic surgery. We also need to show these young kids that looks aren't everything, that chasing perfection can destroy a person, and instead these young people should focus on who they are inside and ignore the façade of their outside appearance. If we as a collective society can overcome these obstacles, this need to look filtered and perfect, then we can help younger generations avoid having to deal with dysphoria like those I experienced and we can avoid future generations making mistakes that many may grow to regret. Instead, we can help these people flourish as the people they were born as.

I certainly grew up in a time before social media was what it is today, before young people had smartphones and an addiction to watching fifteen-second videos on TikTok and scrolling endlessly through Instagram's explore page. Yet even in my time, the age of Myspace and Facebook, I still spent an unhealthy amount of time taking photos, adding filters, and seeking online validation. Now I struggle to think how difficult it must be for children to accept themselves the way they were born, given the tremendous pressure pushed on them from social media, influencers, and celebrity culture. We need to move away from putting these pressures on kids and help them focus on more important things like education, sports, playing outdoors, and reading books. Only then can we overcome the body dysmorphia and gender dysphoria epidemic.

Chapter 14

Warped Expectations

My battle with body dysmorphia was about to get a whole lot worse. Seven days after undergoing my very first surgery, I was ready for the grand unveiling. I was nervous, excited, and optimistic, ready for the first day of the rest of my life as a new person—happy, confident, and beautiful. I headed to the clinic with a sparkle in my eyes, knowing that all my issues would finally be over after this quick fix that would cure all my problems for the rest of my life, or so I was led to believe. Today was the day I would finally prove all the bullies wrong and would finally be able to share the new me with the world. The clinic staff greeted me, and one of the ladies who spoke English said how excited they were for me and how happy they were to see my new look. I walked into the doctor's office and sat down to speak with him. He asked me how my recovery had gone, and I told him it went well, that it wasn't too painful and the medication he prescribed helped a lot. He then proceeded to get his medical tools to remove the cast and started pulling it off. The moment it was off I was anxious to touch it and feel to check how small it was. He told me not to touch, as he had to remove stitches from my nose tip and inside my nose. He plucked each one quickly, with no pause for a break in between each painful pluck. Finally, when the last one was out, he put his hands firmly around my nose bridge and pushed the implant side to side, then did the same with my nose tip, explaining to me that this was to massage the swelling and help it go down. He then reached for the mirror, and I was ready for the moment of truth.

He held a mirror in front of me and I started to cry, though they were much less tears of joy or happiness than tears of shock. I was in disbelief; my nose was much smaller and pointier, but what struck me most was the fact that it was completely crooked—my dream of a straight, beautiful nose was crushed. But then the doctor explained to me that I shouldn't worry, that it was just swelling and it would straighten out over time. His words gave me comfort, and I figured he must be right because, after all, he was a highly respected plastic surgeon and must perform these surgeries all day, every day. He told me not to worry and that when I came back to my follow-up appointment he would give me steroid injections to help reduce the swelling; this was all I needed to reassure me. *Everything will be totally fine*, I told myself, *I should just be happy that my old bulbous nose is gone forever. Surely anything, even a crooked nose, would be better than that.*

A week went by, my nose was still crooked and uneven, the silicone implant inside had clearly been misplaced, and the surgery had gone wrong. When I went to the clinic for my follow-up appointment, I was injected with steroids and offered a new nose surgery for free in six months if I still wasn't happy. As if this wasn't enough to appease me, the doctor offered to give me free laser treatments to remove the moles on my body that I had complained about. Thanks to my body dysmorphia, I had always been highly self-critical of my body and had developed an unusual phobia of skin moles, so the offer to make these disappear forever was too alluring. I took the doctor up on the offer and had several treatments, and he continued to give me steroid injections in my nose, but still it did nothing to fix the botched implant.

As I recovered and the weeks went by, I felt a mixed bag of emotions. On the one hand I was happy that at least my nose was thinner and smaller, but on the other hand my mind became consumed with, and my eyes transfixed on, my crooked nose tip and nose bridge, and I then began obsessing about the next surgery. This was the beginning of my nine-year battle with plastic surgery addiction, spurred on by my first disastrous operation.

Had the procedure gone well in the first place, would I have really developed such an all-consuming addiction with wanting to change every single feature of my face? Or would I have been satisfied, happy, and confident if it had gone right, and never questioned my looks and identity again? In reflection, I think that this one botched procedure definitely contributed to me undergoing an additional five rhinoplasties later on in my life to try and "fix" my nose, yet I wonder if I would have stopped after the first one. Or was the body dysmorphia and the onset of gender dysphoria I would later experience so cemented in my mind that I was destined to continue on my future path to changing everything about me?

This now leads me to question body dysmorphia as a whole and those who suffer from it, the driving force behind the drastic rise in plastic surgery across societies, and whether doctors have a medical and moral responsibility to check if someone is suffering from this before operating. Or is body dysmorphia a benefit to the business models of plastic surgery clinics, helping to drive sales and push more and more young people into surgery? Are the vulnerabilities, self-esteem issues, and identity struggles of younger generations part of the cosmetic surgery's business model and would they lose half of their customer base if they simply decided that those with severe body dysmorphia or gender dysphoria were not suitable

125

candidates for operations, due to their irrational thought processes and mental health struggles?

From my experience, I know that anyone suffering from BDD will stop at nothing until they get what they want. I should know this firsthand, after I traveled to five different countries to have surgery, in search of doctors who would say yes to my often unrealistic and unhealthy demands. Countries such as China and Armenia, where I underwent procedures, have far fewer safeguards for protecting patients and a lower standard and duty of care. So I had gone out of the UK, where many top clinics and surgeons had said no to my demands, to find doctors who would do anything I wanted and just say yes.

We need to protect young people from themselves and from making these difficult, life-altering decisions without a second thought, wanting to follow a trend or look like their favorite Instagram model or celebrity. Having more conversations about self-acceptance, feeling comfortable in your own skin, and more transparency with social media influencers, perhaps requiring a label when a filter or Photoshop is used, could help teens come to terms with much of what they see online and help them to realize that many of the celebrities and influencers we see are presenting an unrealistic and unattainable look.

Chapter 15

Snowball Effect

My dream of becoming a K-pop star was still far away. My first surgery had gone horribly wrong, and my nose was slanted, yet despite this I still felt like it was an improvement on my original nose. Over the next several years, my body dysmorphia became far more severe, and I planned and plotted in my head how I could fix the way I looked and how I could eventually find lasting happiness. After living in Korea for a year, I moved to London, ready to start a new career. I needed to begin a career that would fund my desire to completely alter my appearance. I knew it would be an expensive journey, considering what I had envisioned, and I knew my family would in no way support me with what I had planned, after seeing how upset they were with my first nose surgery in Korea. One of the friends I had at university, Monica, was working in the fashion industry in London and had a high-paying, successful job with her own personal shopping business. I had always had an interest in fashion, particularly women's clothes. From my childhood when I would dress up in women's dresses and wish I was a girl, through my college years when I would read celebrity magazines, paying close attention to what my favorite female celebrity idols like Paris Hilton were wearing, watching *The Devil Wears Prada* on repeat, and binge-watching one of my favorite TV series of all time, *Ugly Betty*. I was never interested in what the men were wearing in any of these magazines, movies, or TV shows—it was always an inquisitive interest in the women. I messaged Monica to see if we could meet for a coffee, as I had just moved to the city and didn't know anyone, and she willingly obliged.

When we met, she told me stories of the high-profile celebrities she had dressed from Kim Kardashian and Demi Moore to Charlize Theron. I was truly enthralled as she recounted each story and how successful she had become. I wanted to do what she was doing, help dress the world's most successful and beautiful women and be around beautiful clothing, which I hoped I could try on and feel empowered by. But there was one problem: I was still shy, lacked the confidence needed for a job like this, and hated when large numbers of people saw my face, even more so now that my nose was crooked. But I needed to do something with my life. I wasn't in Korea anymore, where I had been happy and living a completely different lifestyle; I was back in my home country, and I had to start somewhere. I asked her if she had any job openings at her company for me that she thought would be a good fit. She paused for a moment while I waited with bated breath. "You know, Oli, I have always liked you. You have always been a hard worker, polite, kind, and always friendly. I think you would be great as an assistant to one of the stylists on my team. You just need to follow their instructions, collect various dresses, bring them to the clients, and help organize their daily schedule." I was delighted that anyone would think so highly of me. She then asked me to come in for a trial day the following week, and I willingly obliged.

The trial day was tough because there was a lot of different information to take in, but I was a hard worker, so I diligently tried to do everything correctly. I followed the stylist, Tamara, around for the day. Packing clothing items for her clients, following her as she went to a client's house to dress them for events, and booking taxis for her throughout the day. I felt like it was a job I was well suited to; I was the shadow, not the star, of the show, which is what I wanted. I was just like Ugly Betty, the fashion assistant at *Mode Magazine*. Like Betty, I was an outcast, someone who had been mocked their whole life, but despite all that, someone who did their job diligently and always kept a positive can-do attitude. I wanted to blend into the background, not being noticed while admiring from afar these beautiful women and their dazzling gowns. I felt like I was living inside a real-life fashion magazine.

After the day ended, Tamara thanked me and said she would speak to Monica and get back to me. The next day, I received a call from Monica saying they would be delighted if I joined the team as Tamara's assistant. I immediately said yes, and this led to the next four years of my life in the fashion industry, from 2014 to 2018, where I eventually worked my way up to become a successful personal shopper running my own shopping business. Over the years working in this industry, I met some of the world's most famous women and helped them dress for red carpets, galas, and film festivals. I dressed the girlfriend of the Prime Minister of Thailand, met Queen Beatrix of the Netherlands, Kim Kardashian, African First Ladies, the Prime Minister of Bangladesh, and a variety of successful, powerful women. I was fascinated by this world of glamour, beauty, femininity, and empowerment. I loved being surrounded by so many successful and accomplished women, which led me to wish more and more that I could one day be like them. If only I could rewind the clock and be reborn as a successful woman who could change the world—a woman with so much beauty, grace, and glamour.

During my work as a personal shopper, I met Aliia Roza, who would become and remains to this day my best friend and mentor. She was an ultraglamorous and elegant entrepreneur originally from

Russia who had a successful real estate empire as well as numerous philanthropic organizations. She would shop with me every week, choosing the most dazzling dresses that fitted her supermodel body with incredible ease. Everything looked good on her; she had the body of a goddess and the confidence of a queen. She was a joy to work with, always giving me compliments about how great I was at making women feel good, and how kind I was, always treating her with respect, kindness, and compassion. Not only was she one of my best clients, but she also became my best friend. She would invite me to her philanthropic events and fundraisers sponsored by some of the world's most luxurious brands: Cartier, Chopard, Roberto Cavalli, Damiani, Azzedine Alaia, Louis Vuitton, and so many others. She was an incredible event host, always taking the time to ensure every guest felt welcome and happy. She would always introduce me to her contacts, and thanks to her I was able to meet many future clients for my personal shopping business. She knew everyone, from royalty to billionaires to film stars and beyond, and introduced me to a whole new glamorous world.

Over the next few years my personal shopping business grew, and soon I was working seven days a week dressing some of the world's most beautiful and successful women. I had saved up so much money, and my future was finally starting to look bright. But the more I was around such beauty, where everyone's standards and looks were impeccable, the more I realized I did not fit into this world. I could never look as good as these women, no matter how well I dressed. My face let me down; I was a thorn amongst roses, and something had to change because I wanted to fit into this beautiful elegant world so badly and wanted to be one of them.

As a personal shopper, I would fly around the world and each time try to fix myself along the way, having surgery after surgery in my quest for perfection. I set out on an obsessive mission to fix my nose and fix the rest of my face and one surgery led to another, and each time it would go "wrong" in my mind and I would be forced to fix it. A snowball effect. In psychology the term is used to describe how small actions can lead to bigger and bigger actions being taken, resulting in an unstoppable path and a more extreme result.[1] I was like this ball of snow, rolling down a hill at an unstoppable speed. The more surgeries I had, the more extreme I would want to go each time. I started out with my next two surgeries, both revision rhinoplasties. The first one was in Shanghai, China, in 2015, where I had the silicone implant removed and replaced with cartilage from my own ear. I still wasn't satisfied, so I went for another "fix" in the city of Wroclaw, Poland, in 2016, with a plastic surgeon whom I can only describe as a "butcher." As I entered the Polish clinic there were at least two dozen people sitting in the waiting room, many with casts on their noses, bandages around their faces, or casts on their breasts. At first glance, it looked like I was in some kind of factory, where plastic surgery patients were pumped out at record speeds. A place where profit was put over principles. Still, it was too late for me to turn back; I had traveled all the way here and thought anything had to be better than the current botched nose I had been cursed with. I was ushered into the doctor's office for my first and only meeting with him before the operation. The consultation lasted a meager five minutes. He inspected my nose, looked at each angle, told me what he was going to do to fix it, and then my consultation was over. No in-depth examination, no interest in what my expectations were as a paying customer and as a patient, and no attempt to even ask me what results I was hoping to achieve. It was a factory, and I was just a product that needed to be pumped out of the production line quickly, so that he could move on to the

---

1   Guy, Olivia, and Saul Mcleod, PhD. "Snowball Effect." *Simply Psychology*, 19 July 2022, https://www.simplypsychology.org/snowball-effect.html. Accessed 28 January 2023.

next patient, then the next one. There was simply no duty of care or code of ethics governing this clinic; it was simply about quick profit and then throwing the patient out the door. This doctor and clinic were the very definition of a snowball effect, as they clearly had only one priority—profit. But at this stage I was both naïve and desperate, and I ignored the blatant red flags, took a deep breath, and hoped for the best.

Surgery day came, and after my blood tests were done and my vitals checked, I was ready to go into the operating room—or the butcher's shop, as I would later call it. After waking up disoriented from the anesthesia, I saw that I was in a room with another patient, who had just had a gynecomastia procedure (male breast reduction), something I would go on to have a few years later. I was in pain, and I felt nauseated from the effects of the anesthesia still in my body. After coming round and managing to sip some water, I remember my head throbbing with pain. When I was discharged the next day, I was given just a few Tramadol tablets to ease the pain and told to come back four days later. After what seemed like an eternity of sleepless nights, severe headaches, and swelling, four days passed and I headed to the clinic for a checkup. The doctor said he was going to remove the cast and bandages because he wouldn't be able to do it on another day, as he was going on vacation. From all my research I knew this was a red flag because the dressing was meant to stay on the nose for at least seven days after an operation to help keep everything in place. The doctor didn't seem to care and was in a rush to remove it. I then looked in the mirror and, just like my last two surgeries, I was horrified. But this was by far the worst I had ever had, as my nose had doubled in size, and it was covered in open wounds from incisions that the doctor had made on the outside of my nose. He didn't do a closed rhinoplasty, which is the best method to avoid scarring. Instead, he had butchered my entire nose, and to this day I have cartilage and scarring coming out of the side of my nose. I was horrified, but what could I do now? It was too late to go back in time. After the initial shock and disappointment, I walked through the exit, never to return.

Months passed by, and my nose looked completely destroyed. What had I done to myself? The snowball effect had reached full speed, and it showed no signs of slowing. The clinic and the doctor never contacted me again to ask me about my recovery and whether or not I was happy with the result; they simply did not care. My results and happiness were not of any concern to them. They were too focused on getting the next patients through the door and then the next ones after that. Sadly, we are seeing more clinics adopt this attitude, especially when it comes to gender clinics, where duty of care is often cast aside to focus purely on generating profit and pumping patients in and out of the clinic at record speeds. Greed has become commonplace when patient care should be the first and only priority.

I arrived back in England feeling destroyed and disillusioned after another surgery that had gone wrong. I was hopeless and feeling far worse about myself than I did before; the body dysmorphia only increased each time I underwent surgery and each time it went wrong. It was a repetitive cycle that I never seemed to be able to fully escape. Over the next two years, as I continued with my personal shopping business and continued to be surrounded by beauty and glamour, I felt worse and worse about how I looked after my botched surgeries and became determined to try and fix it.

Around this time, when I began reclaiming old habits and falling back into depression, my father walked out on my family one day, never to return. There was no explanation, no note left on the table, and no reasoning for the abruptness—he simply vanished. This left my mother in despair. Despite his years of abuse, a victim will still mourn the loss of their partner no matter how cruel they were because their whole identity becomes intertwined with their abuser. I was never able to fully process this moment or talk about it openly with anyone. On the one hand, I felt an enormous sense of relief that my mother was free from her oppressor and that I was free from his control, but on the other, I felt like my whole world was collapsing. I always strongly believed in maintaining the family unit and doing whatever it takes to keep a family together, but this was out of my control, and I would struggle to process the moment over the next few years of my life, pushing it to the back of my mind and instead turning to what I always turned to—surgery.

• • •

My next surgeries took place two years later, in 2018. Again, I left the UK to find a surgeon who would say yes to my demands. Many of the UK doctors I had consulted had all told me that they wouldn't operate on me because my nose would collapse. So, I ended up in Yerevan, Armenia. This time I was going for my fourth nose surgery and finally, gynecomastia, liposuction, and areola (nipple) correction. This surgery could have ended my life: the old Soviet-era hospital that used clearly outdated and basic technology; the operating room that looked like something out of a horror story; the recovery period when I was unable to move an inch for days with no one checking to see if I was okay or needed help; and the moment the doctor ripped out the plastic drains from my nipples and left me convulsing in excruciating pain. This experience left me with deep traumas, and I vowed that this was it. This was the final change I would make; I would not risk my life ever again for vanity. Yet just one year later, my promise was undone.

Chapter 16

Korean Clone

It was December 2018, and I was desperate to start a new chapter in my life. I was longing for a new look and to pursue my true passion in life, becoming a K-pop idol. A chance introduction to a top London-based music producer felt like a sign from the heavens that it was meant to be. My friend Aliia had introduced me to the producer, Scott, who worked with Eurovision singers, pop stars, boy bands, R&B artists, and various talents from the nineties and early 2000s. After meeting with him and discussing my interest in making K-pop music, he jumped at the chance, having a passion for exploring new music genres and creating something fresh. I started spending long sessions in the studio, writing lyrics, trying to find the right beat and sound until finally we came up with the right recipe for success—my debut title track, "Perfection."

I gave up my personal shopping career to pursue a career in K-pop, my biggest passion, and hoped I could become a successful K-pop idol. I still didn't have the desired look I wanted, but I couldn't wait any longer for another operation to fail and make me look even worse, so I pressed ahead. I covered myself in layers of makeup, high fashion, peroxide blonde hair, and airbrushed myself to the maximum level until I was finally ready to make my first-ever music video. My dream was coming one step closer to reality. After filming for four days solid and patiently waiting for it to be edited, it was finally ready for release on February 3, 2019. The initial reaction was positive, with many of my fans saying how much they loved it and how the catchy chorus hook, "Pa-Pa-Perfection," stayed in their heads all day long. It felt good to finally be receiving praise and finally be living my dream. But, as I should have predicted, it was short-lived. I was hit with a wave of negativity, mocking the way I looked, tearing apart my vocals and visual presentation, and calling it "the worst song ever made." Most of the comments were focused on my appearance, saying I looked like a "melted candle" or a "wax doll." I then promised myself that I would not release another music video until I changed my entire face, until I could finally look like a K-pop idol and people could appreciate me. While "Perfection" received over 2.5 million views on YouTube and helped launch me as a K-pop artist, allowing me to subsequently launch my own successful merch range including cute K-pop t-shirts, tote bags, signed photo cards, and even backpacks, I knew the only way I would ever be happy was to alter the way I looked more than ever before.

As my song continued to go viral and I became increasingly known in the K-pop world, the barrage of hate regarding my appearance only worsened. So I decided it was time for another change, a completely new face that I hoped would finally remove all my insecurities and make people accept me. I thought if I could look like a K-pop idol and look as good as they did, maybe people would finally love and accept me and maybe the bullying would stop. I also wanted to look more feminine, typical of the K-pop idol look, as I had always felt more in touch with my feminine side and questioned my gender identity throughout much of my life.

I traveled back to Korea in the summer of 2019, ready to undergo five painful and drastic procedures that would change my face forever and even change my bone structure completely. Mandible angle (cheekbone) reduction, T-osteotomy (chin shaving), zygoma (cheekbone) reduction, facial bone contouring, and a revision rhinoplasty. I was having a major identity crisis, and my gender dysphoria and body dysmorphia had kicked in and were telling me I needed to look more feminine, more beautiful, and have the Korean aesthetic, which typically has softer, more feminine features, smaller facial bone structure, and sharper-shaped jaws. I convinced myself again that this was the end game, that after this I would be happy. But I was now starting to question my very own identity: Was I born in the wrong body or wrong country? Whatever I was going through, I was going to the wrong places for answers; plastic surgery was only going to give me a temporary fix to my problems. Maybe I should have seen a therapist or spoken to someone about my issues, but alas I chose not to and continued down my destructive path to erase every aspect of my identity. I never attended any therapy sessions in my life because I never liked talking about my problems to others, instead preferring to keep my feelings bottled up so I alone could have the burden and I alone could deal with it. Had I had the hindsight I do now, therapy would have been the most helpful thing I could have done and could have helped stop my self-destructiveness in its tracks. I didn't even consult with my friends or family for fear of people dismissing me or trying to stop me on my mission to alter myself completely, especially given the fact my family tried, rightly so, to stop my first surgery all those years ago in Korea.

Instead, I went through with the extreme procedures and was unable to talk for two weeks afterward, struggled to drink water without it dripping down my chin and onto my chest, and was on a liquid diet due to my jaw surgery, which had broken my jaw and chin bones to improve my look and make it more of a Korean aesthetic. This time, I was happy with the results. In fact, I was overjoyed. I had a much smaller, cuter face with more symmetry than before. Even my nose was much better, though I was still critical of the shape and still thought I should have made it smaller.

I spent the next two months recovering in Seoul, the Korean capital, enjoying my new-found confidence and new Korean-inspired aesthetic before finally heading back to the UK with my new look. Although again, this would be another short-lived feeling, and soon the elation I felt after the surgery would wear off and I would be longing for more—more extreme, more invasive, and more appearance altering.

After dozens of plastic surgeries and an increasing thirst for more, I was starting to look like a Korean pop idol—or, at least my mind told me so at the time. I felt that after years of trying and years of longing, I had truly taken the necessary steps to assimilate with Korean culture and even look like a K-pop star. I was even releasing my own Korean pop music and becoming an increasingly well-known figure amongst the K-pop community. Maybe dreams do come true. Maybe I could find happiness with my new identity, and indeed my dreams had finally turned into reality. I reminisced about the wishes I had back in 2013, during my first time living in Korea. I had wished for my life to change, I had wished to look like a K-pop idol and wished to exude confidence and become successful. These wishes had finally come true, and my dreams were becoming a reality.

This was a turning point for me, as I had achieved the impossible. I had eradicated the old me, removed all semblance of my old identity, removed all traces of my father, changed my face, changed the way I lived my life, and finally I was a new person, reborn. In 2021 I announced my new identity to the world, using the same logic of the self-identification and nonbinary community, who say you can literally identify as anything and people must respect it. The response to me saying I wanted to have a Korean aesthetic and that I felt like I belonged more in Korean society, more so than my own culture, generated a worldwide response of shock and awe. Those years of chasing acceptance and love were crushed in an instant when I received what seemed, at the time, worldwide uproar and abuse for my new identity. But wait a minute—what was wrong with what I was doing? I was just appreciating my favorite culture; it wasn't appropriation in my eyes. Why didn't people lovingly accept me like they do with everyone else in the alphabet self-ID community who has a different identity? Why were the same people who preach about self-identification and promote identifying as trans or nonbinary turning on me? I thought Generation Z were all about love and self-acceptance, and I had searched my whole life to be accepted and feel valid, yet they had all turned on me. I was painted as a monster.

When I went onstage to perform my K-pop songs, I was jeered at and laughed at. Everyone would film me and post it all over the Internet, saying how ugly I was, how terrible my singing was (that was definitely true, though!), and how I would never be a successful K-pop star. I was treated as a joke, an outsider and loner who did not belong. I was discredited and dismissed simply for wanting to be a different person than who I was born as. The Internet was filled with videos of K-pop fans mocking me, YouTubers doing lengthy videos calling me as many insults as possible and comparing my looks to Michael Jackson, "Catwoman" Jocelyn Wildenstein, and anyone they could compare me to in order to try and break my spirit. The Internet became a cruel, intolerant place for me. TikToks, YouTubers, tweets all directed at me, designed to break me and make me want to go hide under a rock for the rest of my days. I started to hate going out in public, hate performing, and would ignore requests for me to perform at various K-pop festivals due to my insecurities and fear of being mocked. They were absolutely relentless in their pursuit of destroying me. The only thing that kept me going through this time was the thousands of fans I had gained whom I affectionately call the "Oli Squad." These were K-pop fans from all across the world who supported me no matter what and uplifted me with positive comments; thousands of them made fan accounts on Instagram for me and spent hours drawing pictures of me, baking cakes with my face on them, writing songs for me, and even getting tattoos of me. They filled me with so much support and kindness, one of the few things that spurred me on. They made me happy, so I became determined to make them happy by releasing fun songs and YouTube videos designed with the pure intention of making them laugh and smile. The bullies were hard on me, but it didn't mean that I had to be like them; I wanted to spread laughter and joy to my fans and give them a reason to smile, so I would make wacky and crazy videos to make them laugh, even my mock wedding to a cardboard cutout of a K-pop star, Jimin, at an Elvis-themed church in Las Vegas—it wasn't serious, it wasn't a real wedding, but simply a way to make my fans smile, to give them some joy and laughter. In the YouTube age, people enjoy bizarre videos, especially if it can make their day better in this often negative and dark world. These fans, the Oli Squad, gave me purpose, and I am eternally grateful for them in the face of the onslaught from the seemingly endless trolls that continue to try and hurt me to this day.

As human beings we tend to always focus on the negative. Even if we receive one hundred positive messages and one negative, we are drawn to focus on that one negative comment. We analyze and dissect every word, taking it as a reflection of who we are. Despite having so much love and support from my fans, I focused more and more on the negative things people would say about me, especially when it related to my appearance and identity. After being bombarded with negative comments and personal attacks against me every day, I grew disillusioned with the world around me, shifting further from reality and becoming transfixed on changing myself even more radically. I became consumed by it and spent hours of my day watching videos online of other people who had unusual identities and seeing how happy they were—or at least, that's how they tried to come across. I did not see through the façade that most of them were masking their struggles through the veneer of the perfect, happy life. They were masking what they were really feeling inside, just like I was each time I posted a video or photo online. I wasn't the caricature of myself, the happy, comical, goofy person I portrayed online, someone I created to try and help me mask my unhappiness, to erase the real me and replace him with a fantasy character. I had undergone multiple surgeries over the five years prior and finally had undergone my most drastic surgeries ever to get the Korean idol look and try to become someone I was not. I wanted the Korean look and the lifestyle of K-pop idols because it helped me escape the reality of my own existence. I had buried my own identity, Oli the shy boy from England, and reinvented myself as Oli the Korean K-pop star.

I felt trapped with the way I looked and trapped in the wrong body, just like someone who feels they are trapped in the wrong gender. How was what I felt at the time any different from people who transition their gender? I knew deep down it wasn't different, it was essentially the same, and I thought what I was doing was even less extreme than someone who has a full sex change. After all, both changing gender and changing identity or the way one looks involved plastic surgery, so what was the actual difference?

Chapter 17
Canceled & Condemned

Over the next two years, as my K-pop career continued to take off, I was subjected to an increasing barrage of abuse. The more music videos I released and the more TV shows I appeared on, the more I saw an increase in abuse. I had been used to harsh comments about my appearance throughout my life, but now it had become worse than ever. Each negative comment felt like a stab to my heart, and each would open a traumatic wound reminding me of my teen years. That relentless daily bullying, the *Ha Ha Ha Ha* of the bullies jeering at me. Each time it was painful, and each time it would force me into more extreme behavior as a coping mechanism. I didn't search for healthy coping mechanisms like therapy or confiding in a friend about my problems; instead I became destructive to myself and others. The more they trolled me, the crazier I behaved and the more extreme surgeries I would undertake. The more I lashed out and showed my mental health breakdown to the world, the more they tried to cancel and condemn me. It was a daily hate campaign designed to break me; they relished seeing me in such an unstable state and would bait me so I would lash out each time. Whenever I shared images of my new look, I thought that people would finally love me because I looked "beautiful" and had the K-pop idol aesthetic. However, their reaction was always the opposite. They would call me "botched," "a burn victim," and "a horror show." Then the hateful YouTube videos would come in droves, one after another. One YouTuber named iNabber laid into me more than any other. His videos were shockingly cruel and below the belt, and he would use insults designed to make me feel like garbage, comparing me to Michael Jackson and encouraging his hundreds of thousands of subscribers to turn against me. Each time he made a video, I was inundated with thousands of messages telling me to kill myself or encouraging me to commit suicide. All these YouTubers always had a disclaimer on their channel preaching to the "be kind" crowd by saying, "Please do not send abuse or bully the subject discussed in this video. This YouTube is for commentary only and this channel discourages bullying." It was so hypocritical, preaching about being kind and not bullying others yet making hour-long videos causing people to hate me and turn against me. It was only natural that once they were riled up with hatred toward me after watching the video, they would come to my social media and fill it with abuse. The YouTubers knew this and sadistically took pleasure in it.

Trying to change myself to prove the bullies wrong and under-going extreme surgeries became a vicious cycle that only became more self-destructive over time. Each time I would change, I hoped that it would mean that the trolling would stop, but sadly it only worsened.

In May 2021, I was shocked to discover the lengths trolls and YouTubers had gone to make my life a living hell and try to get rid of me forever. As I logged onto Instagram one morning, as I always did as soon as I woke up, to check my latest notifications, likes, and comments, I was stunned to discover I could not even log in. I tried multiple times and thought I had been hacked. I Googled my Instagram from my computer to make sure someone had not hacked it or deleted it. What I discovered was far worse than that and far more upsetting. My Instagram page read, "This account has been memorialized," with a small image of a flower next to it. I was shocked that my own Instagram account was claiming I had died. How on Earth had that happened, and how and why would Instagram have allowed that to be on my page when I am quite clearly alive and well?

I couldn't believe that someone had gone to such extreme lengths to do this to me. How could Instagram have had evidence enough to claim I was dead when I wasn't? I Googled how this could happen, but there were no answers; this had clearly never happened before. This came at a time when certain YouTubers were making increasingly desperate attempts to try and cause me harm so they could make videos about me. I had my suspicions that one of them was behind this, so I searched "Oli London Dead" on Google and it came up with a prank news website announcing that I had died. It wasn't legitimate, it wasn't an established newspaper or anything, and it even said on the website itself that the website was for "pranks." If this was some elaborate prank, it wasn't a very funny one. I tried to piece together what had happened, thinking that maybe the YouTuber I suspected had used this as evidence of my passing and photoshopped photos of me with him to try and prove that they knew me so Instagram would declare my account "memorialized." It still didn't make sense, but this was the best answer I could come up with and the only explanation I could think of. Some sad Youtuber who hated me and wanted views creating a prank news article, coupling that with photoshopped pictures of me and them together, and presenting that to Instagram as "evidence," and Instagram bizarrely not even bothering to do research and falling victim to this person's plan to smear me and cause me problems. Suddenly, before I could continue trying to work out a bizarre theory, my WhatsApp and phone started blowing up with messages. Dozens of texts soon turned to hundreds when Twitter began trending "Oli London Dead." I was mortified; all the other things trolls and Internet haters had tried to do to me before paled in comparison to this. My family and friends all started calling me, desperate to reach me. I assured them I was alive and well and was trying to figure out what had happened to my account. I messaged my Instagram partner manager and asked them to immediately fix my account and make sure this would never happen again to me or anyone else. My family and friends were relieved to hear I was fine, but extremely upset, having believed what they had seen online. While I was trying to make sense of it all and reassure my loved ones, Twitter exploded—my supposed death had become the #1 trend in the world, much to my utter dismay. I attempted to immediately reassure everyone that nothing was wrong and that I was clearly the victim of a prank or a mistake on the part of Instagram. But instead, I was bombarded with hate, all over Twitter, claiming I had faked my own death for attention and that I wanted clout. I was mortified, more so when suddenly the media and newspapers started writing stories claiming the same. It was out of control, and my heart sank. This person I suspected of being behind this prank, this YouTuber who had targeted me for years, had done this to destroy me so they could gain views and notoriety for being the person who caused me such distress. This was one of the lowest points of my life. The whole world was hating on me, saying I had done this to myself for attention or saying they wished I really was dead. It was painful; no words can describe the pain I felt that day. All because of the actions of one person who hated me, one person who wanted to destroy me. And the sad thing is that people fell for it, they immediately made their minds up and went along with the online narrative that I had indeed done this to myself. Out of all the things Internet bullies ever did to me, this had to be the worst. Putting my friends and family through the emotional pain of thinking I had died, and then to add insult to injury the world blamed me for what Instagram did to my account.

This was "Cancel Culture" at its finest, and I couldn't believe the extreme lengths people would go to try to destroy a person whom they disliked or didn't agree with. It was cruel, as cruel as a bull-fighting match. I had been maimed by the sharp spears and swords of these Internet matadors and left to crawl on the floor to pick up the pieces. This wasn't some kind of joke anymore; this Internet hate and trolling had a real-life impact. These people didn't care, they didn't see me as a human being, they just saw me as someone they could push lower and lower until I'd eventually break and maybe then I really would be "memorialized." I felt like quitting everything, giving up on my music, giving up on my dream, and getting more surgery to become so unrecognizable that no one would know me anymore and I could start again. I wanted to delete all my social media accounts, and I deactivated my Twitter and Instagram accounts for a period of time after that traumatic experience.

Weeks passed and I still felt shattered, but a voice inside told me to have courage, to move on, and that I could weather any storm. So I did just that: I moved on, picked up the fragments of my soul and pieced them back together, finding internal strength to rise above these bullies and once again keep fighting to prove myself as the bigger person, to defeat them through winning.

• • •

I continued for the next few years trying to be positive, though it felt almost impossible most of the time, and I tried to be strong, but still these people would chip away at my soul, reminding me of the taunts of teenage bullies and reminding me that I had to change the way I looked, who I was, and my very own identity in order to be less of a target for these people, to be seen as someone to look up to and aspire to be like.

I refused to be the laughingstock anymore and thought that surely if I really did become beautiful or change my identity again, these people would finally accept me and embrace me. I underwent even more surgery to try and achieve this. In 2021, I had a face lift and eye lift in Turkey, followed by new veneers just a few months later, with rhinoplasty and areola correction with a fantastic doctor in El Paso, Texas—"Dr. Worldwide." He was finally able to fix the thing that had caused me the most anguish over the years, my nose, and helped to restore my breathing. Having surgery was always my go-to solution to get a temporary fix of happiness and help me to try and prove the bullies wrong.

But no matter what I did, the bullies continued to harass and attack me. I knew that if the level of bullying continued, I wouldn't be able to weather the storm of abuse forever, but I tried my best to resist it by devoting all my time to fixing my image while focusing my energy on doing something that I loved, making K-Pop music. Writing lyrics for songs, learning how to produce and make beats, and coming up with creative concepts for my own music and that of other artists I worked with. Creativity was my passion, so I invested all my time and energy into coming up with concepts, set designs, custom fashion pieces to wear, and storyboards to make my music videos stand out. This was how I tried to beat the bullies: knuckling down and keeping my mind off of social media. The hard work paid off, my videos became more and more popular, and four of the songs even made it into the top ten on the iTunes K-Pop chart. Additionally, seven of my songs made it to the top forty and sur-passed over 45 million views in total on YouTube over a few short years. This was my way of proving the bullies wrong: success. I had always told myself to fight people through success, from my time at school to those long, arduous days washing dishes in the restaurant kitchen. Proving them wrong was the only way to win and defeat them. It was the best revenge.

During this time, I would spend hour after hour watching YouTube videos of other people who were different, like me. But they were stronger than I, they were happy. The strength of other people who fight for what they believe is right has helped me personally find my own inner strength. I began to feel inspired by the courage of others online who have had to deal with extreme bullying and being canceled, yet have come out on the other side, stronger and tougher. Being true to oneself and staying the course of the journey you are on, despite others trying to stop you, is something that can keep you going in life and make you more resilient. In my case, I used all of this to make myself stronger, and it inspired me to continue on my quest for perfection. I wasn't going to stop at anything until I had done what I had set out to do, no matter how much physical or emotional pain I went through. I reminded myself it would all be worth it.

I started to realize I was not alone in my struggle, that many others struggled with their identity and were bullied for it. I realized that an innumerable group of people like me were subject to horrific trolling and were able to speak openly about it and their other struggles online. Thanks to the actions of those who find the courage to speak up against cancel culture and bullies, the narrative is shifting, and more people are pushing back against the woke mob and cancel culture.

Chapter 18

Identity Crisis

What happened to the old Oli? Where had he gone? I had lost touch with reality and delved into a world of unhealthy obsession, a warped view of my own self, an identity crisis. This had only been made worse by the horrific and never-ending bullying I had become accustomed to online. How did I get to this point, and was there any going back? An identity crisis, or not knowing oneself, has become increasingly common in the modern age with over 1.6 million people identifying as trans or nonbinary across America, according to a 2022 survey by the Williams Institute (UCLA).[1] However, this is only the tip of the iceberg, as we know there are many more millions of people out there who struggle every day. How did they reach that point and how does it compare to my own identity crisis? By this point I was questioning my gender more and more, evoking memories of my teenage years when I was told by others that I was like a girl, I was "too fem," or too passive to be a real boy. This played on my mind almost daily until I eventually

---

1   Herman, Jody L., et al. "HOW MANY ADULTS AND YOUTH IDENTIFY AS TRANSGENDER IN THE UNITED STATES?" *Williams Institute*, UCLA Williams Institute, June 2022, https://williamsinstitute.law.ucla.edu/wp-content /uploads/Trans-Pop-Update-Jun-2022.pdf. Accessed 29 January 2023.

decided the time had come. I was going to give in and listen to all of them. They won; they must have been right, and the way I was made to feel must mean that I was trapped in the wrong body. I began to realize that everything I had done up until this point was misplaced, that I had tried to change the way I looked, but the real reason I had not found contentment was because I was actually the wrong gender. Everything else had been because I was confused and unsure, and the subconscious and repressed memories had finally been reactivated to make me realize everything was down to my internal subconscious struggles with my gender identity.

I had reached the point where I had been told so many times throughout my life that I was a girl and a woman that I was convinced they were right. I had succumbed to groupthink and indoctrination. "Groupthink" refers to an individual choosing to go with the main thought process of a particular group in order to conform, which results in often irrational and dysfunctional decision making. My mind had been molded to the thinking of those around me, I wanted to fit in, and I wanted to conform. Finally, I had found the real reason for my unhappiness and pursuit of perfection—it was simply because I was trans. I couldn't find another logical explanation for it. When you are told so many times you are a certain thing, you start to believe it. Even if it's not true, the human subconscious mind has a habit of going with the crowd and turning something into the truth if enough people tell you it's true.

This is also how indoctrination works, like with the current school system, where children are told by adults so many times that they are the wrong gender, and they should change, that they start to believe it. Children are incredibly impressionable and receptive to ideas taught to them by people in positions of authority such as doctors and teachers. They easily fall prey to ideas, and their minds are altered based on what an adult tells them. Though I was an adult when I transitioned—I was thirty-two—it was the decades of indoctrination that finally got to me and made me change. I was an adult and I still fell victim to this. Yet children are far more susceptible to these ideas than someone like me, who has years of life experience. Children are blank slates, and their minds are easily molded. I fell victim to the mentality, and I took the big step of acting on this, to my later regret. I was ready to undertake a radical change to transform the way I looked and ultimately transform the way I felt.

Chapter 19

Transition

I had reached a point where I still had many daily questions about my identity, I still did not feel complete, and I still didn't feel like my true self. I questioned what was missing in my life, again spending hours upon hours staring in my mirror like I did throughout my teen years, asking the rhetorical question, "Mirror, mirror on the wall, what am I missing from this all?"

Maybe all the kids who bullied me years ago about being a girl were right, and maybe that's the reason I didn't feel fulfilled. I had many questions throughout my life about my gender; I never felt like a real boy or masculine in any sense. I didn't engage in sports, including soccer, or traditional "boy things." I played with Barbie dolls as a child instead of Action Man, and I remember how much I enjoyed putting on women's clothing and accessories from my childhood dress-up box. I had also struggled for years with my sexuality, until eventually coming out at the age of twenty-three in Korea, when I felt free for the first time in my life. I had several relationships after coming out, but they all ended the same way—being cheated on and being told I was "too emotional, like a woman," "too feminine," and not "manly enough." They would cheat on me and say they wanted a real man, not a feminine guy who was far too emotional, not someone like me writing them poems, buying them flowers, and going above and beyond to be romantic. I was far too feminine for them. All these things combined in my mind, and I saw them as signs. Signs that everyone around me had been right and all my misfortunes and struggles were the result of being born in the wrong body. Being a trans woman was the only solution that made sense to me at this time. I had been convinced all my life that I was meant to be a girl, so now it was time to listen to all those voices and follow all the signs that had led me to this path, the path to transition.

I remembered being a child at five years old, and how happy and beautiful I felt dressing in women's clothes and feeling like a glamorous and beautiful girl. Now fast-forward to the Oli in his early thirties . . . I recalled these memories and thought maybe all along I was simply born in the wrong body, maybe I was meant to be a girl. My parents always used to tell me if I had been born a girl my name would have been Alice. Was I Alice in Wonderland? I started to question myself more and more, and after all the surgeries to have the Korean aesthetic I realized that I had perhaps misplaced my identity and been searching for answers and fulfillment in the wrong places—that really, I was meant to be a trans woman.

These thoughts swirled through my mind, so I went where I always went for answers, to the Internet. I saw how happy other trans people seemed to be, how perfect they looked, with their bright smiles, the gleam in their eyes, and I wanted to be just like them—happy, beautiful, and celebrated. I didn't even stop to think that what I was seeing on social media was an illusion and that most influencers only share the best parts of their life, a warped reality, and often these people are very different from what they like to present to the world. I did not consider anything other than what I saw in front of me, the picture-perfect image of happiness. I started doing research in the hope to transition, took steps to look more feminine, and immediately ordered some dresses, heels, makeup, and wigs. This was the first step in trying the new gender I thought I was meant to be, a step to becoming a trans woman. When the clothes arrived, I tried them on, feeling weird at first. Then the wig and makeup followed, and I learned I was terrible at applying makeup. Perhaps that should have been my first clue that this would not work out. I applied the eyeliner, rather sloppily, and then the lipstick and lipliner, drawing the line way too far above the lip, leaving me with what appeared to be clown lips, oversize and bloated and far from feminine looking. It was not the look I was generally going for, but I was happy to be wearing makeup and feeling more feminine. I then put on the heels. I was already five-foot-eleven (180cm), so the heels made me look like an NBA player with a wig and bad makeup. I felt unsure but pressed ahead, giving in to the fact that I was told to become a trans woman by so many people, the fact I used to play with Barbies and dress in women's clothes as a child. I reassured myself that I would get used to this new feeling and in the long run be, happy, content, confident, and an improved version of me, just like all the happy trans people I kept seeing online, especially on TikTok.

After a few months passed, I was ready to make myself look more feminine by feminizing my face. Makeup was not enough to make me look like a woman, especially the way I was applying the makeup, so I had to do something more extreme. Without a second thought, I turned to the thing that I always turned to when I doubted myself or wanted to change: plastic surgery. So I decided the only solution to help me affirm my new gender identity was to go under the knife. I flew to Istanbul, Turkey, to begin my transition. I had been there the previous year for a brow and forehead lift; a dramatic eye surgery called a lateral canthoplasty, to change the shape of my eyes; and veneers, when I wanted the specific Korean K-pop look. Now I wanted to be a woman;

I wanted my face to look more feminine, my eyes to be like cat eyes, my jawline sharper, my face more taut, and my bones softer. I found a fantastic clinic, with an incredible team and a great doctor who walked me through the process. I had numerous appointments, checkups, and pre-surgery assessments to make sure I knew what I wanted. I was in safe hands this time, compared to years ago when I was reckless and took risks with doctors. This time I had the best in Turkey, and they made sure I was confident with what I wanted. My face was drawn up, marks were drawn all over my face on the areas that would be operated on to feminize my face and give me a fresh new look. The surgery went well; I was so used to it by now, it was just like going to the hair salon for me. I was a pro. I had the kindest nurse look after me during my recovery and regular checkups from the doctor while being very well cared for, among the best I had ever experienced in my years of traveling the world on my surgical mission. Three days passed, two days in the hospital and one day in the hotel after discharge, and I was finally able to open my eyes again. Before then, my eyes were stitched and covered with bandages. I was comfortable the whole time and not in much pain. I was more concerned about not being able to check my phone for three days, not being able to post on TikTok, and not being able to spend hours looking in the mirror trying to catch a glimpse beneath the bandages of the brand-new me. I was Oli 9.0 by this point, the ninth version of myself and the ninth time I had changed myself. I had now gone under the knife for a total of nine times with a combined surgery total of thirty-two procedures. This time my facial feminization surgery included eleven areas of my face and neck. I had undergone a 3D face lift with facial feminization consisting of anterior hairline lowering, forehead shaving, supraorbital rim (brow and forehead) shaving, blepharoplasty (cat eye surgery), midface lift, neck lift, chin shaving, lip lift, and buccal fat removal (lower cheeks). All these procedures were to help make my face shape more feminine. My bones were shaved down, fat was removed from my lower cheeks, my chin was shaved and hairline lowered, all to soften my appearance and help me achieve the new me. I was happy, happier than ever; in fact, after a week when my bandages were removed, I really did feel more beautiful than ever. This was different from all the other times that I had surgery, this was a general feeling of finally being perfect and finally being complete. I vowed, as I always did, that I would never have surgery again and this was it—this was the final evolution of Oli. The swelling went down over the next few weeks so quickly thanks to the post-operative care I was receiving including facial treatments and laser therapies. The doctors took great care of me, and I felt grateful for finally finding the right clinic that understood what I wanted, unlike clinics in the past that didn't get the look I was going for or give me the results I was looking for.

As I got back to London, my first instinct was to get human hair extensions to complement my new face. I spent probably five to six hours in the salon having my hair bleached and the extensions taped in one by one, then cut to blend in with my existing hair. When I opened my eyes at the end of the salon appointment, I was truly thrilled. Wow, I had nailed the feminine look and actually looked the best I ever had in my thirty-two years on Earth. I was finally the person I was meant to be. I was showered with compliments from everyone I met, and all my friends said this was who I was born to be. When I finally posted the brand new me, the trans version of me, on Instagram I had thousands of comments saying that I "look better as a woman," and "this is the real you." Positive affirmation, just like every other person who shares their transition online gets. Celebration, applause, and praise.

Many teens simply want to be loved, so when they see others being celebrated for "coming out" and changing genders, they too feel a desire to receive this same positive reinforcement. They feel inclined to change their pronouns or gender so that they too can receive this attention, fawning, and outpouring of love. Quite the contrast from someone who detransitions and is met with the total opposite online response, negative reinforcement that seeks to stop them speaking out and push them back into the shadows, away from the view of the world.

The next step in my journey was to go out in public in a full dress and heels and show off the brand-new look to the world. It was the Cannes Film Festival 2022, I was staying at Hotel Martinez with my best friend, Hollywood actress and entrepreneur Aliia Roza, who always loved me whoever I was and supported me through everything, acting as a rock when I needed one the most. I had known her since my personal shopping days when she used to be my client and we developed a unique and special friendship. She knew how much I had struggled over the years, yet she always stood by me and helped me build my confidence. She never wanted me to have surgeries and always worried, but she was not the sort of person to try and stop someone pursuing their own dreams or living their life in the best possible way. Whatever I did with my life, she stood by me. Her kindness and warmth shone through her radiant energy. She was a real friend and still is to this day, something that is often rare in the modern world. She was also superglamorous, always in haute couture dresses, stunning on the red carpets and at fashion weeks in showstopping looks. She was an inspiration for any woman or any person wanting to look like a woman, like me. We went to a fashion stylist's room at the Hotel Martinez, a room filled with the most glamorous and elegant dresses imaginable. Floral hand-embroidered gowns laden with Swarovski crystals, gold metallic shimmering gowns, and ball gowns laced with intricate beads and diamante details. Aliia dressed in a beautiful and stunning gown that looked so elegant on her slender and perfect body. I knew I couldn't compete and look that good—after all, I was a biological man and always knew I couldn't change my biology and become a full woman. I could simply change the way I looked and the way I lived my life. I had the utmost respect for women, even when I became trans and did not use women's restrooms out of respect for women or change in front of them into my looks for the red carpet. I couldn't fit into any of the elegant size-0 couture dresses, and I knew I could never look as good as a real woman. But still, this was a big day, the grand public reveal, and a pink haute couture custom dress was waiting for me, by a talented Turkish designer, Gulafer Atas. I had a Turkish-made face, and now I was going to wear a Turkish-made dress—how I could have possibly believed my own delusions that I looked like a Korean woman was beyond me. But I now realize what a dark emotional and mental place I had been in for years, that my mind was cloudy, making misjudgments, and I had convinced myself I could be someone I could never realistically be.

I changed into the pink couture dress, despite the fact that it was clearly designed for a real woman and a real woman's body. My shoulders were way too broad, and the designer had to change the way the dress was worn at the very last minute. The part of the dress that was meant to go over my shoulders didn't fit—unsurprisingly. So it was pushed down over my chest area and sewn on in a way to try and make it look like it was meant to be in its new position. I felt ridiculous, I knew I looked ridiculous, and people would laugh at me or judge me. But it was too late to turn back; I had made the decision to become trans, so I'd better get used to this new life. I convinced myself that I couldn't expect to feel more feminine overnight and like anything else in life things would get better over time. There were fewer than thirty minutes left until I had to be on the red carpet for a major Korean film premiere of *Broker*, starring K-pop superstar IU (real name: Lee Ji-Eun). I didn't even have heels, since not a single stylist had heels big enough to fit my feet—my huge manly feet (Size 43 EU/ Size 9 US). I started to panic. This was my first major public outing as a trans woman, and I wasn't prepared. I looked ridiculous, and all I had were some black Saint Laurent Chelsea boots with a slight platform heel. Back in England, I had been struggling to walk in heels and still wasn't used to them, but I deeply regretted not bringing a pair to Cannes. I put on the boots reluctantly, then had to once again have stitches sewn into the back of the dress and the chest area, to stop it from splitting embarrassingly and to save me from having a major wardrobe malfunction on the red carpet. I had to hurry to the car; it was always such a rush heading to a red carpet in Cannes. Hundreds of fans stood outside the Hotel Martinez. Dozens of celebrities stood inches away from me. Viola Davis, Anne Hathaway, Naomi Campbell, Kristen Stewart, and Bella Hadid, to name but a few. How could I compete with their female beauty and elegance? I walked out arm in arm with my friend Aliia, who looked ravishing and radiant. Fans started to scream, and some recognized me despite my new feminine look. It gave me a temporary confidence boost even though inside I was petrified of my dress falling apart and being laughed at on the red carpet. If that happened it would be like being in high school all over again, being laughed at and mocked—I refused to ever have to experience those traumatic feelings ever again. The car arrived on the red carpet after a ten-minute drive from the hotel to the iconic Palais des Festivals. Thousands of people stood outside. I was panicking, I was shaking. I just dreaded being mocked or being laughed at for my new look. It was tough and I knew many other trans people also go through similar nerve-wracking experiences when they first transition, although I'm sure few do this in front of thousands of people. I didn't want to get out of the car; my friend urged me and said it would be fine. Fear gripped my entire body; I felt stiff and rigid and prayed and begged the universe to not let anything bad happen to me. This was my big reveal, please don't let anything go wrong.

The door opened, and a smartly uniformed French man opened the door and grabbed my hand to help me out. I heard the stitches split, one by one. The sound was like chalk being scraped down a chalkboard, excruciating. I thought this was going to be a disaster, but as I stepped out of the car thousands of screaming fans started calling my name, smiling, happy, clapping, and cheering. It was not what I had expected, but it was much needed and a welcome relief. I was finally accepted. I was relieved and thought for once I had made the right decision and people loved the new me more than the old me. Any feelings of worry soon dissipated through the uplifting screams and cheers of my fans in the seemingly endless crowd. I was so grateful to them, so thankful to my fans, the Oli Squad, who had been so loyal to me over the five years since I first became known to the world through social media, my K-pop music, and television. I was truly grateful and appreciative that they had lifted me up when I needed it most. When I walked the carpet, I felt relieved that the dress was still standing and had not split. The photographers went wild for the look, although I still worried that they would put me on the worst-dressed list for my last-minute and disastrous look, with the Chelsea boots and complete change of the original dress design because it didn't fit over my shoulders. I walked up the steps at the Palais, waved at the crowd, and felt relieved as I got through to the upstairs and calmer entrance to the cinema. Aliia came through the door shortly after, smiling and elated that it went so well for both of us. "See, Oli, I told you not to worry, you looked amazing and everyone loved you." She was right; in those few minutes after exiting the car, greeting the onlookers and walking the carpet, I did feel loved, I did feel validated, and I did feel my new identity was the right one for me. It was an electrifying feeling, an adrenaline rush. I was happy to be accepted for the new me in my first public outing. I was finally a woman. This was a very public way of announcing my transition to the world and the way I convinced myself I was finally living my life fully as the person I was born to be, a trans woman.

That was the beginning of the next few months of me becoming more and more feminine and more convinced this was who I was really born to be. Until it wasn't. Until I realized I still felt something was missing. I still didn't feel like me. The incredible feeling I had since transitioning was starting to fade, the serotonin hit was diminishing, and I was starting to want more. The surgery fix time limit had expired, just like every other time, and I started to think about moving on to changing my body. This would be the final surgery, I told myself. Again, this was something I told myself every single time, after each surgery, that it would be the last. It never was, and I feel if I hadn't stopped at this point, I would never stop and would never be truly satisfied with the way I looked. I was always chasing after the unattainable, an unrealistic image, and chasing after things I could never truly achieve. I was even being mocked online and called Jocelyn Wildenstein, dubbed "Catwoman," the infamous American socialite who had numerous surgeries to look more like a cat. I had already had thirty-two surgeries, but I was still feeling it was not enough.

I then began my research into gender reassignment surgeries in Bangkok, Thailand—an apt name for a city where I could have had my penis removed. Bang, and the cock was gone. It would be reshaped and made into a woman's part, and I would be changed forever. I consulted with multiple doctors over video call, and it all sounded so easy and seamless, just as it always did. You come to Thailand, meet the doctor, then they set the date for the surgery, and voilà! you are officially a "woman," albeit a plastic, manufactured one, but still a "real woman." I knew I could never be a real woman, biology and chromosomes could not be changed, but these doctors endeavored to sell me the dream that I could. I was going to start with getting breast implants and then do the rest in a separate surgery, knowing that it would be by far the most excruciating and most painful surgeries of my life. My head told me I had to do it; online influencers, videos, and articles I read told me it was the final process in transitioning. Some videos I saw online said that it was the only way to fully "become a woman." I pondered on this and then booked for December 2022 to get breast implants and then planned to go back to Thailand in 2023 for genital reassignment.

Thankfully, though, I would soon have a dramatic awakening that would save me from disaster and save me from making the biggest mistake of my life. Change was around the corner; I just didn't know it yet.

Chapter 20

Finding God

Having struggled with my own identity for the past decade, I had reached the end of the road. A turning point. I remembered the poem "The Road Not Taken," by Robert Frost, which had resonated with me since my teenage years. We are all presented with a choice in life to take the easy and familiar route or take a risk and go down the road less traveled. I had been on a self-destructive path for the last nine years, since my first transformational surgery back in 2013 in Korea. I had put my mind and body through physical and mental torture with the thirty-two surgeries I had endured, all for the sake of short-term happiness. Who had I become, where was the old Oli? Was he still somewhere trapped inside me? These were the questions I asked myself as I walked home on a cold September evening. Two roads lay ahead of me, and I took a leap of faith and took the one less traveled by. And that has made all the difference.

The road led me to a medieval church. I had passed this church every day without ever wandering inside. However, today was different. Curiosity and my longing for change spurred me to walk through the old wooden door. A choir was singing hymns; the music enchanted me, and I felt as if a magic spell had been cast over me. This powerful energy led me to a seat at the back of the church. I watched intently and listened to the cheerful choir, which was followed by a powerful sermon by the priest. I glanced around. Everyone seemed happy, content. I admired their happiness, wishing I could have just an ounce of their joy, a grain of their good spirit. I pondered for a while. The service ended, and people started to leave their seats and exchange greetings and thoughts with one another. I stared, like a fly on the wall. An old lady with a walking stick smiled at me and greeted me with a warm and tender look. I reciprocated her warm gaze and remarked what a lovely service it had been and that she had a beautiful smile. She then smiled again, nodded her head, and left through the old oak door. I sat alone for a while with a Bible in my hand, and the first page I opened was Matthew 8–10, Psalm 62, the story of Jesus healing a man with leprosy. The leper man was rejected by society, ostracized, and forced to live in the shadows without human love and compassion. Jesus was the only one who approached him and offered him help. Using his own hands, he washed the man and thus cleansed him from his ailment. Reading this for the first time struck a chord in my heart. I was the leper. Or, at least the Internet version. A man who was rejected by society for my identity, a man who was shunned by the whole world for simply wanting to be loved. If Jesus could save a man whom no one else loved, then maybe he could save me. This was a moment of awakening.

They say that God comes into our lives in many different ways. I had attended church during elementary school and again during my time volunteering in Ethiopia, and I had fond memories of these times, except for that one service in Ethiopia that turned out to be an exorcism. I had believed in a higher power throughout much of my life, although I seriously questioned this during my difficult teen years when I felt that if there was a God, he had abandoned me. Despite the ups and downs of my life, I had always prayed to the universe and always believed in the power of thought and energy. Good energy attracts good energy, bad energy attracts bad. This is something that most people generally agree with, that karma comes for those who do bad unto others and good things come to those who give back. The universe had given back to me in many ways throughout my later adult life, but still all my prayers had not been answered. Was it simply because I was asking in the wrong place? These questions ran through my mind as I lay in bed that same night. For hours upon hours, I pondered the very existence of the universe, of life itself and how I had come to become the person I was today.

When I woke the next morning to a cold and crisp autumn day, I felt different. I felt a power had run through my body and enlightened me. I was not Oli London anymore, the crazy K-pop fan and trans-identifying surgery addict—I was just me. It was at this moment I realized in order to be me I had to make some radical changes in my life. I wanted to change, I wanted to be happy, and I knew this was a now-or-never moment. In order to get back to the real me, I had to become a man again; I had to lose the hair extensions, lose the dresses and makeup, and just be my authentic self.

My faith journey over the next several months gave me the guidance and direction I needed to conquer my past demons and to move forward with my life in a positive way so that I could help others suffering with similar identity issues. Reading passages from the Bible each day, I was struck by the compassion of Jesus, how he went out of his way to help others and bring them into the light. The story that I kept going back to was Jesus Cleansing the Leper. The leper was rejected and cast out by people who thought the disease of leprosy was contagious and would spread upon touch or close contact. The suffering man was treated as an outcast, living in a leper colony away from civilization, and these lepers were unable to ever leave the colony or have contact with the outside world. I felt like the leper, like I had been cast out from the outside world my entire life, forced to live a separate life and treated like I had some sort of contagious disease, whether that was the way I looked or because I was different. Jesus heard about the leper man and his suffering, and in order to combat the misconception society held toward leprosy, he paid the man a visit. Jesus didn't like the fact that the law and societal views separated someone from society because they were deemed "unclean." So he went to the man, touched him, and held him while he cleansed him. Jesus healed him out of pity and wanted to change people's perceptions. This is the only instance in Matthew's Gospel where Jesus touched a person out of pity while cleansing them.[1] Soon after, Jesus instructed the man to go to the priest immediately and be examined to be determined as clean. The story, which I found resonated with me so deeply that it was one of the catalysts for me becoming Christian, demonstrates the kindness of God and how He can touch us and come to us in times of need. I was in a great time of need, a lost sheep needing a shepherd, and God had reached out to me and guided me to safety.

The important biblical story also demonstrates how important it is for a member of the Christian faith to reach out and care for those who are cast out or shunned by society. I was shunned and cast out, and yet the Christian community and the members of the Church reached out to welcome me, helped me in my time of need, and helped push me forward through the light to become the man I am today. This is an important message that I urge all Christians and non-Christians alike to follow: Rather than cast out, and shun people who have extreme differences, such as the trans community or those confused with their identity, we should reach out to them and offer them salvation, light, and support to navigate

1 BBC. "A leprosy sufferer (Matthew 8: 1–4)—Jesus the miracle worker—CCEA— GCSE Religious Studies Revision—CCEA." *BBC*, https://www.bbc.co.uk/bitesize /guides/z4h7y9q/revision/2. Accessed 30 January 2023.

through their difficult journey and remind them that they are not alone in the world and that God can help them discover themselves again. Compassion is key to tackling the issue of the rise in teens experiencing gender dysphoria, and we should not vilify those who struggle or condemn those who want to change themselves beyond recognition. We should follow Jesus's example and support those in need and together we can help make the world a safer and more accepting place for all.

Another story from the Bible that resonated with me was Matthew 8:5–13, which is the story of A Roman Officer's Servant. The officer had a high authority and was acclaimed in society for his position, used to having power and giving commands, just like a modern-day celebrity or influencer is seen as a higher authority and put on a pedestal. Yet despite this, he treated his servants with kindness and compassion even though in the ancient Roman Empire, servants were often enslaved peoples from battle conquests and had no human rights or any expectation of being treated with any sort of kindness. Yet this officer was different, and he gave his servants dignity, he gave them respect, and treated them as equals. He also recognized the limits to his own position of authority and recognized that Jesus had greater authority because His authority came from God. From the compassion and respect of the officer, Jesus was able to heal one of his servants from afar. This story demonstrates that with the modern phenomenon of celebrity and Internet influencers, of which I had been labeled as one by the media, people tend to see them as an authority on issues or put their faith in them instead of in the power of God. I had been doing this through my idol worship of Korean pop stars, particularly Jimin of BTS. I had wanted to be like them and in my relentless pursuit of achieving this had failed to recognize that I was funneling all my energy, all my passions and needs, into a false idol. If only I had recognized the higher authority of God earlier on in my life, I could have avoided making many mistakes and decisions that caused harm to myself and to others being influenced by me online. Like the Roman Officer, I had a responsibility and others looked up to me as an "authority," or someone they respected, yet what message had I been sending to the people who followed my unusual journey online? Had I influenced others to question their own identity, gender, or culture because of what I had done? I had been reflecting on these questions each time I attended church or read a passage from the Bible, and it helped me to reevaluate my thinking and follow the motivational teachings of Jesus. By healing others, spreading the right kind of messaging, and wanting to help others, Jesus had changed society's thinking. Lepers experienced less judgment, those with other ailments were treated with kindness, and those with power were taught to treat others without power as equals. While I would in no way compare myself to Jesus, I could certainly learn from his teachings and do better as a person. I could conquer my struggles and then help others conquer theirs, doing it with a sense of duty and tenderness in order to help save lives and make society a better place for all.

By reading these stories and others, I started to see the world more clearly and started to think more logically. Reversing my mistakes of the past and becoming the old me would not be an overnight miracle, but something that would take years to do. But with each day and each visit to church and each interaction with other Christians, I would be able to find the internal strength I needed for my new mission, to save teens from changing themselves beyond recognition before really having time to think about what they were doing. This became my main mission, and I have spent each passing day advocating for these teens, speaking up for parents, speaking up for women's rights, and calling out the direction Western society had been taking as a whole and its future trajectory.

Through pop culture, social media, and entertainment, modern society is increasingly eroding values we once treasured and morals we once held highly. The music industry is pushing more and more demonic messaging, sadistic, sexualized videos and choreography, leading the way to a morally loose society. The social media push is to promote explicit content and gender ideologies to an increasingly younger audience, conditioning them from a young age that all the things once deemed harmful for children are now acceptable, cool, and trendy. Madonna openly mocking Christianity and promoting satanic ideologies, Sam Smith's debauched music videos that push more niche fetishes into the mainstream, or Cardi B's *WAP* video, which made "twerking" a trend. Each music video, each movie, each YouTube video is pushing our society further from God and toward immorality, corrupting the minds of children.

Having grown up in the 1990s, I was lucky to be born in an age when music videos were innocent, costumes covered the bodies, and sexual undertones weren't the main theme of every single music video. Now, with the polar opposite of this, I believe it is causing great harm in shaping the minds of young people and forcing people to think less and less of themselves and become more "experimental," more likely to push boundaries. While it can be good to push boundaries in some senses, it is harmful to young teens whose minds are consumed by what they watch and by following the current trends.

I had witnessed the direction society was going over many years, yet I had been silent, despite my platform. I had been complicit in going along with this, accepting everything as it was, and even pushing ideas through sharing my gender struggles, sharing my plastic surgery journey, and presenting it as normal. It was far from normal, but at the time I believed everything I did was normal. Now through my faith, I am trying to come to terms with who I became and trying to reverse these mistakes and help speak out against what is happening to society, how harmful what we consume online has become for young people's minds, and how we all need to take a step back and remind ourselves that morals, normality, and righteousness are worth fighting for. Every person is worth fighting for, no matter how far astray they are. Every teen that is stuck struggling with their gender, transitioning, or detransitioning and has been led astray by modern society needs to be supported and brought back to the flock, given resources and guidance to ensure they are making the best possible decision for their future and are not being led down a path because of what society has told them.

In the Gospel of Luke, the Parable of the Lost Sheep, a lone sheep becomes separated from the flock. It is lost in the wilderness, wandering aimlessly, and confused. Instead of leaving the lone sheep in the wilderness, the shepherd leaves the ninety-nine other sheep and goes out in search of this lost "child of God." He eventually finds the sheep and brings it back to the flock. The story demonstrates that God does not want to lose a single child and God is not concerned with the Greatest, Strongest, or Best in His kingdom, but He is concerned for all beings. Each person and each child are important to Him. And as a society we should take this lesson and use the analogy to remember that every single child and every single person is important in God's eyes, and those who are lost, no matter how far they stray, can be brought back into the light and brought back to society. We need to help every teen and every child who needs help. While we can recognize that some people generally will want to transition and live their lives that way with no regret, we must continue to fight for the teens that are being pushed each day to undertake a difficult and painful journey that they would have otherwise not taken. After all, as God demonstrates, all of us are important. I had been astray, I had been lost wandering the wilderness for years, yet here I was, back in the flock, reintroduced to society and given a new chance to become a better person and help others. God saved me when I needed Him most, God guided me, and God brought me to where I am today. I am eternally grateful for the grace shown to me by God and the wider Christian community who saved me from myself and saved me from becoming another victim of modern society.

If people can take away anything from this experience and journey, it is that no matter how lost you may feel in life, or how confused you feel, there's always light at the end of the tunnel. Always a chance to change and grow as a human being and change your opinions or your mind about things you once thought of as sacred. While I recognize that many people of different faiths may read this and those who are not religious at all, like I once was, I want everyone to always know that no matter what, there is hope that your life and your circumstances can change, so never give up on yourself or others. Help those who have strayed and help those who need it most. Show the same compassion to others that Jesus showed to the leper and that the Roman Officer showed to the servant.

Chapter 21

Christian Saviors

The only sense of belonging I had felt for the last few years was with the Korean community, who had embraced me with loving arms, made me feel welcome, and gave me a sense of belonging. The Christian community welcomed me equally, with warm open arms. They welcomed me despite my differences, they offered me guidance and support when I needed it most, and I am eternally grateful for the love offered to me in this time of need. I started to attend regular church services several times a week, sitting quietly in the pew at the back along with other members of the congregation. I would listen intently to each spoken word from the priest, memorize each story about Jesus, His disciples, and His teachings. Each time I closed my eyes and prayed, I prayed to God that I could be saved and I could finally be brought back to reality and return to the real me. After each service, I spoke with members of the congregation and on occasion the priest, who wished me well and asked me what I liked about the service. I told him the Psalms were very powerful as was the Gospel of Luke, and that I was a new Christian but found everything I was learning so inspiring and magnificently empowering. He asked me to come again on a Sunday when the congregation would serve cakes and tea and do a workshop on helping others through charity and how to follow in the footsteps of Jesus. I told him I would be delighted to attend.

That Sunday, I dressed up in a smart suit with a shirt and tie—something I had hardly ever done in my life; I was more of a casual dresser, but I wanted to make the effort and wear my Sunday best for this important day. I felt like a man again. Though I still had my long hair, I tied it back into a bun to look more presentable in my suit. I felt great. I hadn't felt this good in a long time, and as I walked through the door I was showered with compliments on my new look and new suit. People were kind, and over the past few weeks I had gotten to know some of them and had begun to develop new friendships. I chatted a while with everyone, discussing the weather (a typical British conversation topic), and then began to discuss the various charitable work the church engaged in. There were projects in Africa, helping to build schools, projects to build hospitals, a Christmas box project to send presents to those less fortunate, and other important charitable causes. This immediately sparked my interest and reminded me of when I volunteered in Ethiopia and helped two hundred vulnerable children get access to school, vocational skill training, accommodation, and health care supplies. It had been a wholeheartedly fulfilling experience, one that reminded me that I had a purpose in life and an opportunity to help make the world a better place.

My experience with the charity project in Ethiopia was over a decade ago, but being back at a church after all these years in England reminded me of the good work I had done and the satisfaction I had felt helping others. I had to become this Oli again, to get back to my roots and get back to the selfless and caring boy I once was. The plastic surgery–obsessed, identity-changing, modern-day Oli was not the person I was born to be, and by speaking with church members and rekindling my old memories, I realized that it was imperative that I unlock the old me once more.

At the Sunday church meeting, some of the church members talked about the projects they were trying to raise funds for and the work that was being done to help communities, particularly in Central and East Africa. I wanted to help, I wanted to learn more and share my knowledge of the situations I had experienced first-hand and the things I had borne witness to while living in Ethiopia, and how the Christian community had helped many people keep faith and get through hard times. Everybody was fascinated to hear my account, and some of them also shared that they too had done projects, either with the church or previously with an organization, and how it had helped them do God's work and build their relationship to God. I agreed that doing these kinds of projects helped bring a person closer to God and helped one achieve self-fulfillment through helping another human being in need. After all, this was following the teachings of Jesus: showing compassion and helping the less fortunate, the people who needed help the most.

This was again another pivotal moment in my detransition and transformation. I had finally opened up to my repressed memories, things that I had not even thought about for years, and I was starting to remember the old Oli and the good, wholesome, and caring person I used to be. The uncorrupted, uncompromising, kind-hearted boy who had devoted much of his time to making the world a better place. I longed to be that person again and reactivate my old memories to help me find myself. I started to do that every day, following that pivotal meeting that had helped spark many memories of the old me, the original Oli. Hearing the stories in the church reminded me of the problems in the world today, from poverty to famine to access to basic education, and how one person can generally make a huge difference. I wanted to be that one person, and I wanted to make a difference. Thanks to my new life within the church community, I was starting to feel like it could be possible, that I could finally rid myself of my internal struggles and release the person trapped inside of me. I was ready to be reborn, through Christ. Reborn again as the real me.

Chapter 22

My Detransition

The moment of reckoning for me in my own detransition journey and where it first started was that fateful day in church that made me wake up and realize I was making a huge mistake. I had mutilated myself beyond recognition, altered every single part of me both physically and mentally, and I was not the same person inside. The once shy, thoughtful, and kind Oli had been cast aside in my endless pursuit of perfection. Yet the day had finally come when I stood up against myself, fought with my own mind, and realized that I had gone too far. Yet, I also came to realize that it was still not too late to change, that it's never too late. Everyone in the eyes of God has a chance to change, redeem themselves, and seek salvation. Even if you don't believe in God or a higher power, you can still find it within yourself through your own internal strength to make drastic changes and sway the course of your life. It's not an easy decision to make; it's an uphill battle that can take much time, energy, and determination. But we all can prevail and find our own internal strength and fight for ourselves, fight for our own validation, and fight for our right to be happy for our short time on this Earth. I was waging a battle and fighting back, after weeks of church visits, sessions with a therapist, seeking detransition resources online (although these were very limited), and seeking strength from other young people who had gender dysphoria or self-identification struggles and later detransitioned, whether medically or socially. I saw the level of willpower of some of these detransitioners, like Chloe Cole, KC Miller, and Cat Cattinson, who were put on hormones and later regretted it, as well as the many other voices sharing their struggles online. Some had experienced severe hair loss and other health-related issues; some had body parts cut up and deemed nonfunctioning. There was the story of Helena Kerschner, who at fifteen transitioned to a boy and later realized she had been pushed into her transition by social media and societal influences. These brave young people fought internally for years in a battle with themselves and with what society had told them to do. They were vulnerable, they were pushed into making life-altering decisions that no child should ever have to make. Children cannot even consent to these procedures and hormone therapy, yet adults in positions of power and authority had convinced them and their parents that this was the only solution, that there was no other alternative. I couldn't believe what these individuals had to go through, the pain they endured, and how after starting their detransition they had no one there to guide them, to support them, or to help them through the extremely difficult process, which takes a tremendous emotional and psychological toll on even the toughest individuals. Online attacks, physical threats of violence from society, being turned away and offered no support from the doctors who were all too quick to transition them, feelings of isolation, being let down by LGBT organizations, and being cast aside as victims of some terrible, irreversible science experiment. These people were made to feel like modern-day Frankensteins, shunned, treated as if they were monsters, and discarded while covered in scars both physically and psychologically. Their bravery pushed me forward and helped me muster the internal strength I needed. I thought if they can do it, if they can transition back to their original selves, then I can, too. I couldn't do it anymore; I couldn't suffer the pain I felt every day, the deep sadness I felt within my heart, my self-loathing, and the erosion of my true identity. I had to escape, and I was finally ready to take that giant leap, to tell myself that it was now or never. Now was my chance to finally find inner peace and be happy with who I am, I was finally ready to accept myself. Just like Houdini, the famed escape artist, I was able to climb out of my box and reveal myself—my real self, not some caricature of Oli, the real Oli—for the first time in over a decade.

• • •

The day had finally arrived: I got some scissors and a razor and decided it was time to remove all my hair, the first symbolic step in making me feel like a man again. I didn't care what it looked like, I just wanted the extensions and my own long hair gone. I didn't want to be reminded of how difficult the last six months had been, living publicly as a trans person, I just wanted it over quick and easy. It was emotional, but at the same time it was liberating; I felt free, like a bird that had been trapped in a cage and finally escaped. I was nearly bald, the scarring in my hairline visible. The scars were deep, and I was covered in them. I had done this to myself, I had wanted this, society had told me I had to do this to feel valid, to feel beautiful, and to feel confident. I couldn't live with regret, and I had to move on and promise myself it was over. I would never again go back to my old ways and would instead focus on self-development, working on my soul and becoming a better person, and learn to feel happy with who I was born to be, the way God had intended me to be. I would find peace within myself and cast aside my internal struggles. After the clumps of my hair lay on the floor, I scooped them up and smiled. I felt happy, I felt an enormous sense of relief and like I could breathe again. I was no longer trapped and breathless—I had escaped my own internal imprisonment. I knew I was doing the right thing.

The next step was to feel more masculine; the hair was simply not enough. It was merely symbolic for me to look and feel more like a man, but I had to act like one. I started working out four to five hours every day, seven days a week. I became obsessed with building muscle mass, obsessed and relentless in trying to get a man's body, in trying to look remotely attractive again and regain the essence of being a man. I would tire myself out, sometimes working out until 2:00 a.m., and do it all again the following morning. Had I replaced one obsession with another? After all, I had a history of obsessing over different things. My nose, K-pop, wanting to look like a Korean pop star, and becoming trans—these were all things I obsessively and relentlessly pursued. Of course, many young people hop onto trends or become obsessed with different things. Some may go through a Gothic phase, some a punk rock phase, and some young kids may even want to be a dinosaur and become obsessed for a period of time with this, but it doesn't mean we should affirm these obsessions and make a decision for these young people to identify as a dinosaur for the rest of their lives. At least my latest obsession, working out and exercising, was finally a healthy obsession and made me feel good, boosted my self-esteem and confidence. When I started to see progress, my confidence skyrocketed, and for the first time in what seemed like a lifetime I felt great again. I felt happy when I looked in the mirror, I felt content. The next step in my detransition was to go back through old photos, open up old memories that had been suppressed in the back of my prefrontal cortex for decades, and to relive childhood experiences. I went to the first church I had gone to as a child, while attending a Church of England school. I went back and walked down paths and through forests I had walked through as a child. I opened up old schoolbooks, my art projects, my old English assignments from high school. I looked through old toy boxes, reminding myself of the many fond memories of my early years. Like with Alzheimer's patients, reminiscing and remembering one's formative years from a happy time with cherished memories can really help to find inner peace and heal. Reminiscence therapy, going back through old memories and reliving experiences from the past and regaining childhood memories, is a technique often used to treat dementia.[1] It is also used to help those suffering with PTSD, helping them to move on from traumas and open up memories in order to heal. I kept reliving my own memories, visiting places where they took place, trying and searching endlessly to unlock the old me. The more I did this, the more it worked and the more fond memories I could recall. Before my detransition I had barely thought about my life in my teen years and early twenties; I had probably only thought about those days less than five times in a decade. It was trauma, repressed memories that once unlocked freed me and gave me the strength I needed to find who I am and bring that person back into the world. The kind, considerate, and thoughtful young man I once was. The person with a passion for helping make the world a better place was back, bigger and better than ever. Now was my time to shine a light on the world and share my lived experience in order to help others. I had to change the narrative and dialogue surrounding detransitioning, self-identification, and gender ideology.

I had lived through many traumas and dealt with them by mutilating myself as a temporary solution to try and fix a far more complex problem. I shared my story online, knowing I had an

---

1   SCIE. "Reminiscence for people with dementia—SCIE." *Social Care Institute for Excellence*, https://www.scie.org.uk/dementia/living-with-dementia/keeping-active/reminiscence.asp. Accessed 3 February 2023.

obligation and an opportunity to help others. In fact, it was more than an obligation; it was a moral duty. If I didn't step in and help, then who would? Who would be there to speak up for other young people who struggle to accept themselves and others going through internal struggles? It was not easy, being so vulnerable and opening up about it, but it felt good to talk about it, a therapy within itself. Talking was healing. I was already having therapy sessions, which is something I would recommend to anyone going through gender dysphoria or questioning their own identity, something for anyone thinking about changing themselves and also for those who detransition. No one should ever feel alone in their struggle, and openly talking about issues can greatly help to improve mental health.

I had to speak up for others, to open up about my own struggles in order to try and warn others, including parents, of the dangers of affirming gender identity without looking at the real reasons for a person's gender dysphoria. When I started to see what was truly going on in the world, the sharp rise in young people being transitioned and how society was complicit in influencing millions of young people across the world to want to medically change themselves, I had to do something. I could not stand idly by and watch so many people who struggle like I did for so many years be manipulated, indoctrinated, and abused by a system that has no real regard for the well-being of these individuals. I started doing endless research into gender clinics and the gender-affirming care system and found an innumerable number of horror stories, which I share in Part Two of this book. There was a deep, dark, and disturbing trend of increasingly younger people being put on hormones and puberty blockers and having plastic surgery to change themselves before they even had a chance to discover who they really were.

In the UK, where I am from, it was much rarer for a teen to undergo gender reassignment surgery or be prescribed puberty blockers and hormones. However, there was one notorious and infamous UK clinic, the Tavistock Clinic, that became synonymous with shocking stories of teens being heavily medicated and kept inside for long periods of time to "help" them transition, and horror stories of teens expressing their regret at ever going there. The clinic was ordered to shut down in 2022 after multiple lawsuits and investigations. Over the years, thousands of vulnerable teens passed through the clinic's doors, with their mental health disregarded and ignored. Instead these vulnerable teens, in desperate search for answers to their internal struggles, were pushed onto medications, questionable medical practices, and a lack of duty of care on the part of the so-called "medical professionals." The charges against the clinic for its reckless handling of its patients included a failure to collect any data on the use of puberty blockers in patients under sixteen, no follow-up or check-ups on patients to see the results of the puberty blockers, doctors completely ignoring the correlation of children with autism and gender dysphoria, and actively prescribing autistic and vulnerable children puberty blockers without consideration for their extreme vulnerability. Doctors willingly provided gender-affirming care to children suffering from eating disorders such as anorexia and bulimia, children with severe depression, and children suffering from past traumas or sexual abuse and put them on hormones and puberty blockers with blatant disregard for the fact their gender dysphoria likely stemmed from these traumas or disorders. Sexual orientation and gender identity issues were blurred, with some children simply identifying as gay, lesbian, or bisexual being wrongly told they are the wrong gender and must transition. All disorders, all mental health issues, all traumas, and autism were treated under the assumption that they were related to the child's gender identity. Transitioning was seen as the only solution, and thousands of innocent teens had their livelihoods stolen by the malpractice of the clinic's staff.

Any staff member who questioned the policies was immediately reprimanded, and basic logic was pushed aside for the extreme push toward transitioning. Many staff, including senior staff, resigned from their jobs over ethical concerns or were called transphobic and forced out of their jobs. In 2021, five thousand referrals to the Gender Identity Development Service at the clinic were made compared with a mere 250 a decade earlier—an extremely sharp rise in the number of teens wanting to transition, just like we have seen across the United States.[2]

The explosive investigation into the clinic unveiled many red flags, and this was just one example of what these clinics do. What else is happening behind closed doors in the one hundred gender clinics in America and what horror stories will be unveiled in the future? The UK was one step ahead with the announced closure of this clinic, but there would be no justice for the teens who now have to live with the results of something that was pushed onto them, or the teens who were misdiagnosed and medically transitioned, never able to get back fully to their old selves even if they did detransition.

One UK clinic was exposed and shut down. Hundreds more still stood across the world. Now it was my mission and the mission of other detransitioners, lawmakers, activists, and concerned parents to help stop other clinics pushing these harmful practices on children. It was also my new mission to speak directly with other detransitioners, to hear their stories, to learn about their struggles, and to find out what solutions there could be for the future and what preventative measures could be put in place to safeguard children and prevent more horror stories while putting an immediate end to any more suffering. We needed to push back against schools

---

2   Society For Evidence Based Gender Medicine. "Clinical Damage: The Tavistock Clinic's closure follows a damning report on ideological malpractice." *SEGM*, 2 August 2022, https://segm.org/Tavistock-closure-the-times. Accessed 3 February 2023.

pushing gender on kids, on literature and books targeting children to confuse them, and push them into the multibillion-dollar gender-changing industry. Why couldn't schools just teach normal subjects like history, geography, religious education, mathematics, and biology? Why was there such a determination for school districts to push gender and other controversial and unnecessary subjects on children, like critical race theory? Or why couldn't schools encourage kids to develop self-confidence, to be themselves and learn to be happy with the way they were born? There is simply no need to teach children about genders, being nonbinary or trans. If they grow up and decide after feeling that way their whole life that they want to be trans or nonbinary, that is a decision solely for them to make as an adult, but we shouldn't have teachers and educators pushing ideas on these kids that they would otherwise not even consider.

I know that if I had grown up in these times, I would have fallen victim much more quickly to gender ideology, given the fact I became trans in much later life. I know that I would have easily ticked the box for puberty blockers, hormones, and gender reassignment, and I would have been pushed through the gender-affirming care system and left to fend for myself and deal with the results for the rest of my life. I don't live with regret with what I put myself through; I am just grateful I didn't go the whole way or didn't grow up in the modern-day school system, as I know I would have been left with severe health problems, extreme depression, and left in a vulnerable state where I could be exploited by the gender system. I had a lucky escape with what I went through and was able to wake up and realize before it was too late. While my face and body are covered with scars from surgeries, scars that will never fade, they are a daily reminder that I almost pushed myself too far, that I am lucky to still be here, and that I need to find inner peace with the real me. I have learned to live with no regrets and instead learn from these past experiences and use them to help make the world a better, safer place for future generations. Everything I have been through up until this point has been a learning journey, but now it has become my mission to help others suffering, to help find solutions, and to help highlight the harm modern society in the Internet age is having on young people and their identities.

Unlike some of the other detransitioners, I was saved before it was too late, saved in the nick of time from going further down the transition route. Although my face, head, and neck are covered in scars that remind me daily of the pain I inflicted on myself during my identity struggles, I've now been saved by my new way of thinking, my newfound faith, and have reached a point where I have much-needed clarity in my life. I was clear about who I really was, and I was able to search deep within my soul to uncover the real Oli that had been trapped inside a prison longing to be freed. I was no longer controlled by the thoughts and opinions of others and the world around me that had convinced me that becoming trans was easy and it was my destiny. The symbolic decision to shave my hair completely to help shed any reminder of my trans identity was something I had never done before; my hair had been my pride and my joy, yet the weight of it on my head had dragged me down and clouded my judgment. My hair was gone, and I had finally been freed to begin my detransition.

Chapter 23

A Voice for Others

We all do things in life we later learn to regret. My case was probably more extreme than others, or dare I say *a lot* more extreme. Upon reflection, I had many sleepless nights feeling guilty for my past behaviors and the message I was sending to the world. What lay heavily on my mind the most was the realization and acceptance over the last few years that millions of young people looked up to me. Millions of K-pop fans, millions of social media users across the world saw me as funny, cool, inspiring, or a trend. I now live with tremendous regret that my actions as an influencer in the Internet age may have led others to go astray, to question their own gender, or may have encouraged them to change their identity.

However, as the Bible teaches us, sins can be forgiven in the eyes of God. We all have a chance to redeem ourselves and seek salvation. I confessed my sins and the troubling things that ran through my mind about my past actions in a confessional at church. The priest told me that God is forgiving, and that Jesus sacrificed Himself for our sins. I needed desperately to hear this, but I also needed it to show myself that despite a person's past actions, they can redeem themselves through helping others. This is what inspired me to use my platform for good, to raise awareness of important issues in the world, to fight for the voiceless, and to fight for the right to be heard for every single detransitioning teen and every single person who has suffered from the effects of self-identification.

My detransition process had been like a rebirth; I was being reborn as myself, the old me, the one who cared more about helping others and making the world a better place, not the vacuous Oli who was obsessed with looking at his own reflection and morphing into someone he was not. I had weathered many storms up until this point, but I was now putting my struggle into perspective.

We all have different journeys in life, and no one can ever fully understand the internal struggles of others, but we can listen to their concerns, we can guide them, and we can speak from our own experiences in order to give them a better future and a better fighting chance to self-love. When I began to fully see the struggles teens with gender dysphoria were facing and the pressures parents were facing just to protect their children, it broke my heart. In many states like Oregon and Washington, parents' rights were being overridden and taken away. Teens struggling with mental health conditions like bipolar disorder, schizophrenia, autism, and other conditions were being taken away from their parents, put into foster care, shelters, or host homes where their minds would be shaped by adults with no blood relation to them, people who did not necessarily have their best interests at heart. Some teens suffering from suicidal thoughts and some from broken families who are put in shelters for their own safety are also vulnerable to being told the answer to all of their problems is to affirm a new gender identity. This caused me great concern, thinking that a child would be separated from their parents and the parents having their rights removed. I learned about cases and spoke with parents across both Washington and Oregon who said the care system had taken away their children, claiming that the parents did not support their child's new gender identity. Government officials, medical practitioners, and the foster care system took these teens away, removing the final safeguard protecting them from undergoing medical transition so that they could become just another number on hospital records and more money in the pockets of doctors and hospitals performing gender-affirming care. I spoke with one brave mother, Julie Barrett, the founder of Conservative Ladies of Washington, a group of thousands of women and mothers concerned with the current system, concerned with the removal of parental rights and that gender dysphoria is being pushed on their children. Parents are the ones who truly care for their children, and they are the only ones who can make the best decisions in the interests of their child no matter how hard that decision may be for the child or how much they rebel. Of course, not all cases are the same and there are kids in the foster and shelter system because of abuse they faced in the home, and it's imperative that they be protected and kept safe from those that hurt them. However, we must acknowledge the growing number of teens who do have loving parents who are against medically transitioning their children, and we must realize that the system is forcibly taking these kids away from these loving parents in the name of forcibly affirming their gender identity. These teens are being taken away from their parents, away from their safety nets, and all protective barriers and safeguarding are being removed. The system conditions these kids to believe their parents are harmful, dangerous, and abusive and that they are now in safe hands. They reinforce that the reason their parents would not accept them is due to transphobia and homophobia and reinforce ideas that the teen was born in the wrong body and now they can change, now they are able to become the opposite gender, the person the education system, hospitals, doctors, society, and social media has been pushing them to become for much of their life. They could now transition and be themselves, and these new "guardians" and supposed protectors would help them achieve their goals. These highly vulnerable teens, torn away from their families, may now end up as lifelong customers of big pharma, being medicated throughout their lives, placed on hormones, estrogen, or testosterone, and even having gender reassignment surgery.

Since my detransition, I was on a mission to be a voice of reason, speak from experience, and help others avoid making mistakes they could well regret for the rest of their lives. Regret can be a heavy burden to carry; it can seem like the weight of the world on a person's shoulders, a pressure that can lead to feelings of considerable guilt. I had many regrets about the past, my actions, my life choices, and who I had become. But I couldn't keep living with this regret, and I needed to change my way of thinking. I knew I had made mistakes, but I had to move on for my mental health, and so I could reactivate my old self, the Oli that helped others like I did years ago in Ethiopia, helping improve the livelihoods and well-being of other young people. This now became my goal, so I would funnel all my energy and thought processes toward this. Not only would it mean I could help others, but it would also divert my thought process that previously had involved constantly thinking about plastic surgery and wanting to change myself. I could finally get over that way of thinking, that repetitive and unhealthy way of life, and be a voice for others confused with their gender and confused with their identity. I could speak out and tell them everything is going to be okay, reassure them that whatever they are experiencing now will likely pass and when they grow up they will be able to learn to self-accept and be happy with the way they were born. A worthwhile mission to save lives so that no one ended up making decisions they would later grow to regret. I couldn't take back my past actions, but I could certainly advise others not to fall for the same mistakes as I did. Soon my regrets disappeared, and I was able to focus on this new worthwhile mission.

PART 2

Chapter 24

Education Then vs Now

I came into the world at a time of great change, socially, culturally, and politically.

Just two weeks after the end of one of the most revolutionary modern decades, the eighties. The eighties saw lightening socioeconomic change across the world, a cultural shift of self-exploration, and the rise of pop culture. The decade also saw a rapid rise in materialism, consumerism, the advent of the MTV era, the rise of the LGBT movement, and the fight for equality as well as the shift in the political climate with President Ronald Reagan's "Reaganomics" policy, building the US economy and democratizing government spending and policies. In the UK, there was a push toward conservatism with Margaret Thatcher, a Jekyl and Hyde character to many, transforming the political landscape of Britain for better or worse. On November 9th, 1989, toward the end of a decade that had seen so much change, the Berlin Wall came crashing down—a turning point in the world of capitalism vs communism. A symbolic shift from the old world to the modern, and into a new decade that turned out to be one of the most notable in modern history—the nineties.

I was born into a new age, an age of meteoric change, where technology became a dominant driving force from video games, movies, music, cell phones, and new electronics designed to make our lives easier. A new age where opinions had become more open, traditional societal values changed, and children were being taught important and thought-provoking subjects about the world in schools.

This was a great time to grow up, a time of change, yet a time where children had the opportunities and tools to thrive and develop into well-rounded future innovators. They often say that the decade of one's childhood is the most important one and the memories from this time are those we cherish until our last breath. Looking back on these periods in our lives draws nostalgia for many along with a vast number of fond memories. We tend to love music, movies, and culture from these periods of our childhood the most. Listening to music from the decades when we grew up, watching films from that era, and surrounding ourselves with reminders from these times can help us reimagine the past and open up memories we may not have thought about in decades.

Part of the care approach for Alzheimer's and dementia patients is to help them recreate memories from their youth through visual and sensory means such as old photos, playing music from that era, and even recreating rooms to replicate the decor of the person's time as a child. This approach, which has been coined Reminiscence Therapy (RT), triggers positive memories of the past to help patients regain memory, calm anxiety, and greatly improve quality of life.[1] This therapy is also used to treat patients with depression, and various studies have shown that helping a person reminisce and remember the good, happy times can improve

---

1   Snelling, Sherri, and Scott Tarde. "First U.S. Dementia Village Recreates a Happier Time." *Forbes*, Forbes, 25 October 2021, https://www.forbes.com /sites/nextavenue/2017/04/26/first-u-s-dementia-village-recreates-a-happier -time/?sh=227684707433. Accessed 30 December 2022.

the overall mental well-being of the patient.[2] As an adult, at age thirty-two, I too used this method while trying to find myself after years of struggling with identity. I needed to unlock memories from my past, recall my childhood, and help figure out why I had taken such drastic life-altering decisions. Using the reminiscent therapy approach greatly helped me in finding my identity and reminded me of the person I once was. I also retraced my childhood, visiting my first school, taking walks down forest hiking trails that I had traipsed through as a child, visiting places I had been all too familiar with in my younger years. Breathing the fresh air of the countryside, taking in the views of the hills and flower-filled meadows, and walking down the same trodden paths I had ventured down many times as a young boy. Each time I did this, I remembered something from my past; it felt familiar, it felt comforting, and it felt like I was slowly rediscovering the old me and all the wonderful memories I had of my time growing up. I began to remember the happy memories of the nineties—a time before gender ideology and before the notion of so many people, like me, being convinced by society that we may be trapped in the wrong body. I was never taught about gender identity, pronouns, being nonbinary or trans in school because it wasn't a mainstream trend back then. We didn't have social media, there was no TikTok, and there were no books in school libraries trying to confuse children like me with their gender.

Despite all the hurdles and struggles I faced in adult life, I was one of the lucky ones. I grew up in a simpler and safer time, a time before ideologies were pushed on children from preschool and kindergarten. Yet the children of today are not so lucky, and they now

---

2   Liu, Zhuo, et al. "The Effectiveness of Reminiscence Therapy on Alleviating Depressive Symptoms in Older Adults: A Systematic Review." *NCBI*, Frontiers in Psychology, 17 August 2021, https://www.ncbi.nlm.nih.gov/pmc/articles /PMC8415872/. Accessed 30 December 2022.

grow up in a very different environment with a variety of pressures that force them to question themselves and experience confusion from increasingly younger ages.

The modern-day school system, particularly in the United States, focuses on teaching such subjects as Critical Race Theory, Gender Ideology, and Sex Education. These have become the priority for school boards in "woke" school districts, taking precedence over the teaching of History, Mathematics, Languages, Geography, and Sports. So it comes as no surprise when we look at the statistics, that in 2022 in both the United States and UK school grades and competency levels dropped dramatically. With such a focus on teaching these new theories and ideologies and less focus on teaching the basics like mathematics and languages, we are seeing an extremely worrying trend across the global education system.

While we have to take into account the detrimental and damaging effect the pandemic and resulting lockdowns have had on children's development for over two years—with many classes being taught online over video and children being forced to wear masks and unable to have social interactions with classmates—we also have to look at what children are now being taught and why such subjects are causing a significant and alarming decrease in academic ability.

According to a 2022 US study by the Annenberg Institute at Brown University, which looked at test scores of 5.4 million K–12 students in grades 3–8, math and reading abilities dropped dramatically across the first two years of the pandemic. Math scores dropped by 0.20–0.27 standard deviations (SDs) compared with same-grade peers in fall 2019, while reading test scores were 0.09–0.18 SDs lower. Students from lower-income families also saw a sharp decrease in test scores, with a comparison between lower-poverty to higher-poverty students showing a 20 percent drop in math and 15 percent in reading ability.[3] But the pandemic is not the only thing that is decreasing test scores; a constant focus on teaching Critical Race Theory and radical gender studies is also to blame. Teachers are increasingly focusing classes on discussing these topics and taking time away from other more pressing subjects like math and reading. The combination of these factors, from the pandemic to the increase in new subjects being studied, sets a worrying precedent for the future. Children *are* the future—they are the future innovators, scientists, doctors, nurses, educators, and engineers. Yet how can we live in hope that the future will be bright, when we see clearly from statistics that the level of education has slid to an all-time low, that test scores are at the lowest in history in both the United States and UK, and children are being constantly pushed to question themselves and prioritize gender and race over everything?

Critical Race Theory examines the history of different races based on the views of social and civil-rights activists and scholars, arguing that certain races are the reason for the oppression of others and that racism is systemic in America's institutions and throughout society. This theory can be harmful in many ways to children, as it teaches them to judge and be critical of people based on their skin color—despite the fact that the majority of people in society today are not racist and don't judge others based on skin color. Children, as we all know from our own childhood experiences, are the most impressionable in society, and they easily mold to views dictated to them by those in authority such as teachers and educators. We also know that children are the least judgmental population group in society; they are born seeing everyone as equals, they are born male or female, and it is the way they are raised, their education, their

---

3   Kuhfeld, Megan, et al. "Test Score Patterns Across Three COVID-19-impacted School Years." *EdWorkingPapers*, Annenberg Institute at Brown University, January 2022, https://edworkingpapers.com/sites/default/files/ai22–521.pdf. Accessed 30 December 2022.

surrounding environment, and the culture they grow up in that ultimately shape their views, mold their prejudices, and manufacture their ideas of gender and identity.

When I went to school back in the nineties, I remember being taught history through an unbiased lens, taught to be free-thinking and form my own opinions about the past, to form my own conclusions on historical figures and events. As Winston Churchill once said, "History is written by the victors," and those who win wars and battles ultimately are the ones who write the history books. But I was taught this from an early age at school and taught to question both sides of the history books, to delve deeper into historical figures and to come up with my own conclusions as a free-thinking child. This is the way it should be. A child should be taught to always question and explore subjects and to form their own opinions—not as we see in schools today where some teachers push woke ideologies with biased opinions onto children and force them to accept that one view without daring to question it or explore alternative viewpoints. The way I was taught, to question everything and to learn all aspects of history and both sides of the argument, is how I believe the education system should be, and indeed this should be the standard across all schools. Children should always be encouraged to think for themselves, yet in 2023, the opposite is sadly the case.

In addition to CRT becoming a widespread part of curricula across America, Gender Ideology or "Radical Gender Theory" has become intertwined with school education syllabi. Over four thousand US schools now teach gender theory under the guise of "Gender and Sexuality,"[4] Kindergarten students as young as four are now being taught about being nonbinary, preferred pronouns,

---

4   Rufo, Christopher F. "Radical Gender Theory Has Now Made Its Way Into More Than 4000 US Schools." *Manhattan Institute*, Manhattan Institute, 24 August 2022, https://www.manhattan-institute.org/radical-gender-theory-made -way-4000-us-schools. Accessed 30 December 2022.

sexual organs, changing gender, and are actively being encouraged to question their birth-assigned sex.

Gone are the good old days of the 1990s and the decades prior, where kids like me grew up excited to learn about the world and excited to study and form our own opinions and views of the world. Now kids are being indoctrinated from an increasingly younger age to feel confused and to prioritize gender and race over learning mathematics and English. We are seeing more children changing gender, falling victim to the pronoun preaching—boys wanting to wear skirts and dresses and identify as girls, and girls wanting to cut up their bodies to become boys. Some children even want to change their race or culture, to erode their birth-given identity to fit in or follow a trend or fit into a social group they identify with. Indeed, I too fell for this culture-adopting mentality after becoming entwined in one of the coolest trends, the K-pop phenomenon. I wasn't taught this at school, like many kids are taught to self-identify these days, but as an adult the world told me it was cool to change and identify in any way you feel. The world also taught me that by self-identifying you will be given praise and positive reinforcement and put on a pedestal while being celebrated as "stunning" and "brave."

Is the current approach of self-identifying, changing gender, and celebrating people for being nonbinary a healthy approach to teach kids? Or is it detrimental to a child's development, abusive in nature, and a form of grooming a child's mind to become something they are not? Comparing this with the time I grew up in, the nineties, I would never have imagined how the world would become so dystopian, akin to George Orwell's visions and accurate predictions in his novel *1984*. And what of the correlation between what is taught in modern classrooms and the "dumbing down" of society proven through the drop in test scores and the constant push for new radical ideas to be taught to children?

The 1990s was a simpler and happier time, a safer space for all. In the span of just a few short decades the world has changed radically. The year 2022 was Orwellian and 2023 even more so, but what about the future, will it only get worse? Or by speaking up against the system, rebelling against the indoctrination of children and the hijacking of the school curriculum by those pushing gender ideology, could we stop this once and for all? This notion of change happening too quickly and how this radical change is endangering education and children's futures is what eventually led me to wake up and speak out and fight for those who have been manipulated and confused for too long. Children need a voice, parents need a voice, and I have come to realize I have a duty to elevate those voices through my own lived experiences to help make the world a better place, to help make it a simpler world for all.

Chapter 25

Gender Ideology vs Parental Rights

At thirty-two, I had transitioned to become a "woman." I didn't grow up in the age of today, the Internet age, the age of woke education and gender politics being pushed on kids, or in an age where gender-affirming care was a prolific system exploiting teenagers. I was lucky to grow up just before all of this became the norm, yet I still fell victim to many of the influences of modern gender ideology and still generally believed at the time that I was a trans woman and that I could change my gender. I was an adult living in the new age of self-identification and gender ideology that targets the minds of millions of easily influenced people across all walks of life. I was a lamb to the slaughter, like the millions of others across the world who are currently considering or undergoing surgery, socially transitioning, and those trapped as victims of the gender-affirming care system—the umbrella term for teens and young people being prescribed puberty blockers, hormone replacement therapy, and being encouraged to transition.

Gender-affirming care, despite the pleasant-sounding name, is another term for what many would call "genital mutilation," or a term for undergoing irreversible procedures and taking hormones that can have devastating consequences. Of course, there are cases where people have gone through this and lived happy lives, confident in their decision to change. I have always advocated for people doing what makes them happy as long as they can consent and have undergone the right checks and balances, and as long as they alone make the decision as an adult without being influenced by others. It is hard to understand someone who spends their entire life feeling trapped and unhappy with the way they were born, and I and many others feel strong compassion for the struggles of these individuals. But we know in today's world, most of these individuals, even adults, are being coerced, sold a false dream, and being indoctrinated to believe changing gender is the solution to all of their problems and that they will be happy for eternity once they transition. We know now that this is a false dream being peddled by the medical system, LGBT organizations, Planned Parenthood, and other stakeholders who seek to profit and gain from increasing numbers of patients in the gender-affirming system.

In 2022, few checks and balances were in place to protect the growing number of teens being pressured into having this "gender-affirming care" as a minor. In states like Oregon, teens are allowed to "consent" as young as age fifteen to undergo gender reassignment surgeries, without even the permission of their parents. A CHILD having surgery to cut up their entire body and change their anatomy! It sounds like a horror movie, but sadly this has become a reality.

In the case of Oregon, these surgeries in minors without the parents' knowledge are also taxpayer funded. A female-to-male transition can cost around $70,000, while male-to-female costs between $40,000 to $50,000, and this does not include the lifelong health implications these surgeries can have on people's bodies as well as the lifelong cost for prescriptions, hormones, and medications. There is also little long-term data or studies to show the health implications for these procedures. I had undergone facial feminiza-tion surgeries as an adult, yet fifteen-year-olds were able to undergo full-body surgeries. How was this normal?

In 2017 there were 15,172 cases of children between the ages of six and seventeen being diagnosed with gender dysphoria, yet by 2021 this had sharply risen to 42,167.[1] These figures represent the children and teens who visited a doctor to receive a medical diag-nosis and do not take into account the many thousands of others who experience gender dysphoria yet never get an official medical diagnosis or visit a medical practitioner. So we can assume, based on growing trends across schools, social media, and society that the number of gender-dysphoric children is significantly higher than the medical research data present.

California has seen the highest uptick, along with New York and Washington state, with California alone rising to over three thou-sand medical diagnoses in 2021, compared with just over a thou-sand in 2016. In 2022, California passed Senate Bill 107, which will give legal sanctuary to any one parent or child who decides to flee a state such as Alabama, Idaho, or Texas that has laws to prevent gender-affirming care in minors. What this means is if one parent decides that their child is "trapped in the wrong body," or wants to be the opposite gender, they can flee to California, where the gender-affirming care process can begin—overriding the paren-tal rights of one of the parents who may object to the decision. Minors are also able to flee to California to undergo puberty block-ers, hormones, or in some cases genital reassignment without their parents' consent. The bill passed by Democratic California State Senator Wiener, the BDSM- and bondage-gear–loving senator,

---

1   Respaut, Robin, and Chad Terhune. "Number of transgender children seek-ing treatment surges in U.S." *Reuters*, Komodo Health, 6 October 2022, https://www.reuters.com/investigates/special-report/usa-transyouth-data/. Accessed 2 February 2023.

who has posted topless images of himself in leather bondage clothing on Twitter, and who aside from creating this bill has pushed to relax laws for sex offenders, pushed to decriminalize people with HIV+ from disclosing their diagnosis to their partners, and to place biological men who identify as trans into women's prisons.[2] Not only this, but Wiener has been calling for gas stoves to be banned, claiming they are toxic to health, and passed legislation for "Safe Consumption Sites," to allow drug addicts to be injected with heroin and other dangerous substances in legally designated areas in California.[3] States like Alabama currently have laws in place that punish parents and health-care providers with up to ten years in prison for providing gender-affirming care to minors.[4] So the new California law provides sanctuary for any teen or parent from these states that outlaw gender surgeries being performed on anyone under the age of eighteen and allows one parent who chooses to allow their child to have body surgery or hormones a free pass, giving California courts jurisdiction over each case and overriding other state laws, even if the child is a resident of one of these other states. The bill, which went into effect on January 1, 2023, now means a child can travel out of state, with or without their parents, and go to California to undergo gender-affirming care such as

2   Haworth, Ian. "California's New Year's resolution: Let transgender youth suffer irreversible harm." *Washington Examiner*, 3 January 2023, https://www.washingtonexaminer.com/restoring-america/community-family/californias-new-years-resolution-let-transgender-youth-suffer-irreversible-harm. Accessed 2 February 2023.

3   Wiener, Senator Scott. "Senator Wiener's Safe Consumption Sites Legislation Passes Assembly." *Senator Scott Wiener*, 30 June 2022, https://sd11.senate.ca.gov/news/20220630-senator-wiener%E2%80%99s-safe-consumption-sites-legislation-passes-assembly. Accessed 2 February 2023.

4   Reuters. "Fact Check-California law gives courts clear jurisdiction over minors seeking gender care in the state." *Reuters*, 30 September 2022, https://www.reuters.com/article/factcheck-explainer-california-transgend-idUSL1N3111JR. Accessed 2 February 2023.

hormone therapy, puberty blockers, and gender reassignment surgery. If one of the parents opposes this, then Californian courts and authorities can take action against that parent for denying the child gender-affirming "care."[5] This not only puts children in harm's way by allowing them to make decisions they may have been coerced into making by educators, medical professionals, social media influencers, and other pressures that could have influenced their decision, it also takes away the rights of parents and sets a dangerous precedent for using the law to stifle parents who may object to gender ideology or their kids being put on hormones. Whatever state they may be from, those laws will become void if the child goes to California, putting the parent under immense emotional distress.

It is simply unthinkable to remove the rights of parents, particularly for something so life altering as changing gender. We are sadly seeing more and more parents losing their parental rights, especially since the beginning of the COVID pandemic, where many parents were forced to comply with mask and vaccine mandates or their child would be expelled from a school. In addition to this, with gender ideology, like with the new California law, we are seeing parents being thrown out of school board meetings simply for voicing their objection to certain topics being pushed on children such as sex education for kindergarteners, allowing boys into girls' restrooms and locker rooms, Drag Story Hours, or critical race theory classes. Whatever anyone's beliefs, whether someone is supportive of trans people, open-minded, or opposed to the idea of people living as the opposite sex, every parent still has the fundamental right that is enshrined in the Constitution to decide what is best for their child and to speak out and voice their opinion on matters that

---

5   Woods, Norman. "California's S.B. 107 threatens children and parents in South Dakota." Family Heritage Alliance, 13 September 2022, https://www .familyheritagealliance.org/californias-s-b-107-threatens-children-and-parents -in-south-dakota/. Accessed 2 February 2023.

concern their children's education. It's a basic parental right, yet these rights are being taken away more each passing day.

In 2022 in the state of Vermont, a fourteen-year-old girl was suspended from Randolph Union Middle School and her father was fired from his role as the school's much-loved sports coach simply for complaining about a boy undressing in front of teenage girls in the girls' locker room. Decades ago, this would have provoked outrage and protests from parents and activists for putting teenage girls at risk—the boy would have been the one suspended and teachers would have made strict policies to ban males from female spaces in schools. Yet in this case, thanks to the wokeness of modern society, the girl was suspended. Not the boy who had violated the female safe spaces. It sounds like a story right out of George Orwell's *1984* dystopian novel, a future where extreme ideologies and completely ludicrous scenarios were the norm. Common sense had become heresy and outlawed. In the *1984* novel, in an authoritarian society void of reason, those in authority tell you 2+2=5 and you are made to believe that even the most ludicrous falsehoods are in fact the truth. The brave Vermont schoolgirl, Blake Allen, who simply voiced her concerns to a group of friends (who later reported her to a teacher for being "transphobic"), was forced to write a letter of apology to the boy stating how she was wrong to criticize him being in the locker room and wrong to misgender him. Her father, Travis Allen, then wrote a Facebook post criticizing the school for the way they treated his daughter, and he was then suspended without pay for expressing his concerns as a parent and defending his daughter's safety.[6] To most people this sounds like insanity, yet sadly it

---

6   Carnahan, Ashley. "Dad, daughter rip suspension for complaint on trans female in girls' locker room: 'Male shouldn't be allowed.'" *Fox News*, 28 October 2022, https://www.foxnews.com/media/dad-daughter-rip-suspension-complaint -trans-female-girls-locker-room-male-shouldnt-allowed. Accessed 2 February 2023.

has become the norm, and the example of Blake Allen's story has become a reality for many students in the American school system. Many are fearful of speaking out about males in their locker rooms or gender-neutral restrooms being introduced in schools. Parents are also being threatened or silenced about speaking about these issues, which has a detrimental impact on their children, all for fear of having their child suspended and being smeared or labeled "transphobic," or a "bigot."

In another case of school boards putting the rights of trans and nonbinary students over the rights of girls, in May 2021, in Loudoun county, Virginia, a fifteen-year-old boy wearing a skirt entered a girls' restroom and raped a teenage girl.[7] After the horrific violent assault, the victim's father was treated worse than the rapist. The school board had been pushing transgender policies for a number of years and denied the assault took place, claiming their policies of respecting people's identities did not have any correlation to what happened. When the father was initially called to be alerted to his daughter being attacked and arrived at school in distress, a natural reaction for any parent, he was later arrested, even though his daughter was the victim. The school board called the police on him and had him arrested and later prosecuted after trying to tell his daughter's story at a school meeting. He was the victim's father, he had been traumatized and had his world ripped apart, his daughter had been violated, and yet the school board treated him like he was the criminal. Another page straight out of George Orwell's novel, where criminals are treated as victims and the actual victims treated as criminals. The boy who was arrested

---

7 Warren, Steve. "VA Judge Finds Trans Teen Guilty of Sexual Assault in Loudoun County High School Girl's Bathroom Case." *CBN.com*, 26 October 2021, https://www1.cbn.com/cbnnews/us/2021/october/va-judge-finds-transgender -teen-guilty-of-sexual-assault-in-loudoun-county-high-school-girls-bathroom -case. Accessed 2 February 2023.

and charged for committing the assault was eventually convicted but faced no jail time after the court ruled that he would change and never reoffend.[8] This was despite the fact that the skirt-wearing boy had been arrested for sexually assaulting another girl at a different high school. How on Earth was the victim treated worse than the criminal? And how could a boy who had assaulted two girls be free to walk away from his crime, with no justice for the victims? He identified as "gender-fluid," so his rights were automatically put above the rights of the victims. The school board protected him, they pushed for boys to be in the girls' restroom, they tried to cover up the severity of the assault and punished the father as well as the girl, even though she was the victim. This is an extreme example of a miscarriage of justice, but how many more cases like this are we going to see in the future if more and more schools put gender-ideology policies in their schools? Whether that means gender-neutral restrooms or allowing boys into locker rooms, it puts girls at risk. We should not and cannot allow this to become the norm, even if it just saves one child from being assaulted. Society has a duty to protect every single child in an environment like a school. School is supposed to be a safe and nurturing place. Until then, we are sadly going to see more of these terrible cases happening unless we push back, unless parents continue to fight back, unless policy makers and lawmakers enact laws to prevent this happening. The children of the world deserve better.

---

8   Standing For Freedom Center. "Skirt-wearing male student is found guilty of raping a 15-year-old girl in a school bathroom in Loudoun County, Virginia." *Standing for Freedom Center*, 26 October 2021, https://www.standingforfreedom .com/2021/10/skirt-wearing-male-student-is-found-guilty-of-raping-a-15 -year-old-girl-in-a-school-bathroom-in-loudoun-county-virginia/. Accessed 2 February 2023.

Chapter 26

Gender-Affirming Care

Gender-affirming care refers to a range of medical, psychological, behavioral, and social interventions used to support a person's gender-identity transition. This can range from medical interventions such as hormone replacement therapy, puberty blockers, double mastectomy for girls, and genital reassignment. The behavioral part involves "specialists," psychologists, and medical "professionals," helping a person adopt the behaviors of the opposite gender, guiding them on how to identify as male or female and how to behave and feel like the opposite sex. The social part refers to how the person can live in society and integrate as the opposite gender, from using women's restrooms (in the case of men who identify as female), dressing more feminine, and fitting in with their new gender by imitating feminine mannerisms and behaviors.

When it comes to gender-affirming care in children, doctors and medical practitioners are supposed to thoroughly examine a child's mental and physical health, their cognitive development, the rate of their physical development during the period, and based on parental consent. However, parental consent can be overridden in some instances such as the case in Oregon, where fifteen-year-olds can have surgery without the parents' consent or knowledge.

We also see, like in California, states supplanting parental rights to allow the teen to decide for themselves if they want to undergo gender-affirming care. Other states are also attempting to follow suit, with Washington state and the introduction of SB 5599, which will allow teenagers to undergo gender-affirming care under the guise of "protected healthcare services" and "inclusivity." Washington state has also introduced HB 1469, which would make it a sanctuary state for teens traveling from other states to undergo gender-affirming care and receive access to hormones and surgeries. This bill, like the law passed in California, means that the laws of the state in which the teen resides are overridden and a parent is unable to take any legal action if their child goes to a sanctuary state to transition. Again, like California's law, this would seek to stop parents in other states from taking legal action to block their child from undergoing gender-affirming care in Washington and would also leave taxpayers with the burden of paying for these treatments and surgeries. I testified before both Senate hearings about my opposition to these new bills, along with countless parents who simply wanted to retain their right to protect their children. In each Senate hearing, an overwhelming number of people testified against the bills being passed, citing concerns for children and parents, yet the bills were pushed through regardless of these concerns. What also raises alarm bells with the Washington SB 5599 bill is how it has an emergency clause that means if it passes through the Senate, it immediately becomes law, surpassing the usual ninety days or longer it normally takes for a passed bill to become law after being signed by the state governor.[1]

---

1   Barrett, Julie. "WA Dems Go All-In ON Gender Transition of Minor Children." *Conservative Ladies of Washington*, 27 January 2023, https://conservativeladies -ofwa.com/wa-dems-go-all-in-on-gender-transition-of-minor-children/. Accessed 2 February 2023.

With more states pushing for gender-affirming care to become accessible to teens, often going against the wishes of parents, we are seeing the numbers of teens undergoing full transitions on the rise. Over the past five years, the number of adolescent teens (under eighteen) on the record for having puberty blockers was 4,780 according to a Komodo Health Research study. [2] However, the number will be significantly higher given that this study only considers pediatric patients with a gender dysphoria diagnosis and does not include teens whose puberty blocker prescriptions were not covered by medical insurance.

Puberty blockers are a type of medication, also referred to as GrNH diagnostics, that suppress and limit testosterone and estrogen. They are administered normally via injection every few months or in some cases via an implant placed in the upper arm that aggressively stops the growth of breast development in girls, attempts to halt the menstrual cycle and halt the natural female growth of a woman. In boys, the puberty blockers stop the onset of an Adam's apple, block a male's voice from getting deeper, limit the growth of facial and body hair, and limit the growth of male genitalia. The drugs used to transition a person lack long-term clinical trials and were not even originally intended to treat gender dysphoria. The FDA approved the use of GrNH diagnostics to treat prostate cancer, endometriosis, and central precocious puberty, and they were not originally intended for use suppressing puberty and a teen's physical development. We do not know the consequences of these treatments ten or twenty years down the line, nor what health conditions a person may develop as a result of being administered such strong drugs. We see cases of detransitioners discussing side effects

---

2   Respaut, Robin, and Chad Terhune. "Number of transgender children seeking treatment surges in U.S." *Reuters*, Komodo Health, 6 October 2022, https://www.reuters.com/investigates/special-report/usa-transyouth-data/. Accessed 2 February 2023.

of these drugs from hair loss, bone development issues, and issues with reproductive organs. However, because this is a new phenomenon, there is no real research on the side effects or research on what these puberty blockers do for reproductive health.

Hormone replacement therapy takes place after the teen has been on puberty blockers for a period of time, and after the teen's puberty process has been blocked, the hormone medication changes the body of the teen into the gender of their desired new identity. There are 14,726 teens under the age of eighteen on record for having HRT from 2017 to 2021 according to the Komodo Health Inc. study. Girls are prescribed testosterone to transition their bodies while boys are prescribed estrogen. The girls will notice muscle development in their arms and leg areas and hair growth on the face and other body areas. They will also develop male features like stronger jawlines and masculine bone structures. Boys transitioning to girls will experience development of softened facial and body features, fat distribution more to the buttock and hip area, and their genitals shrink, leading to issues in later life including reduced sex drive and urinary incontinence.[3] There are no long-term studies on the effects these hormones have on trans patients, but in a study of 1,208 women by Steinauer et al., 64 percent of women taking HRT reported incontinence issues during four years of treatment.

In a 2014 study in The Netherlands of seventy adolescents undergoing affirmative care, one of those patients died during surgery and several others developed obesity from the hormones.[4] The fact that one person died undergoing gender reassignment surgery

---

3   Lofthouse, M. "HRT can cause urinary incontinence in older postmenopausal women." *Nature.com*, Steinauer, JE, et al., February 2006, https://www.nature.com/articles/ncpendmet0093-nrendo. Accessed 02 February 2023.

4   Gender-affirming" Hormones and Surgeries for Gender-Dysphoric US Youth." *SEGM*, Society for Evidence Based Gender Medicine, 28 May 2021, https://segm.org/ease_of_obtaining_hormones_surgeries_GD_US. Accessed 2 February 2023.

during this study alone is beyond shocking and heartbreaking. But how many other young people are dying that studies don't know about, and how many more will tragically lose their lives undergoing these extremely risky surgeries? We should not be allowing a single person to lose their life because they are unhappy with the way they are, whether society told them to change or they generally felt like that. But tragically we will only hear more of these horror stories thanks to the dramatic increase in young people undergoing these procedures.

We also cannot take all the data and stories of detransitioners and simply ignore what is going on, as to do so would be abandoning our principles and morals. Turning a blind eye to what is going on with these children, how they are being indoctrinated and pushed into their decision to change their bodies, and how as a society we are allowing this is unacceptable. We also must acknowledge and sympathize with the real struggles these teens face and look at gender dysphoria as a mental health issue, taking away the stigma by talking about it and being more vocal on the harm the gender-affirming care industry is having on kids.

There are now over sixty pediatric gender-affirming clinics across America, up from a mere handful of clinics just ten years ago.[5] With the rise in these clinics we are seeing increasing numbers of teenagers undergoing gender-reassignment surgery; the Komodo study found 776 double mastectomies were performed on girls between age thirteen and seventeen in the united States from 2019 to 2021.[6] The study only took into account surgeries

---

5   Bazelon, Emily. "The Battle Over Gender Therapy." *The New York Times*, 24 June 2022, https://www.nytimes.com/2022/06/15/magazine/gender-therapy.html. Accessed 2 February 2023.

6   Respaut, Robin, and Chad Terhune. "Number of transgender children seeking treatment surges in U.S." *Reuters*, Komodo Health, 6 October 2022, https://www.reuters.com/investigates/special-report/usa-transyouth-data/. Accessed 2 February 2023.

performed on girls using an insurance claim and those who had an official medical diagnosis of gender dysphoria. Teens who paid for themselves or whose families paid did not make up these statistics, so there will likely be thousands of other teenage girls having these "top surgeries" and removing their chest areas that the data and studies don't even know about.

In order for a teen to be considered for any of the affirmative-care procedures, the normal requirements are a medical professional finding that the individual experiences several of the symptoms of gender dysphoria for at least six months, which can include feeling trapped in the wrong body, wanting to look like the opposite gender, dressing in girls' clothes if a boy or vice versa, and using pronouns for the opposite sex. Also required in standard practice is a letter from a professional therapist and ongoing psychotherapy sessions.[7] So a teenager can just question their gender for six months and display the symptoms of feeling confused with the way they were born and technically fit the criteria to be prescribed these treatments. As we know from our own teenage years, when any teen goes through puberty and goes to high school; they often go through phases, questioning their identity and feeling confusion about who they are. This is typical of growing up, and we have all experienced these feelings. Many of these teens may just be confused with their sexuality, some may be gay, some may be lesbian, and some may be bisexual. But because it is such a confusing time for these teens, they may mistake their struggle and confusion with their sexuality with being the wrong gender. For example, if a teen boy is attracted to other boys, they may not realize they are gay and may mistake this for thinking that they are meant to be female. If

7   Boyle, Patrick. "What is gender-affirming care? Your questions answered." *AAMC*, Association of American Medical Colleges, 12 April 2022, https://www .aamc.org/news-insights/what-gender-affirming-care-your-questions -answered. Accessed 2 February 2023.

a boy then has these feelings for six months and a therapist gives them a gender-dysphoria diagnosis based on what this teen is experiencing, the teen then qualifies to be put on hormones, puberty blockers, and even undergo surgery. We therefore cannot discount that there could be many of these teens thinking they are the opposite sex when they are simply misplacing their confusion with their sexuality.

We also cannot discount the fact that many teens go through phases. Some may go through a goth phase, where they listen to heavy metal, like wearing eyeshadow, dye their hair black, and wear heavy eyeliner. Yet it doesn't mean they will feel or identify as a goth for the rest of their life; indeed, many will grow out of this phase. Similarly, many young people through their teenage years do question life and feel convinced they are different and feel trapped, yet many of them grow up to be perfectly happy with the way they were born. Of course, we must consider both sides of the spectrum. There are teens who feel trapped in the wrong body their whole lives and eventually transition and live that way for the rest of their lives, and generally do feel confident in their decision to transition. We have to respect the decisions a person makes as an adult if they have felt unhappy with being a certain way their whole life. Yet at the same time, we know that decades ago the rates of transitions were much fewer. Of course there were trans people, of course there were men living as trans women and vice versa, but the numbers were much lower. Now we are seeing 1.6 million people aged thirteen-plus in the United States alone identifying as trans, according to a 2022 census study.[8] This is a significant rise from a similar study published in 2017, which examined data from 2006 to 2016

8 Herman, Jodie L., et al. "How Many Adults and Youth Identify as Transgender in the United States?" *Williams Institute*, UCLA, June 2022, https://williamsinstitute .law.ucla.edu/publications/trans-adults-united-states/. Accessed 2 February 2023.

and found that 1 million Americans identified as trans.[9] So in just a few short years an additional six hundred thousand people are now identifying as trans, a staggering 60 percent increase.

---

9   Meerwijk, Esther L., and Jae M. Sevelius. "Transgender Population Size in the United States: a Meta-Regression of Population-Based Probability Samples." *NCBI*, AM J Public Health, February 2017, https://www.ncbi.nlm.nih.gov/pmc /articles/PMC5227946/. Accessed 30 April 2023.

Chapter 27
The Challenges
Detransitioners Face

If my detransition and finding myself again taught me one thing, it is to question and challenge gender and identity as a whole. Many share the simple scientific and biological belief that there are only two genders reflective of the two sexes, while others argue that there are three: male, female, and transgender. However, there are also more extreme examples where activists and advocates for gender ideology argue there are up to seventy-two genders ranging from "alexigender," a person who cannot identify their identity and switches between different genders based on their mood, to "demifluid," a gender identity for nonbinary people who partially identify with female and partially with male, and even "domgender," an identity where a person has multiple gender identities but one identity is more dominant.[1]

When I first shared my story online and during media appearances across America, I was met with two polarized responses. One side was people praising me for speaking out to help others and for

---

1 Allarakha, MD, Shaziya, and Pallavi Suuyog Uttekar, MD. "What are the 72 Other Genders?" Medicine Net, 2/2/2022 February 2022, https://www .medicinenet.com/what_are_the_72_other_genders/article.htm. Accessed 12/17/2022 December 2022.

sharing my story so openly and honestly. The other side consisted of those who vilified me, who tried to shut me down and silence me. I was called a "monster," a "traitor," and a "troll," with these people trying to discredit my lived experience and "gaslight" me (a term they frequently like to use when someone criticizes them). The irony was that these were the same people who preach about acceptance and about respecting people's identities however unusual they may be, yet I was suddenly cast out and they were turning on me. However, I took the high road and the moral one, knowing that by sharing my story I could help the millions of teens across America who also struggle with identity and gender. I had to weather the storm of abuse to help give a platform to others who had detransitioned and others who wanted to share their story. These kids needed me to be their voice, to bear the brunt of the attacks from the woke warriors, and to be a beacon of light and give them hope. Hope that they could weather any storm, hope that they could swim across any raging sea, and hope that they too could have their voices heard. They too could be validated, recognized for their struggles, and given the opportunity to speak freely and openly about their struggles and their detransition. For years these teens felt rejected, alone in their struggle, scared to even utter a word against the trans cult. For if they dared to speak out, they were met with a torrent and hailstorm of condemnation, called transphobic, with endless tirades aimed at them from anonymous social media accounts and online bullies. There was no one out there to look up to or anyone to speak with about their struggles, and they were left isolated and alone. Part of my activism since my detransition is to help open the barriers that have held detransitioners back from speaking out. To take away the stigma and shame they may feel and to let them have their voices heard loud and clear. Because they are valid. They need to be heard and listened to. Their voices are extremely important to help the thousands of other teens and young people who are going through the same process of regret, of struggling with the decisions they made or were forced and coerced to make as teens. They shouldn't have to feel this way, and they should have a support system in place to help them. While there are thousands of LGBT organizations across the world to support people who transition, there is virtually no support and no resources out there for those who detransition. Very few organizations exist to offer guidance, information, and a care system for those who have decided that changing gender wasn't right for them personally. We need to support all teens in their journey and their struggles. Regardless of what anyone's viewpoints are on the issue of transitioning, everyone deserves support, validation, and help to navigate through their gender dysphoria and identity struggles and come out on the other side, learning to accept themselves and find happiness from within.

Thankfully, in 2023 we are now seeing a number of organizations like Gays Against Groomers, for which I am a proud ambassador, offering a support system for detransitioners as more and more teens come out and bravely share their detransition stories on social media. In 2023 we also saw the first major Detransition Awareness Day being held outside the Capitol building in Sacramento, California, where a group of brave detransitioners including Chloe Cole, Abel Garcia, Cat Cattinson, and Prisha Mosley spoke up and shared their stories to raise awareness of the harm the gender-affirming care industry had inflicted on them, during a time when they were feeling extremely mentally vulnerable. While this peaceful rally and public speech went ahead, extreme trans activists violently attacked onlookers with clubs and assaulted four journalists, including a Turning Point USA reporter, to try and intimidate and scare away media from reporting on the rally.[2] Any detransitioner

---

2   Brown, Jon. "Detransitioning rally turns violent when Antifa shows up, participants left 'afraid' to speak out: organizer." *Fox News*, 15 March 2023, https://www.foxnews.com/us/detransitioning-rally-turns-violent-antifa-shows-up-participants-left-afraid-speak-out-organizer. Accessed 17 March 2023.

who bravely speaks up in public or anyone who speaks publicly on the harms of gender ideology is met with the same extreme response. In March 2023, Turning Point USA Founder Charlie Kirk delivered a speech at University of California, Davis, where the prominent conservative speaker spoke on the dangers of pushing gender ideology on children.[3] Kirk was simply exercising his right to free speech, as anyone does when speaking on gender ideology, yet he was met with a massive hate campaign: protesters smashing windows outside the venue and trans activists assaulting police officers. We are seeing this level of violence every single time anyone dares to exercise their right to free speech and dares to question the irreparable harm modern society is having on young teens. As George Orwell once said, "If liberty means anything at all, it means the right to tell people what they do not want to hear." The fight to silence critics of transitioning children has become so virulent and extreme as to strike fear into any detransitioner who thinks about speaking out. For simply sharing their truth and their heartbreaking story, detransitioners must consider the targeted hate campaigns and relentless harassment they will receive from trans activists. This puts many of them off from going public and sharing their story. If we all come together as one and continue to speak up and push back against those attempting to cancel free speech, then eventually we can encourage the many other detransitioners hiding in the shadows to come out and share their cautionary tales in order to help others.

We are finally starting to see a shift in the narrative online and across society of people speaking up against the indoctrination of children and against the recent drive for gender ideologies pushed

---

3   Richard, Lawrence. "Elon Musk, others respond after protesters smash windows, hurl eggs at Charlie Kirk event on college campus." *Fox News*, 15 March 2023, https://www.foxnews.com/us/elon-musk-respond-protesters-smash-windows-hurl-eggs-charlie-kirk-event-college-campus. Accessed 17 March 2023.

on increasingly younger kids. More people are fighting back against woke ideologies and standing up to defend children and parents who have for too long felt powerless, unable to share their concerns or express their opinions openly for fear of school boards and activists retaliating against them. The momentum is rising and will continue to rise the more we see gender ideology being pushed on kids, and we all have a moral and social responsibility to figure out a solution that is best for all parties and foster an inclusive environment that allows dialogue and debate from both sides of the argument to allow real change to occur. We need solutions that ensure every child is protected and safeguarded from doing something that could cause long-term harm to their physical and mental health.

Changing gender and pronouns is a recent phenomenon spurred on by various factors including social media, the education system, TV, and media normalizing children transitioning, and of course the real driving force behind it all, the multibillion-dollar pharmaceutical and medical institutions that stand to profit from children transitioning.

If we look at the statistics from the CDC's Behavioral Risk Factor Surveillance System (BRFSS) and Youth Risk Behavior Survey (YRBS), one in five people across the United States who identify as trans are between the ages of thirteen and seventeen, out of an estimated 1.6 million Americans identifying as trans. That is a staggering three hundred thousand-plus children and teens wanting to change their birth-given gender. This is also a sharp increase in just a few years from 2016 to 2017, when the Williams Institute research center at UCLA estimated that the number of teens identifying as trans was half the current figure (Herman et al.).[4] In a

---

4   Herman, Jody L., et al. "How Many Adults and Youth Identify as Transsexual in the United States?" *Transgender people in the US*, Williams Institute, UCLA, 06/01/2022 June 2022, https://williamsinstitute.law.ucla.edu/publications/trans -adults-united-states/. Accessed 17th December 2022.

study published by Cedars-Sinai, the research suggests that children who experience the modern phenomenon of gender dysphoria, being confused with the gender assigned at birth, begin to start experiencing these feelings at age seven.[5]

As any parent reading this will know, and if all of us look back to our younger years, we can see that it is completely normal for a child to experience confusion about their identity and anxiety from a young age. This is a perfectly normal part of growing up, questioning oneself and wanting to fit into society and fit in with the cool kids at school. Based on the statistics, social media trends, and what schools are teaching kids, the number of children feeling confused is going to continue to grow unless a new approach is implemented to protect children from gender ideology. We need to approach this issue with kindness and compassion. Having gone through being trans, I understand the many daily struggles feeling trapped in the wrong body brings. It is an issue that requires understanding from both perspectives. Women need their voices amplified, and parents of children being taught gender ideology in kindergarten need their concerns addressed in order for any change to occur.

The current status quo is that anyone who dares question the narrative of becoming trans, or anyone who calls into question the sharp increase in teens receiving gender-affirming care is called "transphobic," "bigoted," and "hateful." This rhetoric does not in any way help the trans activists or their cause. In fact, by shouting down anyone with a different opinion to them it actually pushes people away from their message. What happened to having open and sensible debate? Debate is healthy in any form of democracy and a vital part of helping to address societal issues.

---

5   Garcia, MD, Maurice. "Most Gender Dysphoria established by aged 7." *Cedars-Sinai*, Cedars-Sinai, 16th June 2020, https://www.cedars-sinai.org/newsroom/most-gender-dysphoria-established-by-age-7-study-finds/. Accessed 17th December 2022.

There are also many members of the LGBT community who feel that the vocal trans activists and predominantly men who self-identify as women and encroach on women's rights are causing tremendous harm to the community. This harm has caused extreme division with groups and has resulted in the LGB-only acronym popping up across the world, dropping the "T" for the trans people in the community.

Chapter 28

Challenging Gender Ideology

I didn't know there were others out there in the world who had also detransitioned and experienced extreme gender dysphoria, the term I had finally come to accept as the reason for my years-long identity crisis and the term used for the thousands of people who also experience issues with their gender identity.

I suddenly began to see other voices on social media sharing their brave stories, many of them teens who had undergone full gender reassignment surgery and had lived to regret it. Despite seeing their suffering and identifying with it, through the suffering I had endured as well, I saw that what stood out the most was their bravery. Their strength and courage to challenge the gender-ideology narrative. Their courage to fight back against the status quo. But sadly, they were not being heard; on the contrary, they were being silenced. Silenced by the extreme trans activists, the woke mob, and the keyboard warriors who all too often like to target vulnerable individuals with abuse.

I was no stranger to receiving abuse from these people. Over the years, I had been trolled to a level unseen by many—death threats, extreme threats of hate, false stories being spread—there was no limit to their cruelty and inhumanity. I had lived through this, I had experienced it, and I was, sadly, used to it. Although no person should ever have to get "used to" being bullied and trolled, I had developed such thick skin, like a plate of armor that deflected all negativity and hate. But the brave people sharing their fearless stories of detransitioning were being pushed into a corner, being bullied into submission. I could not allow that.

One thing going to church and reading about the teachings of Jesus had taught me was always to be kind to others, to "do unto others as you would have them do unto you" (Luke: 6:31). This is the Golden Rule to a happy and fulfilling life. Spread kindness, and help others when you see them in need. I knew I had to do something, as a bullying victim myself, and as a person with a large platform I had the power to help them. I started speaking out about my own detransition and sharing stories of others who had done the same. I started speaking on how there are thousands of people out there, if not millions, who changed gender and later regretted it and now wanted to try and find themselves and get back to their biological selves. It has become a more recent phenomenon, because, as we have seen, there has been a sharp increase in teens being taught about genders and pronouns and being sold the dream of how easy it is to transition. So even without looking at statistics, we know as a fact that whenever people embrace or adopt a trend such as transitioning there will always be a high probability that a number of people will change their minds and realize they had gone down the wrong path. Yet with something as serious as having genital reassignment, double mastectomies, puberty blockers, hormone replacement therapy—all being administered to kids—we cannot simply ignore what is going on or not even have a conversation. These kids have not been allowed to have a voice about their regret and subsequent detransitions. Just look at the case of famous reality star Jazz Jennings, a transgender male to female who has shared her story since childhood on her reality series, *I am Jazz*. At age five, Jazz was declared transgender; at age eleven, they were put on puberty blockers to suppress the male hormone testosterone. Once Jazz started high school, she was then put on a course of estrogen before having a full gender reassignment surgery at age eighteen, all while being documented on a TV show. Viewers got to witness firsthand the ups and downs of a child transitioning and one thing became extremely apparent: Jazz's mother, Jeannette, was the one pushing for her son to transition into a girl. Jeanette Jennings has been an advocate for transitioning children for years and founded the Trans Kid Purple Rainbow Foundation, an organization that coaches parents on socially and medically transitioning their children, even pre-school children who have absolutely no concept of gender identity.[1] Fast-forward to 2023, and in the latest episodes from Jazz's reality show we see her struggle and regret her changes, saying, "I just want to feel like myself . . . all I want is to be happy and feel like me and I don't feel like me ever." We have also seen Jazz struggle with a binge-eating disorder and gain significant weight from years of hormones changing her body while struggling with numerous mental health issues. Would Jazz be struggling with all these things had her mom not pushed her to transition from a young age? Critics argue that Jeannette Jennings simply exploited her child for profit and gain, while making her child famous and getting lucrative endorsements and a long-running TLC reality series. Jazz thought she was trans at age five, and even if she had not had any influences on her identity, at age five a child has no real concept of identity, so the sad reality is that Jazz was pushed into changing and is now, in adult life, having to suffer with the consequences and the mental health and physical struggles associated with years

---

1   Landreneau, Avigail. "Jazz Jennings' Mom Jeanette Helps Parents Transition Their Preschoolers." *All About The Tea*, 15 February 2023, https://allabout-thetea.com/2023/02/15/jazz-jennings-mom-jeanette-helps-parents-transition-their-preschoolers/. Accessed 17 March 2023.

of taking hormones, puberty blockers, and medically transitioning her body. Yet those who question the decisions of Jazz's family in transitioning Jazz from a young age are labeled transphobic, just like anyone who asks logical questions about why we as a society are allowing this to happen.

And why is that? Why has society suddenly gotten to such a point where no one is allowed to have open and fair discussion for fear of being canceled? There are many trans organizations and prominent gender activists who deny the very existence of those who regret transitioning or struggle with the long-term consequences, and there are those who refuse to accept that detransitioning is a real thing. In December 2022 before the House Oversight Committee Hearing on the increasing violence against the LGBT community, Representative Michael Cloud [R-Texas] quizzed a prominent LGBT organization leader on detransitioning, and she completely denied its existence.[2] She responded to the congressman's questioning by saying that these kids don't exist, everything is a lie, and they are not real. So, with this in mind and the struggle for detransitioners to even be allowed to exist or allowed to share their struggles, how can we ever expect to advance as a society when the very existence of people is denied?

The gender clinics also go out of their way to control the studies, research, and data in order to mask the true rates of detransitioners. However, one major study published in 2011 found 84 percent of transgender children stopped identifying as transgender once they became adults.[3] In the long-term study, participants said that between

---

2   Keene, Houston. "LGBT advocate claims in House hearing 'detransitioning' is not 'a real thing.'" *Fox News*, 14 December 2022, https://www.foxnews.com /politics/lgbt-advocate-claims-house-hearing-detransitioning-not-real-thing. Accessed 17 December 2022.

3   Steensma, Thomas D., et al. "Desisting and persisting gender dysphoria after childhood: a qualitative follow-up study." *PubMed*, Clinical Child Psychology and Psychiatry, 7 January 2011, https://pubmed.ncbi.nlm.nih.gov/21216800/. Accessed 30 April 2023.

the ages of ten and thirteen they experienced severe gender dysphoria and began to believe they were transgender. Researchers linked the time period in their lives with the significant changes to their social environment, the changes to their bodies through puberty, and the first experiences of falling in love and developing sexual attraction, all of which combined to produce feelings of gender discomfort and feeling that they identified as the opposite gender.

We cannot simply continue allowing children to suffer. Whatever side of the argument people are on, whether they support transitioning or not, the main issue is that these are children. In the United States, teens are not allowed to drink alcohol or buy cigarettes until age twenty-one, unable to get a tattoo until age eighteen, and unable to drive a car until age sixteen to eighteen, depending on their state laws. Armed with this knowledge, how on Earth could a child possibly consent to undergoing gender reassignment surgeries? How could they give their informed consent to being pumped with puberty suppressors and hormones when they don't truly know their lifelong effects?

This is more of a question about protecting children, preserving the innocence of youth, and allowing them to develop fully into well-rounded adults than it is about whether someone agrees with changing genders or not. I transitioned as an adult yet still grew to regret it. My face is incapable of much movement, I feel numb, my muscles are paralyzed, I have no feeling in my chin or cheeks, I have deep scars running through my forehead, nose, and hairline, and I regret it. I regret all of it. Yet again, my point is, that I made this decision as an adult and, ultimately, I consented. As much as I could blame society, or the people who told me to do this to myself, or the social media trends that normalize this behavior—ultimately, I consented and made the decision myself. Yet kids don't have that option; whatever factors they have around influencing their decisions, whether good or bad, they cannot consent.

We all have a moral obligation to protect the vulnerable. Children are the most vulnerable and impressionable in society, and if we do not start taking real-life action now to speak out for them, then the situation is only going to get worse. We will see an increasing number of kids being mutilated and living to regret it, oftentimes being left alone to suffer and struggle and come to terms with the decisions made for them by adults when they were too innocent and too naïve to understand the devastating long-term consequences.

Chapter 29

Detransitioning

"Detransition" is defined as the reversal of a transgender identification or gender transition by either social, medical, legal, or psychological means, or a combination of these factors. Detransitioning has become increasingly common in the last few years, and we have seen numerous cases of teens expressing their sincere regret after undergoing the gender transition process, from taking hormones to having gender reassignment surgery. One such case is Chloe Cole, an eighteen-year-old who, at fifteen, was medically transitioned with puberty blockers and a double mastectomy. Chloe has recounted her gender dysphoria and identity struggles by sharing that her struggle began at age eleven, after being exposed to gender ideology via the Internet and social media.[1] She became convinced that she was a boy, leaving her parents feeling "scared and desperate for answers." They took her to a gender clinic where medical professionals convinced her parents that if they didn't transition her, she could end up dead, using the

---

1   Heipel, Edie. "Meet the 18-year-old leading the fight to protect children from transgender surgeries." *Catholic News Agency*, 20 September 2022, https://www .catholicnewsagency.com/news/252376/chloe-cole-leading-fight-to-protect -children-from-transgender-surgeries. Accessed 3 February 2023.

much-used claim that if you don't transition a child it can lead to suicide. Many clinics and trans activists tend to use this analogy, claiming that if you don't transition a teen they are more likely to want to take their own life. While we cannot discount the correlation between suicidal tendencies and severe depression, with trans and detransitioners, we have to realize that many of those with gender dysphoria and confused with their gender are already struggling with severe mental health issues, and we should be addressing these issues and finding ways to support their mental health rather than offering a temporary fix of "transitioning." Many teens are pushed into switching gender after being sold a dream that this will be the end of all their problems, and they will suddenly wake up feeling happy for the rest of their lives. Sadly, it's not a quick fix, and what the clinics and activists don't tell these teens is they will likely only experience temporary happiness. Just like the temporary happiness I received every time I had surgery, every time I went under the knife and woke up thinking I would be happy with the new me forever. It's temporary, a quick fix with no lasting solution to a problem. We also have to consider the effects taking such strong hormones and puberty blockers has on both physical and mental health. We know there are side effects and that the hormones lead to chemical imbalances in the brain. Like Chloe, whose doctors sold her a dream and offered a quick, temporary solution with permanent consequences to the feelings she was going through. Instead of being responsible and giving Chloe counseling and therapy to try and guide her through her identity struggles, which for many teens is a phase and just part of teenage life, doctors instantly insisted that she be fast-tracked and transitioned immediately—before it was "too late."

Chloe is now taking legal action against the doctors who did this to her, with the support of the Center for American Liberty and a lawsuit led by Dhillon Law Group in the Chloe Cole v. Kaiser Permanente suit.[2] The detransitioner-turned-activist has described the immense physical and emotional pain she has endured due to the transition process and how she and her parents were coerced into the medical transition in the state of California. The gender clinic actively promoted, advertised, encouraged, and targeted teens and their parents by selling false promises and overselling the procedures as easy and as the only solution to their complex problems. In Chloe's case, like with many teens and parents coerced into transitioning by gender clinics, her parents were not even offered the option of psychological treatments that would have gotten to the root cause of her issues and helped her navigate through her gender dysphoria and conquer it. They did not even offer her hope for the future with her identity struggle or even mention how most teens grow out of these feelings; they instead sold her a "false dream" and said that it was the only solution if her parents wanted to keep her alive.

As we have seen, dozens of these gender clinics have popped up across America over the last few years, with at least sixty pediatric gender hospitals and clinics, according to the Human Rights Campaign, although now there are even many dozens more.[3] The vast majority of these clinics are in states with liberal governments and liberal policies. California has at least nine of these clinics, New York has three, Pennsylvania has five with more added every single year.[4] Unsurprisingly, correlating with the rise in gender clin-

---

2   Dhillon, Harmeet. "Chloe Cole v. Kaiser Permanente." *The Dhillon Law Group*, https://www.dhillonlaw.com/lawsuits/chloe-cole-v-kaiser-permanente/. Accessed 3 February 2023.

3   Society for Evidence Based Gender Medicine. "'Gender-affirming' Hormones and Surgeries for Gender-Dysphoric US Youth." *SEGM*, 28 May 2021, https://segm.org/ease_of_obtaining_hormones_surgeries_GD_US. Accessed 3 February 2023.

4   Human Rights Campaign. "Interactive Map: Comprehensive Care Programs for Gender-Expansive Children and Adolescents." *Human Rights Campaign*, https://www.hrc.org/resources/interactive-map-clinical-care-programs-for-gender-nonconforming-childr. Accessed 3 February 2023.

ics is the rapid increase in the number of teens transitioning. It's big business and big money. As we have seen from the Komodo Health study, the leading study on teens transitioning, the number of children who started on puberty blockers or hormones totaled 17,683 over the last five years, a sharp and significant rise from 2,394 in 2017 to 5,063 in 2021.[5] In reality, however, the numbers are much bigger than reported in this study and don't include those whose families pay out of pocket and those not paying on an insurance claim. It's clear and blatantly obvious that the numbers are rising because the clinic numbers have increased to exploit these teens' struggles and turn their suffering into profit and business. Big pharma tactics—create the problem and offer the solution. These clinics push for kids to be confused, they create the studies, they do the research, they control the LGBT organizations and their messaging, and hence they control the narrative.

The tactics these clinics use to advertise and promote transitioning are becoming more and more targeted to increasingly younger children. Take for instance Dr. Sidhbh Gallagher, a Florida-based gender doctor who uses TikTok to promote transition procedures to minors by making fun, trendy videos.[6] As we know with TikTok, many teens and even young children use the app and spend hours a day on it. Senator Marco Rubio and others even described the Chinese-owned social media app as a digital fentanyl because of its addictive nature and the harm it causes from molding the minds of

---

5   Terhune, Chad, et al. "As children line up at gender clinics, families confront many unknowns." *Reuters*, 6 October 2022, https://www.reuters.com/investigates /special-report/usa-transyouth-care/. Accessed 3 February 2023.

6   Tighe, Mark. "Irish gender affirmation surgeon based in Florida is reported over 'false promotion' in TikToks." *Independent.ie*, 9 October 2022, https: //www.independent.ie/irish-news/health/irish-gender-affirmation-surgeon -based-in-florida-is-reported-over-false-promotion-in-tiktoks-42051361.html. Accessed 3 February 2023.

children politically, socially, and culturally.[7] So is it any wonder kids are thinking about transitioning when they are being targeted by doctors, clinics, and LGBT organizations to transition and develop gender dysphoria from increasingly younger ages?

This particular Florida-based doctor, who performs over five hundred gender reassignment surgeries a year and operates on at least one or two under the age of eighteen years old each month, has amassed hundreds of thousands of TikTok followers and millions of views and was even the subject of a Federal Trade Commission (FTC) complaint over her unethical and aggressive marketing and advertising practices that targeted teens. The doctor, in her own words, has also said that her younger patients are usually fifteen, but she has even operated on one thirteen-year-old and a fourteen-year-old and performed painful and irreversible double mastectomies on their chests to "treat" their gender dysphoria.[8] Shockingly but unsurprisingly, the doctor claimed that she got most of her clients and patients from TikTok. After seeing her fun, engaging, and targeted videos on how easy and life-changing it is to change gender and how she alone can offer a quick and seamless solution to an extremely complex problem, many of these teens and adolescents booked procedures with her.

One of Dr. Gallagher's former patients later detransitioned after undergoing a breast removal with the doctor. Grace Lidinsky-Smith, who transitioned as an adult in her early twenties, said that the doctor presented a warped reality of the gender reassignment process and sold it as a "falsely rosy picture." The detransition activist said that after suffering from a combination of depression and gender

7 Rubio, Senator Marco, and Rep Mike Gallagher. "Rubio, Gallagher Introduce Bipartisan Legislation to Ban TikTok." *Senator Marco Rubio*, 13 December 2022, https://www.rubio.senate.gov/public/index.cfm/2022/12/rubio-gallagher-introduce-bipartisan-legislation-to-ban-tiktok. Accessed 3 February 2023.
8 Ghorayshi, Azeen. "More Trans Teens Are Choosing 'Top Surgery.'" The *New York Times*, 3 October 2022, https://www.nytimes.com/2022/09/26/health/top-surgery-transgender-teenagers.html. Accessed 3 February 2023.

dysphoria, which only worsened over time, instead of seeing a therapist and getting treatment and support with these mental health issues, she opted to book surgery with Dr. Gallagher and thought that gender reassignment would be the solution to her problem. She was sadly misguided and made an irreversible decision and now lives with deep regret. After just a year since surgery and being placed on the hormones, she realized she had made a big, irreversible, and regrettable mistake. [9] Grace, just like Chloe and other detransitioners, was subjected to brutal online attacks, character assassinations, and targeted harassment and intimidation campaigns in an attempt to stop them speaking out. Grace, who appeared on an episode of *CBS 60 Minutes*, said that she was targeted with a coordinated hate campaign from trans activists after a trailer for her appearance on *60 Minutes* was released. Why wasn't she allowed to tell her story? Why couldn't she be hailed as "stunning and brave," as trans activists like to declare anyone who changes their gender identity?

With each detransitioner who speaks out, we see relentless attacks against them via social media and also by liberal mainstream media outlets who attempt to discredit these brave and inspiring individuals and scare them from ever speaking out again. What does this tell us? It tells us just how strong the grip is of the trans industry, big pharma, LGBT organizations, pediatric clinics, and those in positions of authority who push this agenda on society. People are not willing to accept that there are a huge growing number of cases of teens who live with regret, who realized they were pushed to do something that manipulated and exploited their vulnerability.

Back to the case of Chloe Cole: she also shared she has autism and ADHD, which she was diagnosed with aged seven, and was

---

9   Lidinsky, Grace, et al. "There's No Standard for Care When it Comes to Trans Medicine." *Newsweek*, 25 June 2021, https://www.newsweek.com/theres-no -standard-care-when-it-comes-trans-medicine-opinion-1603450. Accessed 3 February 2023.

thus clearly a very vulnerable young girl, yet doctors took advantage of her vulnerability to exploit her, mutilate her, and profit off her suffering. A cruel and unimaginable thing to do to a child, to target the most vulnerable and exploit them for greed and to push a dangerous and harmful agenda.

According to a study from research at the University of Cambridge, there is a clear link between autism and gender dysphoria, revealing a high rate of autistic children also struggling with gender dysphoria.[10] The research found gender dysphoric people, those thinking they were the opposite gender, were three to six times more likely to be autistic. Additionally, the study also found that a large number of those with gender identity issues had autistic traits and are likely to have undiagnosed autism. The researcher combined the data from five different datasets with the data of 641,860 people. Out of the total number of people, 30,892 had autism and 3,777 identified as a different gender from their gender assignment at birth. So 5 percent of the 641,860 of those studied were autistic, yet when we break down those that identify as a different gender of that 3,777 number, 895 of them had autism. Meaning a startling 24 percent of those with a different gender identity were autistic, a much higher number compared with the males and females who did not have any gender identity issues. The gender dysphoric people on average also experienced autistic traits, meaning many of them were undiagnosed so the number of gender dysphoric people with autism would in reality be far higher.

The researchers also studied the correlation between those with gender identity issues with six other mental health conditions

---

10 Dattaro, Laura. "Largest study to date confirms overlap between autism and gender diversity." *Spectrum | Autism Research News*, 14 September 2020, https://www.spectrumnews.org/news/largest-study-to-date-confirms-overlap-between-autism-and-gender-diversity/. Accessed 3 February 2023.

including depression, schizophrenia, and attention deficit hyperactivity disorder (ADHD). Those with autism also have a higher likelihood of having a combination of different mental health issues too, such as depression or others listed above, so are thus much more likely to be easily influenced and manipulated into going forward with transition.

When we look at these diagnoses and recognize that people seeking to transition are more likely to be autistic and have other conditions, and seeing that these are extremely vulnerable individuals, it is thus morally completely irresponsible for anyone to take advantage of this and push or encourage a person to change gender because they feel that way. If we could actually treat gender dysphoria as a mental health condition and recognize these clear correlations, we could prevent the growing trend of teens being pushed to transition and later detransitioning and living their whole lives with medical or psychological health issues because of what they were pushed to do as a teen. As the above study suggests, there is a correlation between autism, those with autistic traits and undiagnosed, with an increased rate of gender dysphoria.

In one of the few studies on detransitioning, twenty-eight adults who had undergone their transition at a young age, 56 percent between ages eighteen and twenty-four, were studied over a period of a year through their detransition to understand the reasons for choosing to go back to their biological self and the issues they faced with doing this. Sixty-four percent were born female and wanted originally to become trans male; 36 percent were born male and wanted to be female.[11] In many of the subjects, detransitioning

11 MacKinnon, PhD, Kinnon R., et al. "Health Care Experiences of Patients Discontinuing or Reversing Prior Gender-Affirming Treatments." *JAMA Network*, JAMA Network, 25th July 2022, https://jamanetwork.com/journals/jamanetworkopen/fullarticle/2794543. Accessed 03 Februry 2023.

occurred due to health concerns and mental and psychical reasons. Many of these participants spoke on the stigma associated with detransitioning and the lack of health-care professionals out there who were trained or even willing to help them through their detransition. The study concluded that there is a great need for more research and studies into detransitioning and the long-term consequences of a person taking puberty blockers and hormone replacement therapy as well as the effects this has on the body and one's health. There is also very little support in terms of health care to guide people through returning to their birth-assigned gender. In another study conducted in Canada, the research concluded trans patients need "close scrutiny" when seeking hormonal and surgical treatments.[12] The lead researcher of these studies, Kinnon MacKinnon PhD, who is transgender, acknowledged that many parents sign consent forms for their teen to undergo gender-affirming care without acknowledging the unknowns and without knowledge of the long-term consequences. Indeed, as we see with the parents of many detransitioners, like Chloe Cole, they sign consent forms almost under duress, being told only the benefits of the surgeries with no regard to the negative impacts; and, in Chloe's case, doctors said to her parents before signing the consent form, "Would you rather have a dead daughter or an alive son?"[13]

We cannot simply offer a quick-fix solution to teens wanting to transition and then be surprised when thousands detail their pain

---

12 MacKinnon, K. R., et al. "Preventing transition 'regret': An institutional ethnography of gender-affirming medical care assessment practices in Canada." *Science Direct*, December 2021, https://www.sciencedirect.com/science/article/pii/S0277953621008091?via%3Dihub. Accessed 03 February 2023.

13 Heipel, Edie. "Meet Chloe Cole, the 18-year-old leading the fight to protect children from transgender surgeries—EWTN Global Catholic Television Network." *EWTN*, 24 September 2022, https://ewtn.co.uk/article-meet-chloe-cole-the-18-year-old-leading-the-fight-to-protect-children-from-transgender-surgeries/. Accessed 3 February 2023.

and suffering and announce they are detransitioning. We cannot allow these vulnerable individuals to feel helpless, to have no one to talk to, to have the same doctors who were so quick to sell them the dream and to sign off and perform their gender surgeries, then dismiss them and refuse to help or treat them. This is more than neglect; this is abuse of vulnerable persons, and the doctors and medical institutions doing this to teens should be held legally accountable. Society cannot continue to push this agenda on kids and expect them to be okay and happy for the rest of their lives. We all have a duty to protect the most vulnerable in society, and we must uphold and protect the moral duty we have to every single person who is pushed into doing something they would not have considered by themselves.

Chapter 30:
Self-Identification

We live in an age when self-identification is heavily promoted, pushed, and encouraged across society, where people are given praise and encouragement for having unique and unusual identities. Some people are now identifying as fairies, some are identifying as clowns, and some adults are even identifying as animals, such as the case of thirty-two-year-old Japanese man Toru Ueda, who identifies as a wolf and spent over $20,000 on a custom realistic-looking wolf costume. The world of self-identity seems to have no limits, with the boundaries being pushed to the extreme.

In 2022, we saw the rise of a new identity, one of the most harmful and dangerous, of grown adult males identifying as "transage" and as babies. Wearing diapers, sucking pacifiers, playing with baby toys, and demanding everyone around them respect their identity. Yet at what stage does an identity become dangerous, such as this case of men saying they are children, and at what point do we stand up and say enough is enough and realize that the more we try to normalize these identities, the more extreme they will become? We have even seen extreme cases of men being convicted of a crime using self-identification as a way to get more lenient sentences or in an effort to be imprisoned alongside women.

The subject of allowing anyone to self-ID with any identity they feel is definitely a slippery slope and can lead to many dangers, as we are seeing today. If society has been pushing to accept transsexual as acceptable and normal within society, will transage acceptance be next? Anyone with a logical mind can see the clear and present dangers with this, how it puts children at risk and allows adult males to try to normalize their unusual fetishes. In a shocking case in Scotland, a convicted murderer became trans so he could be around women in an all-women's prison. Soon after, he changed his identity to become a "baby." As astonishing as this story may be, the prison officers and the justice system in Scotland "respected" the killer's new identity and provided him with diapers, pacifiers, and even held his hand like a baby when he left his cell.[1]

Scotland is probably one of the more extreme examples of a country that has allowed self-identification to take precedence over society. In 2022, the Scottish parliament, led by First Minister Nicola Sturgeon, passed a new Gender Recognition Reform Bill. The new law allows those sixteen years and older to change gender and be given legal recognition of their new gender after living as trans for three months, or six months for sixteen-year-olds. However, the law allows sixteen-year-olds to begin the process of changing gender starting three months before their sixteenth birthday—effectively giving fifteen-year-olds the right to start the process of changing gender or identity. Because of this law, biological men would now be able to use women's restrooms as they saw fit, as well as women's locker rooms, spas, and other areas that are normally reserved only for women. These people could also participate in women's sports

1   Bracchi, Paul. "Killer was born a man, became a woman and now identifies as a BABY." *Daily Mail*, 27 January 2023, https://www.dailymail.co.uk/news/article -11684997/Read-killer-born-man-woman-identifies-BABY.html. Accessed 29 January 2023.

and, if convicted of a crime, go to an all-women's prison, where they could put female inmates at considerable risk as well as psychological distress. Prior to the passing of this bill, an average of just thirty Gender Recognition Certificates were being granted to people legally changing their genders.[2] This figure is in a country of 2.7 million women. The new law, which passed with majority backing in parliament, will now help two- to three-hundred people legally change their gender and obtain a Gender Recognition Certificate. Just a handful of people out of the 2.7 million women whose rights, livelihoods, privacy, and safety will be pushed aside for such a minority of people to feel "happy." How could such a small minority be able to dictate the lives and rights of millions? The bill, which passed with eighty-six votes in favor and thirty-nine against, became Scotland's most debated and controversial bill ever and was consulted on and lobbied for five years prior to passing. Outrage ensued, and many women including prominent feminists like JK Rowling spoke out condemning the bill and the harm it would cause to women. Yet Scottish members of parliament demonstrated how out of touch they were with the majority view and that they were siding with a tiny fraction of people. Trans people already had rights, trans people were already living in Scottish society, and many people didn't have a problem with them or with respecting their decisions. The bill only sought to sow the seeds of discontent, outrage, and objection due to the many concerns raised. The bill was originally meant to protect trans people's rights but actually made their lives far more difficult. Before the bill, they were living their lives, doing as they pleased, and not the subject of fierce debate. Now they are often vilified and ostracized because of the

---

2   Brooks, Libby. "Scotland's proposed gender recognition laws explained | Scotland." *The Guardian*, 21 December 2022, https://www.theguardian.com /uk-news/2022/dec/20/scotland-proposed-gender-recognition-reforms -explained. Accessed 29 January 2023.

actions of the few radical trans activists who use the new law to infringe on women's rights and intimidate feminists for speaking out. In January 2023, one month after the controversial bill passed, a scandalous story hit the headlines of a twice-convicted male rapist who had gone on to become trans, after committing his crimes. Whether he was looking for a softer sentence and better treatment for being "trans" and thus considered more vulnerable, or he was hoping he would be sent to a women's prison so he could commit his crimes on at-risk female prisoners, this alarmed many. After the story hit headlines and after the man was incarcerated for three weeks in an all-female jail, outrage ensued, and thanks to media pressure, social media response, and the work of women's rights activists, the decision was taken to transfer the "trans" rapist to a male prison. This all happened within one month of the new gender bill being passed into law.

We need to consider the perspective of the individuals identifying as the opposite gender and try to understand their argument and need for legal recognition in order to try and come up with a better solution that protects children and women. Pro self-ID activists argue, based on the fact that in the UK sixteen-year-olds can have babies, if you are old enough to have a baby and bring life into the world and consent, then you can be old enough to know who you are and how you identify. These people argue that it can seem patronizing to allow one thing but not the other and is hypocritical in the eyes of people identifying as trans. But at the same time we must consider that whatever the law says in Scotland, these are still teenagers and not yet fully developed adults (no one is an adult until eighteen) and therefore should not be making any of these life-altering decisions. In the United States, most state laws have eighteen as the age of consent or the age someone can have a baby, when a person has matured and become an adult.

The vast majority of countries agree that eighteen is the age when a teen becomes an adult, though UK laws may differ to allow certain circumstances. It is one thing for a teenager to say how they identify and to want to live that way, but it is a completely different debate as to whether or not that teen, that sixteen-year-old, should be able to undergo genital reassignment surgery, be put on life-altering hormones, and take puberty blockers. We know that they are still not adults and the human body doesn't stop growing until at least twenty-one, some parts of the body even older than that, and that puberty doesn't end for most teenagers until at least eighteen. So, it is one thing to argue for a teen to live their life the way they choose, but it is another thing for that teen to undergo double mastectomy and other invasive procedures.

We need to have serious conversations, roundtable discussions, research studies, and long-term scientific data to discover what is really the best solution. Protecting women's rights is paramount. In Scotland, women represent over 2.7 million people, yet only thirty individuals legally transitioned on average over the last few years. We need to be sensitive to all but go with the majority consensus. After all, democracies are based on voting, and the majority vote becomes the rule of law. We also need to offer teens struggling with their own identities support, love, and acceptance to help them navigate through adult life while ensuring that those who choose to identify in different ways respect the rights of others, such as women, and that women's safe spaces and prisons are kept strictly for women in order to safeguard this. If all of this happened, the trans debate would become less loaded and less controversial, and people would be more willing to accept others for their differences. The issue is, like in Scotland, having a policy and agenda forced on the majority of the population and telling them what they have to do, and stifling debate (as anyone who criticizes these policies is labeled as transphobic) is harmful. It harms women greatly and harms actual trans people because the loud voices of the few trans activists become the representatives of the entire community—when in reality, many trans people don't want to cause a problem for others and simply want to go about living their lives.

Chapter 31
The History of Transgenderism

There have been instances throughout history, from Ancient Egypt to Ancient Greece, of men and women identifying more with the opposite sex, feminine men living as women and vice versa. Byzantine Kings and Ancient Roman leaders were reported to keep the company of biological men living as women. Indeed, throughout Ancient China and the Byzantine Empire, eunuchs were at the center of each royal court. These were men who had genital mutilation—back then without even anesthetic—so they could serve in the royal palaces and not be a threat to the alpha male Kings and Emperors and their hundreds of wives and concubines. Many of these eunuchs developed same-sex attractions as a result of being forced to be "feminine and submissive," and indeed many of them would have felt more like a woman due to the circumstances and environment surrounding them. In Ancient Rome, Emperor Marcus Aurelius Antoninus, known widely by the nickname Elagabalus, who ruled Rome from 218 to 222 BC was known to have worn female clothing, acted effeminate, and expressed a desire to have his genitals removed to become more feminine. According to the Ancient Roman writer Cassius Dio, the emperor shaved his body hair, wore makeup, and even dressed up as a woman while prostituting himself in Rome's brothels. He would stand naked in the palace soliciting passersby who had to refer to him as "mistress." The writer also noted how Emperor Elagabalus offered a huge sum of gold to any physician who could perform genital removal on him. Elagabalus also referred to his wife as his husband, and his wife referred to him as wife. A complete gender role reversal in his marriage and his life, driven by his obsession with sexualization. This, paired with scandalous stories of his sexual escapades in Rome's brothels and the royal palace, ultimately led to his assassination at age eighteen.[1]

Other examples throughout history include Albert Cashier, born female as Jennie Hodgers, a US Civil War soldier from the Union Army who made up one of 250 women who dressed as men to fight in the Civil War. From a young age, she dressed as a boy and assumed a male identity using the name Albert D. J. Cashier. Joining the army as a man, she went unrecognized by other soldiers and went on to fight as an infantryman in forty battles.[2] Her true gender was only discovered one fateful day while working for an Illinois state senator, when she had her leg run over by Senator Lish accidentally driving into her. After receiving emergency medical treatment from the local town doctor, it was only then that it was discovered Albert was in fact a woman. Yet instead of ostracizing Albert and exposing her secret to the world, the doctor listened to her pleas and agreed to keep it a secret. She was later placed in a home for veterans to recover, and all the staff, while fully aware of Albert's real gender, never broke her confidence or spoke out. In later life, however, she was confined to a mental institute where staff

1   Brigden, James. "Was Elagabalus Rome's first transgender Emperor?" *Sky HISTORY*, History Channel, https://www.history.co.uk/articles/was-elagabalus-rome-s-first-transgender-emperor. Accessed 8 February 2023.

2   U.S. National Park Service. "Albert Cashier." *National Park Service*, 13 January 2022, https://www.nps.gov/articles/000/albert-cashier.htm. Accessed 8 February 2023.

leaked Albert's lifelong secret and Albert was subsequently charged with defrauding the government to receive a military pension, by lying about her gender to get into the military. However, she was never convicted after soldiers from the same unit attested to her bravery and courage. Albert Cashier was an American hero; after serving in forty battles and devoting her life to her country, she should be celebrated for her courage. While she likely suffered from a rare example of gender dysphoria in nineteenth-century America, she sacrificed her entire life in service admirably and courageously to the very end. Could it be that Albert was what we could today call transgender and that she generally did feel trapped in the wrong body? Or if we look at the historical side of the story, the nineteenth-century Civil War era was a time when women were not equal to men and were not able to join the army and serve their country, as they are today. Could Albert have adopted a male identity and dressed up as a man simply because she wanted to serve her country and was not able to as a woman? If we look back across history, there are numerous examples of women dressing up as men in order to live a life other than being a housewife; as we know, for centuries women had very few rights and were not even able to work in most fields due to the patriarchal nature of the time. We will never fully know the truth to Albert's stories, but nonetheless we should celebrate her lifelong sacrifice to serve her country despite so many obstacles being against her at the time.

If we go back to the 1900s, when the term transgender was first coined, and to the 1920s, when the world's first gender reassignment procedures were carried out, we can start to see how we got to where we are in today's society, and how medically transitioning came about and has grown to what is today a multibillion-dollar industry that has become mainstream and part of a popular and growing trend. In 1910, German doctor Magnus Hirschfeld coined the term transgender, long before society and popular culture even heard it. The doctor, who specialized in gender studies, became the first ever to perform sex change surgeries on men wanting to become women. The doctor and the institute he later founded, the Berlin-based Institute for Sexual Research (German: *Institut für Sexualwissenschaft*), was the first to perform gender reassignment surgeries on patients and the first to use hormone therapy to try to manipulate an individual's hormones and prescribe a man with estrogen. The very first gender reassignment patient ever was German-born Dora Richter, born male as Rudolph Richter, who went from male to female during the world's first-ever sex change. At the institute in 1922, under the care of Magnus Hirschfeld, Dora underwent testicle removal, a world first, followed by penis removal and vaginoplasty in 1931. Dora had identified as a girl throughout much of their life and was reported at the age of six to have attempted to remove his penis with a tourniquet, a device used to stop the blood flow to limbs, and was also noted to wear dresses as a teen and display predominantly feminine mannerisms.[3] After being arrested several times for cross-dressing, Dora was referred to Doctor Hirschfeld and given employment as a maid. During his employment, he and five other transgender people at the institute were able to dress as women while they worked without fear of persecution during a time when wanting to dress in women's clothes and cross-dressing were considered a crime. While living at the institute for years, the doctors studied Dora and the other transgender individuals living there in order to research the impact hormones and removal of testicles and genitalia had on a person's sex.

Much of the research on becoming transgender that medical institutes use today came from this Berlin institute that performed

---

3 Providentia. "Dorchen's Day—Providentia." *Providentia*, 5 December 2010, https://drvitelli.typepad.com/providentia/2010/12/dorchens-story.html. Accessed 8 February 2023.

the world's first sex change operations and vaginoplasties. Another patient at the institute, Lili Elbe, one of the world's first to receive gender surgery, died in 1931 after undergoing a failed uterine transplant and succumbing to health complications. Lili was later depicted in the Hollywood blockbuster *The Danish Girl*, starring Eddie Redmayne.[4] After the death of Lili Elbe under the care of the institute, major public backlash arose, and when the Nazis came to power, they sent a mob of Brownshirts to the institute in 1933 to shut it down. Much of the research and data were lost, yet what remained laid the groundwork for gender reassignment surgeries that we see today. However, because much of the research at the institute was destroyed, we still don't fully know what other factors may have led these particular individuals, like Dora and Lili Elbe, to feel trapped in the wrong body. Dora Richter disappeared the night the Nazis came, never to be seen again, likely killed by the Nazi mob or imprisoned; no one has any answers to this day.

In 1952, before the word transgender ever appeared in popular culture, there was the curious case of a U.S. Army veteran who shocked the world after becoming the first American to undergo gender affirmation surgery to transition medically into the opposite sex. Born George William Jorgensen Jr. in the Bronx, New York, in 1926, he served in the U.S. Army during and after WWII. As a child, Jorgensen reportedly expressed feminine tendencies and was bullied for being too feminine and too "girly." During high school, Jorgensen developed same-sex attractions, something that has been found to be common with teens experiencing gender dysphoria. While he claimed he was not gay and instead trapped in a woman's body, and asserted that he was in fact a woman, this draws parallels

---

4   History vs Hollywood. "The Danish Girl vs the True Story of Lili Elbe, Gerda Wegener." *History vs. Hollywood*, 2015, https://www.historyvshollywood.com /reelfaces/danish-girl/. Accessed 8 February 2023.

with modern society, where many teens mistake their sexuality for their gender identity and thus feel trapped in the wrong body while the issue has more to do with their sexuality. However, in the case of Jorgensen, he continued to feel trapped in the wrong body until adulthood, unlike many teens today who outgrow their gender identity issues after puberty.[5] In the early 1950s, after returning from the military, Jorgensen still continued to feel like a woman and wanted to physically become one, so he began taking estrogen in the form of ethinylestradiol, a medication that was widely used for birth control, the treatment of menopausal symptoms, and gynecological disorders.[6] Following this, he underwent hormone replacement therapy in Denmark with Danish endocrinologist Christian Hamburger and experienced significant changes in his body including enlargement of the mammary glands and bodily changes to look and appear more feminine. A year later in 1951, he underwent his first surgery, an orchiectomy, removal of the testicles, followed by penis removal surgery in 1952. Then in 1954, he underwent a vaginoplasty in the United States. After writing a letter to explain his sex change to his parents, it was leaked to the media and stoked much controversy and bewilderment across the world.[7] While a private letter on such a private and emotional subject was only intended to be a family matter, it opened the world to

---

5   Wallien, Madeleine SC, and Peggy T. Cohen-Kettenis. "Psychosexual outcome of gender-dysphoric children." *National Library of Medicine*, Journal of the American Academy of Child and Adolescent Psychiatry, December 2008, https://pubmed.ncbi.nlm.nih.gov/18981931/. Accessed 8 February 2023.

6   Stewart, Michael. "Ethinylestradiol. menopausal symptoms; menstrual disorders." *Patient.info*, 24 August 2020, https://patient.info/medicine/ethinylestradiol-for-menopausal-symptoms-or-menstrual-disorders. Accessed 8 February 2023.

7   Jorgensen, Christine. "Christine Jorgensen who Achieved Fame by Undergoing a Sex Change." *Web Archive*, UCO College of Liberal Arts, 22 February 2009, https://web.archive.org/web/20090222002724/http://www.libarts.ucok.edu/history/faculty/roberson/course/1493/supplements/chp27/27.%20-Christine%20Jorgensen.htm. Accessed 8 February 2023.

a whole new idea—transgenderism and changing gender. The doctor who administered the hormone therapy in Denmark, Christian Hamburger, later claimed that after Christine Jorgensen's (formerly George William Jorgensen Jr) story was spread across the world, he received more than four hundred letters of appeal from people wanting their own sex change. While Christine was not the first person in the world to undergo a sex change, after surgeries were first performed in 1919 in Germany at the Institute for Sexual Research under Dr. Magnus Hirschfeld, they set a precedent into research into changing genders, the use of estrogen and hormone therapy in changing the body from male to female or vice versa, and the use of surgery to transform sexual organs.[8] Now fast-forward to the present day, and there are over 1.6 million people aged thirteen plus identifying as trans in the United States alone and thousands undergoing hormone therapy and gender reassignment surgeries every year.[9]

Looking back through history tells us that while transgender people did always exist and while there were cases in the early twentieth century, there were far fewer people identifying as trans than there are today. This could be put down to a variety of reasons, and of course we have to consider that a hundred years ago, being homosexual or bisexual itself was considered a crime, let alone someone being transsexual, so people were unable to express themselves openly; hence, we have very limited data and few case studies. However, while we can generally acknowledge that there have always been people who have felt trapped in the wrong body,

8   Blakemore, Erin. "How historians are documenting the lives of transgender people." *National Geographic*, 24 June 2022, https://www.nationalgeographic .com/history/article/how-historians-are-documenting-lives-of-transgender -people. Accessed 8 February 2023.

9   Herman, Jody L., et al. "How Many Adults and Youth Identify as Transgender in the United States?" *Williams Institute*, UCLA, June 2022, https://williamsinstitute .law.ucla.edu/publications/trans-adults-united-states/. Accessed 8 February 2023.

men feeling more feminine or women feeling more masculine, the main cause for concern with today's society is the issue of children who would never have considered they were the wrong gender, being taught or pushed ideas that convince them to think they are transgender when they are simply not. This is the real issue. We should always be sensitive and understanding with people who identify as transgender, and if history teaches us anything on this issue, we can learn that there have always been cases of people being transgender, or feeling different to the body they were born with. While we can acknowledge this, we must also acknowledge that the recent huge spikes in children being transitioned is not a normal phenomenon, rather a man-made one whereby society is pushing children to change gender. We simply cannot allow children to become science experiments, for vulnerable people to be convinced and coerced into surgeries and hormone therapies, or for other mental health issues to be ignored. While Christine Jorgensen was a pioneer in the 1950s and extremely brave for being able to live her life the way she wanted to, despite society and advanced technologies being against her and the unimaginable hurdles she faced in order to achieve their goal of becoming trans, we must recognize that not every person that is convinced they are trans actually is, and that many become trans because of societal and environmental factors that convince them to change. We have to take all of these factors into account and apply them to the current situation, where we are seeing a growing number of young people becoming trans, many because society, educators, and their surrounding environments mold their minds into doing so.

These examples throughout history spark interesting debate, as these individuals who preferred to live as the opposite sex went against society to become who they wanted to be. At the time, this was far from normal and indeed extremely frowned upon in society. LGBT organizations would argue this proves the existence of trans people throughout history and that they always existed. I do agree with this statement and acknowledge there have been cases of people wanting to be the opposite gender throughout history, and my argument would be as long as they were happy and not harming anyone, then that is all that matters. While these individuals throughout history made their own decisions, we will never know which factors may have influenced them to become the person they became. Whether their parents told them constantly as a child that they wished they had a daughter instead of a son, whether they had suffered abuse or traumas as a child, whether they were actually gay, lesbian, or bi and didn't understand the concept of sexuality at the time, or whether through sexual fetish they decided to dress up as the opposite sex. But one thing is for certain: we will never know for sure and we will never know whether perhaps none of these factors influenced them and they simply felt different from birth, which is something we know some trans people do feel for their entire lives. This book is not about discounting the experiences and lives of trans people. It is certainly fascinating to look back through history and compare a handful of examples to the millions of people who within the last ten years have gone on to identify as trans as part of a growing phenomenon and trend.

Chapter 32

State Laws: For & Against

The transitioning of teens is arguably one of the most controversial, debated, and talked-about topics of our time. But with considering any argument, it is important to look at both sides, to examine the arguments both for and against gender-affirming care. Being armed with this knowledge helps us better understand the other viewpoint, why they speak so passionately and intensely on it, and why they get so defensive and confrontational around being questioned on pushing transitioning on teens. While we can acknowledge every single child's story is different and while some generally feel they are a different gender from an extremely young age, many are simply being pushed into it through societal and environmental factors.

Some proponents and supporters of gender-affirming care argue that the reason gender-affirming care is performed on teens is to stop the development of male or female sexual organs, to stop masculine features like strong jawlines developing in biological boys, or help stimulate hair growth and muscles in girls wanting to become boys. They will argue that if this is not done during puberty, it makes it more difficult to transition that person as an adult and they will likely not be able to look and live as the opposite sex as easily. They also argue it is cruel and immoral to allow a person to feel trapped in the wrong body, in the wrong gender, and thereby prolong their suffering. With LGBT organizations arguing that if GAC is not provided to teens, then it will result in severe mental health issues, depression, and a higher risk of suicide. They also argue that not performing medical procedures on these children will lead to greater risks in adulthood if they choose to take hormones and surgeries at that time. However, supporters of this current system fail to acknowledge the increasingly high detransition and regret rate, as well as the health implications of taking long-term hormones such as bone density growth issues, increased risk of heart problems, and increased risk of many other major health problems in later life. They also fail to look at data that show over 80 percent of teenagers grow out of gender dysphoria into adult life, and therefore putting them into the gender-affirming care system is the completely wrong approach. Despite the increasing push to medicalize teens and to push this multibillion-dollar industry, numerous states are not passing legislation or are in the process of restricting gender-affirming care in minors in order to safeguard children from being harmed.

According to The Williams Institute at UCLA, fifty-eight thousand teens will lose access to gender-affirming care across sixteen states that have banned or are currently proposing legislation to ban gender-affirming care.[1] Half of the bills across these states would ban insurance providers from paying for transitioning teens. Missouri introduced bill SB 843 in the state senate, adding to a pre-existing bill on gender transitioning of minors, which would ban all health-care providers and physicians in the state from providing gender

---

1   Conron, Kerith J., et al. "Prohibiting Gender-Affirming Medical Care for Youth." *Williams Institute*, UCLA, 11 March 2022, https://williamsinstitute .law.ucla.edu/publications/bans-trans-youth-health-care/. Accessed 8 February 2023.

reassignment and cause them to face discipline and the potential to have their medical licenses revoked.

The Bill stipulates:

> Under this act, no physician or health care provider shall provide gender transition procedures to any minor or refer such minor to another health care provider for such procedures. This prohibition shall not apply to services for minors born with medically verifiable disorders of sex development; treatment of any infection, injury, disease, or disorder caused or exacerbated by gender transition procedures; or procedures undertaken because the minor suffers from a condition that would place him or her in imminent danger or death or impairment of a major bodily function unless surgery is performed. Any health care provider referring for or providing gender transition procedures for minors may be subject to discipline by his or her professional licensing board for unprofessional conduct. The provision of gender transition procedures to a minor in violation of this act shall be considered grounds for a cause of action against the health care provider, as described in the act.[2]

The bill makes it clear there are exceptions for any child born with the wrong genitalia, based on their biological sex, and those with verifiable medical disorders related to sex development, and also makes provisions for detransitioning teens who need urgent medical care to reverse health complications from previous transitional surgeries, hormones, or puberty blockers. While trans advocates

---

2   Haskins, Sarah. "SB843—Modifies provisions relating to gender reassignment treatment for children." *Missouri Senate*, Missouri State Senate, 13 May 2022, https://www.senate.mo.gov/22info/BTS_Web/Bill.aspx?SessionType=R&BillID =71259876. Accessed 8 February 2023.

argue states like Missouri are cruel to deny children medical transitioning, we see here that the law is simply protecting teens with gender dysphoria from undergoing gender reassignment and still allows medical interventions for children born with real medical conditions, such as intersex individuals who are born with the sexual organs of both male and females.

Similarly in Texas, senate bills were proposed and went to hearing to take steps to further prevent minors being transitioned and to prevent and deter hospitals and physicians from performing these dangerous and life-altering operations. Texas House Bill TX HB672 seeks to criminalize gender-affirming care and categorize it as child abuse and revoke liability insurance from medical institutes that prescribe medication to treat gender dysphoria.[3] The legislative proposal would act as a strong deterrent for physicians and parents wanting to transition children. In addition to this, Texas has also been at the forefront of taking on criminal proceedings against those who push for medical transitions on minors. In 2022, Texas Governor Greg Abbott ordered state agencies to open criminal investigations into parents who have medically transitioned their children.[4]

On the opposite side of the fence, other states are passing laws or proposing legislation to make it easier for teens to get access to gender-affirming care without parental consent. In Washington state, senate bill SB 5599 passed adding provisions to an already existing bill to make it easier for homeless teenagers in foster care or shelters

---

3   Hefner, Rep. Cole. "88(R) HB 672—Introduced version." *Texas Legislature Online*, 14 November 2022, https://capitol.texas.gov/tlodocs/88R/billtext/pdf /HB00672I.pdf. Accessed 8 February 2023.

4   Migdon, Brooke. "Texas bills seek to add criminal penalties to gender-affirming health care, drag performances." *The Hill*, 16 November 2022, https: //thehill.com/homenews/state-watch/3738737-texas-bills-seek-to-add-criminal -penalties-to-gender-affirming-health-care-drag-performances/. Accessed 8 February 2023.

access to gender-affirming care under the guise of "Protected Health Care" with a "Compelling Reason." This means that teens who were extremely vulnerable and had been separated from their parents whether by force, choice, or other reasons would be able to "consent" to changing their gender medically without their parents or caregivers being informed. In January 2023, I testified before the Washington State Senate my opposition to the bill, knowing that it would leave the most vulnerable teens in the state open to exploitation by physicians, health-care workers, trans organizations, and gender clinics. I joined concerned parents from across the state who wanted to protect their children, some of whose own kids had been taken away from them and put into shelters, and even a trans person and members of the LGBT community who expressed opposition to the bill, knowing it would only allow vulnerable teens to be exploited for profit. It was moving to hear the testimonies of so many others and to hear their genuine and valid reasons for opposing such a measure. Those who argued for the bill, on the other hand, used insults and critiques toward the testifying parents, trying to discredit them and blame them for "bad parenting" without knowing the reasons why their children had been taken away from them. They immediately judged these parents without knowing the full circumstances, trying to paint them in a certain light, when in reality these parents spoke from a place of pure love and devotion in trying to help their children. They also tried to discredit me; the Chair of the Senate Hearing, Senator Claire Wilson, laughed after my speech, mocking my accent because I didn't sound American. I ignored this blatant attempt to try and discredit me, despite the fact the senate hearing was open to anyone. I wondered if I spoke with a Spanish accent or had been a person of color would they have mocked me or tried to discredit me because of the way I spoke? It became clear to me that this was a biased hearing, that the powerful trans groups, hospitals, and Democratic senators sponsoring this bill would not stop until they achieved their agenda: to put vulnerable teens into the gender-affirming care system. They had already decided and had no real regard for those with real concerns, parents, mothers, teachers, concerned citizens, and even LGBT members who opposed the bill. The bill later passed and was signed into law by Gov. Jay Inslee.

The bill followed closely in the footsteps of California bill SB 107, which passed and was signed into law by California Governor Gavin Newsom to make the state a sanctuary city for teens to have gender-affirming care without parental consent.[5] Washington had seen the success of this bill and was clearly trying to replicate it. It was a domino effect; once one state successfully passed a law, another would follow and then another.

The same could be said for the dozens of states opposing gender-affirming care and the bills and laws introduced to stop procedures being performed on minors. Once one state banned it, others followed. It was a battle pitting half of America against the other. Democratic states vs Republican, and Parents vs the Medical Establishment. America was built on unity and freedom, not division, yet sadly, thanks to the constant push to transition vulnerable children, America has become more divided each day. As of May 2023, sixteen states have now banned gender-affirming care for minors: Arkansas, Florida, Georgia, Idaho, Indiana, Iowa, Kentucky, Mississippi, Missouri, Montana, North Dakota, Oklahoma, South Dakota, Tennessee, Utah, and West Virginia.

In neighboring Oregon, a state that requires health insurers like Medicaid and Medicare to provide gender-affirming care as a

---

5   Wiener, Senator Scott. "SB 107." *California Legislative Information*, CA Senate, 10 March 2022, https://leginfo.legislature.ca.gov/faces/billTextClient.xhtml?bill _id=202120220SB107. Accessed 8 February 2023.

health necessity,[6] children can undergo double mastectomies and gender reassignment surgery without any parental consent at age fifteen due to the law stating that the age of medical consent in Oregon is fifteen.[7] One gender clinic in the state, Doernbecher Children's Hospital, went from having just sixteen children being treated annually in 2013 to 724 being treated in 2021, a sharp and alarming rise of 4,500 percent.[8]

This law and others passed, like the one in Washington, simply offers genital reassignment as the solution to a much greater problem. We know from studies like the 2008 study published in the *Journal of the American Academy of Child and Adolescent Psychiatry* that most children with gender dysphoria do not remain dysphoric after puberty ends.[9] The study also found that many of these teens grew up to have either a homosexual or bisexual sexual orientation and many had mistaken their gender identity for their sexuality. The study concluded that the most likely outcome of children with gender dysphoria was that they would be gay, lesbian, or bisexual as opposed to being trans or wanting to transition. These data and those of other studies suggest far more complexities to gender dysphoria than meets the eye and that many of these states and physicians diagnosing children with gender dysphoria are ignoring

---

6   OHSU. "Transgender Health Program: Insurance Information." *OHSU*, https://www.ohsu.edu/transgender-health/transgender-health-program-insurance-information. Accessed 8 February 2023.

7   Springer, Dan. "Oregon allowing 15-year-olds to get state-subsidized sex-change operations." *Fox News*, 2 May 2016, https://www.foxnews.com/politics/oregon-allowing-15-year-olds-to-get-state-subsidized-sex-change-operations. Accessed 8 February 2023.

8   Terhune, Chad, et al. "As children line up at gender clinics, families confront many unknowns." *Reuters*, 6 October 2022, https://www.reuters.com/investigates/special-report/usa-transyouth-care/. Accessed 21 March 2023.

9   Wallien, Madeleine SC, and Peggy T. Cohen-Kettenis. "Psychosexual outcome of gender-dysphoric children." *National Library of Medicine*, Journal of the American Academy of Child and Adolescent Psychiatry, December 2008, https://pubmed.ncbi.nlm.nih.gov/18981931/. Accessed 8 February 2023.

many other factors and the fact that after puberty, many children do not continue to have gender dysphoria into adulthood.

States like Oregon, California, and Washington, passing bills and laws to make it easier for children to have GAC without parental consent are completely sidestepping and ignoring all of the other factors that contribute to a child having gender identity issues, such as mental health conditions like autism, the fact that gender dysphoria may be misdiagnosed, the fact a child may be confused because of their sexual orientation, or even the blatant fact that they will grow out of these feelings by the time they reach adulthood. During the Washington State Senate hearing where I testified, the testimony that stood out to me most was an older trans person who said that as a teen they went through all the feelings of feeling trapped in the wrong gender and desperately tried to change gender. They begged their parents to transition, they tried everything, but couldn't medically transition. In later life, they said that they were extremely grateful and glad the medical laws allowing teens to have GAC were not available when they were growing up, as they would have undergone these irreversible medical procedures and lived with regret. Having trans people and LGBT people speak out on the harm society is doing to vulnerable teens is a powerful and important step in defeating this gender ideology. The more LGBT members who speak up about their own community, the more likely the rest of their community will listen and heed their warnings.

Chapter 33

The World Is Waking Up

Outside the United States, the conversation is finally shifting, and countries like Finland, Norway, Sweden, and the UK have shifted their policies on transitioning teens and backtracked on previous rules. In Finland, despite passing a gender recognition bill in 2023 that made it easier for trans people to legally self-identify—removing the need for a medical diagnosis or hormone therapy to be legally declared the opposite gender—the conversation has slowly been shifting. A bombshell insight into transgender treatments and the harm they are causing to young people was exposed by the country's top transgender expert. Dr. Riittakerttu Kaltiala is the chief psychiatrist at Tampere University Hospital Department of Adolescent Psychiatry, one of only two gender clinics in Finland. The doctor, who had been in charge of youth transgender treatments at the clinic since 2011 and a leading authority on transgenderism, conducted a study on gender dysphoria in the adolescent population. The five-year replication study found startling results.[1]

---

1 Kaltiala-Heino, Riittakertuu, et al. "Gender dysphoria in adolescent population: A 5-year replication study." *Gender dysphoria in adolescent population: A 5-year replication study*, vol. 24, no. 2, 2019, p. 379, https://journals.sagepub.com/doi /10.1177/1359104519838593?url_ver=Z39.88–2003&rfr_id=ori:rid:crossref .org&rfr_dat=cr_pub%20%200pubmed. Accessed 2 March 2023.

The study examined whether there had been an increase in the prevalence of sex changes and gender dysphoria in Northern Europe between 2012 and 2017. The study examined a variety of factors including comparing gender dysphoria in childhood vs during puberty and comparing the difference over a five-year period. In a 2012 study of youth, 2.9 percent of teens displayed signs of clinically significant gender dysphoria. In comparison, in a 2017 study, 5.9 percent of youth expressed signs of gender dysphoria or gender identity issues—an almost doubling of the number of teens questioning their gender in the space of just five years. This certainly supports the explosion we have seen in the last decade in the numbers of young people with gender dysphoria and identity struggles across the world.

In addition to this, the study and research from Dr. Kaltiala noticed a sharp rise since 2011 of teenage girls with no history of gender dysphoria during childhood being referred to her clinic. In a separate 2015 study by the same doctor and research team, 75 percent of those referred to the Tampere University clinic had severe psychopathology issues prior to any issues with their gender. Teens on the autism spectrum being referred for gender transitions were also found to be extremely common.[2] Of this 75 percent, all of them were undergoing child and adolescent psychiatric treatments prior to being referred to the gender clinic for multiple psychological disorders and issues. The majority of these children had more than one mental health issue; 64 percent of them undergoing gender-affirming care were diagnosed with depression and were

---

2   Kaltiala-Heino, Riittakertuu, et al. "Two years of gender identity service for minors: overrepresentation of natal girls with severe problems in adolescent development—Child and Adolescent Psychiatry and Mental Health." *Child and Adolescent Psychiatry and Mental Health*, BioMed Central, 9 April 2015, https://capmh.biomedcentral.com/articles/10.1186/s13034–015-0042-y. Accessed 2 March 2023.

undergoing treatments for this; 55 percent had anxiety disorders; 53 percent had suicidal self-harming behaviors; 13 percent had psychotic symptoms; 26 percent had autism; and 11 percent had ADHD. These children were extremely vulnerable prior to referral to the gender clinic and had multiple conditions that severely impacted their mental health, yet were still considered ideal candidates for a medical transition.

The study even concluded that based on the findings of gender dysphoria appearing, in many cases, only in teenage years and disappearing in later life, as well as the incidence of a staggering 75 percent of patients having other severe psychological conditions, treatment guidelines for teens with gender dysphoria need to be carefully reconsidered. The findings also highlighted that the commonly accepted idea of gender dysphoria of being something a person was born with or experienced from a young age until teenage years was incorrect, and in actuality many of these individuals only developed signs during puberty or as a response to developmental difficulties.

While these statistics alone should be enough to alarm people and make parents think twice about medically transitioning their child, the study also found a staggering 85 percent of children studied who had severe gender dysphoria and cross-sex identification did not develop a transgender identity in adulthood. All of these children in the 85 percent group reverted back to their biological sex and the gender they were assigned at birth after becoming adults. Meaning that the vast majority of those with even the most extreme form of gender dysphoria as teenagers grow out of it, adding huge credit to the theory that in many cases it is a phase, something that is normal for all teenagers to experience. Of course there are still cases of someone generally feeling they are in the wrong body their whole life, and as an adult they may make the decision to live as the opposite gender, and they may generally be happier changing themselves, but these instances are rarer and the majority of young people do not keep these feelings in later life.

The study also found 62 percent of those examined only started to experience gender dysphoric symptoms at age twelve or later, at the onset of puberty, and had never questioned their gender or experienced dysphoria during childhood. Nineteen percent of girls had displayed tomboyish behavior as young children, yet neither they nor their parents had ever questioned their gender identity during their pre-teenage years. Other factors that may have influenced these children to want to change their gender during their teenage years were also found, including a high correlation between children who had been severely bullied at school and as a reaction to this started to experience gender dysphoria symptoms. Of those studies, 57 percent of those studied said they had experienced severe bullying in elementary school and 45 percent in high school; 73 percent of study participants said they had been bullied prior to questioning their gender; and only 8 percent thought about their gender identity before experiencing bullying. Children who had felt socially isolated during school were more likely to begin to develop gender dysphoria, according to the study's findings.

In a separate long-term study conducted between 1976 and 2011, backing up the Finnish research team's findings, researchers from Ontario, Canada, noted several key observations: the number of adolescents and teens being referred to gender clinics far exceeded the number of adults, and the number of teens being referred to clinics sharply increased toward the end of the study, between 2004 and 2007.[3] The early 2000s showed the biggest increase in gender clinic referrals and correlates with societal shift, with the advent of

---

3   Wood, Hayley, et al. "Patters of Referral to a Gender Identity Service for Children and Adolescents (1976–2011)." *Taylor & Francis Online*, Journal of Sex & Marital Therapy, 29 May 2012, https://www.tandfonline.com/doi/abs/10.108 -0/0092623X.2012.675022. Accessed 2 March 2023.

cell phones and early social media platforms as well as a shift in new concepts of gender ideology beginning to emerge across society.

What this teaches us is that, as we have seen in the past fifteen years with the sharp rise in the number of pediatric gender clinics springing up across the world, there are many factors behind the sudden rise in medical transitions, including a huge push to misdiagnose children with pre-existing conditions and convince them to change genders; the impact of bullying in influencing a child to want to change their identity in order to "fit in"; the masses of social media videos encouraging children to be confused about gender; and the inescapable pop culture landscape that pushes ideologies on young people from increasingly younger ages. Even in the 85 percent of cases from this study of teens with severe forms of gender dysphoria and strong feelings they were the opposite gender, this eventually disappeared in adulthood. Further, the 75 percent of teens that had multiple pre-existing conditions including severe depression, suicidal and self-harm tendencies, and anxiety disorders were being misdiagnosed with gender dysphoria or offered gender-related treatments as a quick fix to their other mental health issues.

Following the new research published on the harm of misdiagnosing teens or medically transitioning them rather than looking at more appropriate solutions for a child's health, Sweden, the Scandinavian country once considered by trans activists as a pioneer in transitioning treatments, recently changed its policies when it comes to minors. In 2022, the country did a U-turn by restricting hormone replacement therapy in minors and limiting double mastectomy procedures on teenage girls.[4] The Swedish health

---

4   Min, Roselyne. "As Spain advances trans rights, Sweden backtracks on gender-affirming treatments for teens." *Euronews*, 17 February 2023, https://www.euronews.com/next/2023/02/16/as-spain-advances-trans-rights-sweden-back-tracks-on-gender-affirming-treatments-for-teens. Accessed 2 March 2023.

authority, which had previously deemed gender-affirming treatments "safe" and "effective" back in 2015, had completely changed its course, citing the lack of long-term data and research into the risks of transitioning minors. The National Board of Health and Welfare even went as far as to say that with gender-affirming care "the risks outweigh the benefits." The health authority cited a 1,500 percent increase in teens aged thirteen through seventeen with gender dysphoria in the decade between 2008 and 2018, an alarming rate that forced the country to realize that gender identity issues were part of a recent trend, never before seen throughout history. Sweden's announcement was completely unexpected, but welcomed, for a country that was once at the forefront of the gender-affirmative care industry in Europe.

The United Kingdom's health service, the NHS, also did a sharp U-turn in 2022, announcing the closure of notorious gender clinic Tavistock and putting an end to the "Gender Affirmative Health Care Model" for youth across England. The change in policy means that England will end using gender-affirming care, including hormones and puberty blockers, and instead health-care providers will focus more on psychotherapy and psychoeducation in treating adolescents with gender dysphoria.[5] Puberty blockers will no longer be used in teenagers, except in cases of research and clinical trials, and clinics like Tavistock will no longer be able to put children through harmful medical processes. After conducting a major review and examining substantial stakeholder evidence, the NHS decided to change the UK's approach to gender dysphoria. This change occurred after the health service saw a significant and worrying rise in referrals in recent years, inconclusive and limited research and

---

5   Society for Evidence Based Gender Medicine. "The NHS Ends the "Gender-Affirmative Care Model" for Youth in England." *Society for Evidence-Based Gender Medicine*, 24 October 2022, https://segm.org/England-ends-gender-affirming-care. Accessed 2 March 2023.

evidence into the harmful long-term effects of hormone treatments, extreme concern with clinical approaches to treating children, and the harm the health-care system had on fast- tracking children without having proper checks and balances in place, normally used to ensure a patient is making an informed decision. Adding further to this new direction, the health service also highlighted the tremendous harm even socially transitioning a child can have, stating that it is "not a neutral act" and can cause significant psychological harm to a child's or adolescent's development and mental well-being. The new rules also mean the shutdown of the Tavistock and Portman NHS Foundation Trust, a clinic that whistleblowers claimed had no duty of care or concern for the well-being of its patients. Patients being referred to the clinic had risen to a startling five thousand per year, up from just 210 patients a decade earlier. The clinic was found to offer no long-term support, checkups, or research on patients who had received hormones or puberty blockers at the clinic.[6]

In 2023, another European country known for its pioneering gender reassignments suddenly reversed its approach to treating gender dysphoria in teens. The Norwegian Healthcare Investigative Board (UKOM) published a report calling puberty blockers and hormone therapy "experimental" and noting that these treatments were not "evidence based" and needed urgent revision.[7] Norway, which, like many other Western countries, had seen a sharp rise in teens being placed on testosterone or estrogen, is now looking at alternative ways to treat gender dysphoria, and the Norwegian medical board has come to a realization that many young people

6   Rigby, Jennifer. "Exclusive: NHS drafts stricter oversight of trans youth care." *Reuters*, 14 October 2022, https://www.reuters.com/world/uk/exclusive-nhs -drafts-stricter-oversight-trans-youth-care-2022–10-14/. Accessed 2 March 2023.
7   Norwegian Healthcare Investigative Board. "Patient safety for children and young people with gender incongruence." *UKOM*, UKOM, 9 March 2023, https: //ukom.no/rapporter/pasientsikkerhet-for-barn-og-unge-med-kjonnsinkongruens /sammendrag. Accessed 21 March 2023.

are being wrongly diagnosed with gender dysphoria when in fact they have other conditions that lead to their identity issues.

In Canada, while the country's liberal government run by Justin Trudeau pushes transitioning teens as something that is "normal" and "essential," the tide is starting to change. In 2023, a prominent Canadian psychiatrist and pioneer in child gender dysphoria treatment who performed medical transitions on teens since 1975, suddenly admitted what we all knew—hormones, puberty blockers, and reassignment surgeries cause irreparable and unimaginable harm. Dr. Susan Bradley, who founded one of the world's first gender clinics, The Gender Identity Clinic for Children and Adolescents at Clarke Institute of Psychiatry, now an octogenarian, has finally admitted that gender-affirming care is harmful to children. In a 2023 interview with the Daily Caller Foundation, Dr. Bradley admitted that she and her colleagues "were wrong" to prescribe puberty blockers and hormones to minors.[8] In a complete about-face, the psychiatrist and gender pioneer said that hormones are "not as reversible as we always thought and they have longer term effects on kids' growth and development, including making them sterile and quite a number of things affecting their bone growth." A shocking but welcome admission from a woman who has been behind thousands of children being pushed into taking experimental drugs to alter their bodies forever. Many of these children and this doctor's own patients could go on to develop issues with their bone development; thinning out of their bone density, which could lead to arthritis; bone cancers; and pain and issues with mobility. In a research paper published by Dr. Bradley, researchers found that

---

8 Bell, Brandon. "'We Were Wrong': Pioneer In Child Gender Dysphoria Treatment Says Trans Medical Industry Is Harming Kids." *The Daily Caller*, 11 March 2023, https://dailycaller.com/2023/03/11/pioneer-in-child-gender -dysphoria-treatment-says-trans-medical-industry-is-harming-kids/. Accessed 17 March 2023.

87.8 percent of boys referred to her clinic for gender dysphoria treatment eventually came to accept themselves and be happy with their biological sex. This backs up the Finnish study, which found an 85 percent rate of teens growing out of gender dysphoria. It also gives significant credit to the argument and other research that suggests that the majority of teens grow out of gender dysphoria in adulthood and that putting them on hormones and puberty blockers is completely the wrong approach and treatment method for these teens.[9]

While the UK, Sweden, Norway, and even Finland had reversed certain policies and changed their approach to treating teens with gender dysphoria, other European countries have gone in a completely different direction and instead have pushed for it to be easier for people to transition.

In 2014, Denmark became the first European country to adopt a law to make it easier for anyone to self-identify and change their legal gender while removing the need for an official gender dysphoria medical diagnosis. The law also allows for individuals to be medically castrated in order to affirm their new gender.[10] While the law was praised by trans and LGBT activists, it sparked serious concerns about women's rights and safety, as the new law allows biological males to use women's spaces and biological women who identify as men to use men's spaces. The law also paved the way for other countries to pass similar laws including Ireland, Luxembourg, Malta, and Portugal which have removed the requirements for legal

9   Bradley, Susan, et al. "A Follow-Up Study of Boys With Gender Identity Disorder." *National Library of Medicine*, PubMed, 29 March 2021, https://pubmed .ncbi.nlm.nih.gov/33854450/. Accessed 17 March 2023.

10 Danish Parliament. "June 11, 2014 the Parliament decided in favour of this: Proposal for Law about change in the law about the National People's Re." *Equal Rights Trust*, 11 June 2014, https://www.equalrightstrust.org/ertdocument -bank/Amendment%20to%20Danish%20Registration%20Law%20on%20 -Gender%20(English)%20v2.pdf. Accessed 2 March 2023.

gender recognition, making it much easier for anyone to self-identify without a medical certificate or psychological evaluation.[11]

Scotland, while part of the UK, has its own government and own parliament that can pass its own laws. In December 2022, a law was passed, similar to Denmark's, that allowed people to self-identify. Anyone aged sixteen and older could legally identify as the opposite gender, and biological men were able to legally use women's spaces. The law sparked intense scrutiny and eventually led to the resignation of Scotland's leader, First Minister Nicola Sturgeon, after it was revealed dozens of biologically male convicted sex offenders were being housed in women-only prisons because they had self-identified as trans. In almost all of these cases, the male prisoners only changed their gender identity after committing the crime in attempts to get reduced prison sentences and be housed in facilities with women. This prompted intense outrage across the UK and highlighted the harm of allowing anyone to legally Self-ID.

Spain has made it easier for children to transition and for people to self-identify in a bill similar to the Gender Recognition Reform Bill that was passed in Scotland in December 2022. The bill makes it easier for anyone age sixteen and older to change their legal gender on their ID. Prior to the laws passing, trans people had to get a medical diagnosis of gender dysphoria and proof of hormone treatment for at least two years in order to legally be determined as trans and thus change their gender. Additionally, fourteen- and fifteen-year-olds can now apply to change their gender, with their parent's or guardian's consent, and even twelve- and thirteen-year-olds could be able to change gender, if a court judge agrees to it. The law was pushed by the country's equality ministry run by the far-left

---

11 Bentz, Jan. "The Transgender Bark Is Bigger Than its Bite." *The European Conservative*, 18 March 2023, https://europeanconservative.com/articles/news /the-transgender-bite-is-louder-than-its-bark/. Accessed 21 March 2023.

political party, Podemos, part of the Socialist coalition controlling the Spanish parliament. Upon the announcement of Spain's new law, the United Nations Rapporteur on Violence Against Women, Reem Alsalem, expressed concern on allowing anyone to self-identify and the implications it has on women. Speaking with Spanish newspaper *El Mundo,* she said, "Nations need to reflect on whether someone with a male biological sex, once they have acquired their female gender certificate, should be able to access all programmes and categories designed for biological women."[12] The concern expressed by the UN official and many others is that without a specific medical diagnosis and checks and balances that someone generally had been living as the opposite sex for two years, anyone could now self-identify and be able to use women-only spaces, thus putting women at considerable risk while taking away women's rights.

While we have seen several European countries push further with self-ID laws and give easier access to gender-affirming care or make it easier to transition, we have finally started to see countries that have been offering transgender health care and laws for Self-ID starting to completely reverse their decisions after realizing the immense harm being caused. We have seen this with the UK health service highlighting the worrying spike in teens with gender dysphoria in recent years, and compared with the Finnish research state showing that 85 percent of teens with gender dysphoria grow out of it and 73 percent had pre-existing psychological conditions. This study and its findings are also backed up to the Canadian research showing 87.8 percent of boys grow out of gender dysphoria in adulthood, so that putting kids into the gender-affirming care

12 AFP. "Spain passes trans law allowing gender self-determination." *France 24,* AFP, 16 February 2023, https://www.france24.com/en/live-news/20230216-as -spain-advances-trans-rights-other-early-adopters-hesitate. Accessed 2 March 2023.

system is both alarming and wrong. We can finally bear witness to the fact that health-care services and government health agencies in a growing list of countries are finally starting to realize that transitioning teens is not the solution.

We know that it is harmful, and we know that many teens are having gender dysphoria during puberty, a time when they are confused and trying to work out who they really are. We know that many of these teens have been bullied and are trying to fit in, and are seeing the growing trend of "self-identifying as a different gender" as a way to fit in at school and in peer groups. We see that many of the adolescents being referred to clinics have a lot of worrying pre-existing issues including suicidal tendencies and self-harm and that many struggle with severe depression. We see that many of these young people only develop questions about their gender after age twelve, during the most difficult period in puberty when they have to navigate through the challenges of being socially accepted at school and when they are susceptible to outside influencers, teachers, social media, friendship groups, and books that may convince them they are the wrong gender. We know all this, we see the data, we see the research, we see the thousands of detransitioning youth who have been left traumatized by the system that exploits their vulnerabilities, misdiagnoses them, and offers affirmative care as a quick-fix solution. While we can hail the great leaps the UK has taken to reverse its policy on affirmative care and the research from Finland and Canada, we know in America this conversation is far less advanced. We know most of the teens being medically transitioned are in the United States, the number one country for gender-affirmative care, and we know all of these teens are being exploited by the multibillion-dollar medical establishment. We also know that America is where this war on children, this culture war, is most severe with Drag Story Hours teaching children about gender identity, where school libraries are filled with books that encourage children to become confused with their gender and sex, and where the entire TikTok homepage is littered with videos of trans and nonbinary influencers, whom kids look up to, pushing videos that are designed to target children's vulnerabilities and make them question themselves. We see all this, we know it's going on, and we need to focus all of our efforts on bringing common sense to this issue, by speaking up, by sharing the data and research that exposes the exploitation of affirmative care, and by proving how countless vulnerable teens are having their lives destroyed in the name of gender "care."

Chapter 34

The War on Women

In the early twentieth century, the Suffragettes movement was founded by women in England to campaign for women's rights, a woman's right to vote and for women to be treated equally to men. Founded by Emmeline Parkhurst in 1903, the Women's Social and Political Union (WSPU), which was later dubbed the Suffragettes movement, quickly grew the support of thousands of women across the United Kingdom, women who had for centuries been treated as lesser than men and treated unfairly throughout history. Women had risen up together in unity and found their voice despite many of them being arrested for protesting for their rights, many being vilified by the media, and countless women being silenced. Women took to the streets and stood outside Parliament demanding politicians give them equality and the right to vote. Many were arrested, many were assaulted by police officers, and subsequently many of these women went on hunger strikes, determined with their sheer willpower to demand equal rights. They were fearless, they were warrior women who did not give up despite the constant attacks they faced, without fear of becoming social outcasts—they had one goal: to obtain equal rights. It was a hard-won fight. It took until 1918 for their first major victory, with the passing of the Qualification of Women Act in the British parliament, which allowed women the right to be elected to parliament. An additional act was passed the same year, the Representation of the People Act 1918, which allowed some women over thirty to vote, although they had to be property owners and meet certain requirements. This helped 8.4 million women become eligible for voting. Then in 1928, all women over the age of twenty-one won the right to vote and thus women finally began to achieve equal rights. After decades of campaigning, women had a voice; they had fought long and hard but finally had achieved a landmark change.[1] For decades after, and still to this day, women across society, feminists, and activists have had to fight for equal treatment, equal pay in employment, the right to be respected and treated equally to men, and for women to not have to fear being shut down by patriarchy and misogyny. All of these hard-earned victories of women demanding to be treated fairly are now rapidly being undone.

In the last decade we have seen men who identify as women clawing away at women's rights, taking away women's voices, silencing any woman who dares question them, and taking away women's spaces, their sports, and their rights to fair treatment. In sports, we are seeing biological males who identify as women competing against women, such as the case with University of Pennsylvania swimmer Lia Thomas, who ranked 554th on the men's team and achieved the number one rank while competing against women. While Lia is an adult and is responsible for making her own life decisions on how she identifies, when it comes to women's sports it is undeniable that a biological male has a significant advantage. Stronger muscles, larger biceps and calf muscles give those born

---

1   Holborn, Margaret. "Women's suffrage—February 1918, first women gain right to vote." *The Guardian*, 5 February 2018, https://www.theguardian.com/gnmeducationcentre/2018/feb/05/womens-suffrage-february-1918-first-women-gain-right-to-vote-in-parliamentary-elections. Accessed 3 March 2023.

male a competitive advantage over women. Even after hormone therapy during a transition, like with Lia Thomas, who has been on testosterone blockers and estrogen, studies have shown that men will always have an advantage while competing against women. In a 2020 study of U.S. military personnel who underwent medical transitions while in service, researchers found that trans women still have a competitive edge over women even after one year of hormone therapy. The study, conducted by Dr. Timothy Roberts at the University of Missouri-Kansas City, found that during a running race, biological males who had undergone hormone therapy to become trans for a one-year period still outperformed biological women. Additionally, even after receiving hormones over a two-year period, the trans runners still ran 12 percent faster.[2] In a separate study conducted in Sweden by researchers at Karolinska Institutet in Stockholm, they found the muscular advantage of biological men competing in sports is only minimally reduced by taking testosterone and hormone medication.[3] The lead researcher in this Swedish study, Tommy R. Lundberg PhD, also stated that there is no sufficient evidence that two years of taking hormone medications would be enough to suppress an athlete's biological advantage.

Women who speak up for fairness in their sports, such as University of Kentucky swimmer Riley Gaines, who competed against Lia Thomas, are being labeled "transphobic," "bigots," or "hateful" for daring to question the unfairness of what is going on right now. Women, who had for centuries fought for their rights

---

2   Roberts, Timothy A., et al. "Effect of gender affirming hormones on athletic performance in transwomen and transmen: implications for sporting organizations and legislators." *British Journals of Sports Medicine*, 2021, https://bjsm.bmj .com/content/55/11/577. Accessed 3 March 2023.

3   Lundberg, Tommy R., and Emma N. Hilton. "Transgender Women in the Female Category of Sport: Perspectives on Testosterone Suppression and Performance Advantage." *PubMed*, February 2021, https://pubmed.ncbi.nlm.nih.gov/33289906/. Accessed 3 March 2023.

beginning with the Suffragettes, who launched a movement that helped women gain equality, are now having all of their hard work unraveled.

Sports is just one area where women are losing their rights. Additionally, biological males who become trans are now using women's locker rooms, restrooms, spas, and other spaces once designated for women only. Women are being marginalized, silenced, and made to fear speaking out and standing up for their rights. We are also seeing women being erased from dictionaries, changing the definitions of a woman to "anyone that identifies as female," and we are even seeing organizations like the United Nations Women's campaign, Amnesty International, Human Rights Campaign, and numerous others attempting to redefine women and take away their fundamental rights to their own spaces and their own protected rights.

It is possible for all of us to live in a world where everyone is treated with respect, where everyone can exist with equal rights and equal opportunities but without the need to take away from another group's fundamental rights, in this case the rights of women.

The suffragettes fought hard for the rights that women have today, and we owe it to them and to all women to ensure a future where all women can feel safe using female-only spaces, where all women can have the chance to shine in women's sports, and all women can speak out and not have to fear their voices being stifled by trans rights activists who, just like men in the early twentieth century, did everything in their power to try and silence them, to belittle them, and to demean their very existence.

Chapter 35
Social Media Contagion

We are all influenced by something in life, whether that be celebrities, pop culture, the movies we watch, fashion choices, political opinions we form, or entertainment we consume. But how do these influences shape our lives and how can certain influencers directly impact our decision-making process, push us into doing something we would have otherwise not considered, and lead us to become completely detached from who we are?

In the age of social media, we all strive to feel validated, to get attention, to get a high "like count," high engagement, and become an "influencer." Indeed, many young people aspire to become influencers. According to one report by think tank Morning Consult, 86 percent of young Americans aspire to become influencers and another 12 percent already believe they are influencers.[1] In a similar study in the UK, one in five children aged eleven to sixteen surveyed said their dream is to grow up and become a social media influencer. The top five professions listed by these same children as

---

1   Morning Consult. "86% of young Americans want to become a social media influencer." *CBS News*, CBS, 8 November 2019, https://www.cbsnews.com /news/social-media-influencers-86-of-young-americans-want-to-become-one/. Accessed 17 January 2023.

an aspirational career included both "influencer" and "YouTuber" ahead of professions like veterinarians and teachers.[2] So what is behind the trend in kids aspiring to be influencers and what are these kids hoping to get out of this? Validation? Fame? Love? Praise?

As human beings we are social creatures, and part of what we require is to be validated, accepted, and receive recognition. Many kids, whether because of repressed memories, difficult childhoods, or a need and desire to feel loved turn to social media platforms for attention. The more likes, followers, and comments one receives, the more serotonin is released in the brain. If we receive limited interactions, only a handful of likes, and have a smaller following, we tend to use that as a reflection of our character. This then makes us question our self-worth, with thoughts like "No one likes me, my followers aren't going up, maybe it's because I am ugly or worthless." I am sure many of you reading this can identify with these feelings; social media has a profound effect on our mind and psychology. We shouldn't look at our social media accounts and the interactions or engagements we have and see it as any reflection of who we are, yet so many of us do.

So many compare themselves with influencers and celebrities like the Kardashians, who use filters and plastic surgery as well as wealth to try and present an ideal goal for social media users to emulate. There is nothing ideal about what celebrities like the Kardashians present to us, as it is unattainable to most people. We should simply aspire to be ourselves, aspire to be kind and spread love, and work on our own self-confidence without the need and desire to constantly seek validation from others.

---

2   Papadatou, Aphrodite. "1 of 5 British children want a career as social media influencers." *HR Review*, AWIN, 31 January 2019, https://www.hrreview.co.uk /hr-news/1-of-5-british-children-want-a-career-as-social-media-influencers /114597. Accessed 17 January 2023.

For many years, I became addicted to social media, wanting to grow my following, always checking views and likes, and seeing that as a reflection of myself. On days when my likes were low, I would feel bad, feel depressed, and judge myself harshly. I would rekindle thoughts about my childhood and teenage years, difficult memories of feeling invalidated, hated, and being targeted with hatred and cruel insults. On days when my engagement was way up and my views were receiving millions of views in a twenty-four-hour period, I would feel on top of the world and loved. This constant back-and-forth had a detrimental impact on my brain, as it does with many young social media users, and I believe it played a significant role along with trying to deal with my repressed memories in making me become addicted to becoming someone I was not. Thirty-two plastic surgeries, wanting to be a Korean pop star, and eventually thinking I was a trans person, all because I wanted to be validated, I wanted to be loved and celebrated, which in turn led me on a toxic path that I am slowly still recovering from today. I was a grown man, yet I fell victim to the power of social media. Many kids are also now following this route, through no fault of their own, and limiting the time kids spend on social media and what kind of content they have access to could be a great solution in helping beat this toxic cycle.

With an estimated 90 percent of teens between thirteen and seventeen using social media and two-thirds of US teens owning a cell phone and spending an average of nine hours a day online, teens are being heavily influenced by the videos and information they consume.[3] When we look at the number of users on social media as a whole, Facebook comes on top with 2.9 billion users; YouTube at

---

3   American Academy of Child and Adolescent Psychiatry. "Social Media and Teens." *AACAP*, American Academy of Child and Adolescent Psychiatry, March 2018, https://www.aacap.org/AACAP/Families_and_Youth/Facts_for_Families/FFF -Guide/Social-Media-and-Teens-100.aspx. Accessed 3 February 2023.

2.2 billion; Instagram at 1.4 billion; TikTok at 1 billion; Snapchat at 500 million; and Twitter at 300 million.[4] The United States has over 130 million users on TikTok, with ages ten to nineteen accounting for 32.5 percent of users.[5] These young users spend on average ninety-five minutes per day on TikTok, opening the app an average eight times to consume the fast-format, fifteen-second videos on the FYP homepage (For You Page).

TikTok, which is owned by Chinese conglomerate ByteDance, has been under increased US government and congressional pressure due to the concerns of the Chinese government having access to the data of US users. In addition to this, senators and members of congress and even FBI Director Christopher Wray have noted how the Chinese version of TikTok, named Douyin, shows completely different content to Chinese users. Concerns have also been raised regarding the Chinese Communist Party's influence on the app and its content, with pro-China propaganda being pushed to users and alleged interference with US elections and a drive for certain ideologies to spread in the minds of American users.[6] On the Chinese app, users are presented with videos encouraging patriotism, education, skill sharing, strong work ethic, and other good character-building types of videos. In stark contrast, TikTok in Western countries displays twerking, numerous videos of nonbinary adult men telling children to transition, men advertising tampons, drag shows with sexually suggestive dance routines, and other content designed to

---

4   Doyle, Brandon. "TikTok Statistics—Everything You Need to Know [Jan 2023 Update]." *Wallaroo Media*, 20 January 2023, https://wallaroomedia.com/blog /social-media/tiktok-statistics/. Accessed 3 February 2023.

5   Nover, Scott, and Taryn Rade. "TikTok Is Growing Up, and So Are Its Users." *Adweek*, 26 May 2020, https://www.adweek.com/performance-marketing/tiktok -is-growing-up-and-so-are-its-users/. Accessed 3 February 2023.

6   Suciu, Peter. "Is TikTok Really A National Security Threat?" *Forbes*, 11 July 2020, https://www.forbes.com/sites/petersuciu/2022/11/18/is-tiktok-really-a -national-security-threat/?sh=f7dfe474ade3. Accessed 3 February 2023.

"dumb down" a population in comparison to Douyin, which pushes strong masculine and feminine societal ideals, celebrates the traditional family unit, and pushes more intelligent content.

We see TikTok influencers like Dylan Mulvaney, who has over ten million followers, becoming amongst the most popular influencers on the app, generating billions of views, while Dylan, who was born biologically male, parades around in comedy videos using typical stereotypes of women being "ditzy blondes." Many of his videos sexualize the messages, such as proudly encouraging his trans and nonbinary followers to "celebrate the bulge" and show their penis bulges in public by wearing tight women's dresses and going to the mall to show them off. In addition, Dylan and other influencers claim that "trans women can menstruate" and are regularly seen promoting tampons for trans people. Children see this, each video has millions of views, and over time this behavior of mocking women and confusion with gender identity shapes and influences the mind of the teens who consume this content on a daily basis. The more they watch, the more they start to want to emulate this behavior. Dylan is celebrated on TikTok, validated with millions of views per video, huge brand partnership deals, millions of likes, and thousands of positive comments on each post. Any teen who sees this level of success and attention would surely want to emulate it, especially given the fact that so many young people these days aspire to be famous and become influencers. An estimated one in four American teens plans to choose influencer as a future career.[7] So when these same teens see people like Dylan, when they see men dressed as women being given positive reinforcement, praised, and idolized, they want to become just like them. And when they see

---

7 "Young People Want To Be Influencers Even As Older Americans Say It Isn't A Real Job!" *Forbes*, Forbes, 20 October 2022, https://www.forbes.com/sites/petersuciu/2022/10/20/young-people-want-to-be-influencers-even-as-older-americans-say-it-isnt-a-real-job/?sh=5424d3285f04. Accessed 03 February 2023.

doctors, like the case of Dr. Gallagher in Miami, who makes fun, entertaining videos on her gender reassignment surgeries at her clinic, they buy into that and want to be a part of that culture.[8]

Teens and children are the most easily influenced in society. They often base their own beliefs, interests, preferences, and identities on what they have seen online, what the current trend is, and emulating those who become famous, like Dylan Mulvaney, who in the eyes of many is causing irreparable damage to the subconscious minds of teens.

An influencer by definition is a person with the ability to influence potential buyers to buy a product or service or to buy into an idea that this influencer suggests or pushes. With this in mind, we see the influencers promoting the products "Gender Ideology" and the service "Gender-Affirming Care," and, whether knowingly or unknowingly, these influencers are selling young teens the idea that it's easy and cool to change their gender and puts the idea in people's minds that if they somehow question their own identity, based on the indoctrination from what they have mostly consumed online, then they must join the cult, and use the product and service to change their own gender in order to fit in and become an influencer themselves. When they do this, they are accepted into the cult, given praise and positive reinforcement, and thus renounce their biological gender and past identity to become a clone of someone they have seen on the Internet and a clone of an influencer they aspire to follow. Just like a cult leader, influencers have the power to alter opinions and indoctrinate a person into their own belief system.

---

8   Reinl, James. "Campaigners urge Florida health chiefs to probe Miami trans-op doctor." *Daily Mail*, 19 December 2022, https://www.dailymail.co.uk/news/article -11533471/Campaigners-urge-Florida-health-chiefs-probe-Miami-trans -operation-doctor-TikTok-scandal.html. Accessed 3 February 2023.

With over 2.3 million followers across my own social media platforms, with 1.2 million followers on my TikTok, and over 2.3 billion views, I came to realize during my transition that I had the power to influence millions of people around the world, and these people who have followed me for years may have altered their thinking or questioned their own identity because of my very open struggles and by sharing my journey online. I had a responsibility to them; I could use my platform for good, or I could continue to air my identity struggles online and cause harm to others who may also struggle with their own identity issues. I couldn't live with the thought of influencing others to be confused or to become transgender or a clone of a K-pop idol or adopt a completely different identity to the way they were born. I had to be a role model, I had to help my followers go on a path that was positive and the best possible route for them. While I cannot control the path and decisions others take, for the millions who consume and watch my videos each day on TikTok, I was responsible for influencing their thinking and molding their minds. I felt guilty for my past actions, when I was so consumed with my own self-loathing and wanting to be a completely different person that I projected this out into the world through my videos, through sharing my surgical journey, through sharing my new trans identity. I had many sleepless nights because of this during my detransition until I came to the realization that whatever I was in the past and however I acted, I had the power to change myself and do a 360-degree turnaround. I could make up for past wrongs and help influence my audience in a more positive, motivational, and inspiring way. I could speak up and be a voice for the millions of teens who struggle each day with being bullied online or in school, who struggle to accept themselves, who go through phases where they question their identity. Just like the first time I decided to detransition, again I took the path less followed, and it has made all the difference.

I chose to be a fighter, to be a REAL influencer, and actually influence people with a positive mindset, encourage them to be free-thinking, and encourage them to learn to love themselves for the way they are. I wanted those who looked up to me to find confidence from within and not have to feel a societal pressure to change the way they look, to change their pronouns, or to change their gender. We need more influencers to move away from their constant focus on self, which some may call narcissism, or self-obsession. Or maybe, like me, these influencers simply wanted to feel validated. They want attention, they want likes, praise, and adoration because it makes them feel worth something, gives them a temporary confidence boost, and makes them feel special.

Social media can be both positive and negative, yet too much time spent on it, too much time wanting to be like the people we see online, can lead to self-doubt, questioning of one's identity, and can encourage a person to want to change who they really are. We need to move away from the focus on likes and move toward a push for self-acceptance and learning to love ourselves for the way we are.

In 2022, in a controversial move, Instagram gave users the option to hide likes. At first, many Instagram users objected; there was outcry and condemnation for the move, with influencers claiming it would damage their brand deals and image. I, too, thought it was a bad idea at first, thinking that likes were so important in showing how popular a person was. After several months of the move being implemented, I grew to understand it and actually think it was the right move. Like most other people on the platform, I was completely obsessed with how many likes I got. I would refresh my app every few minutes each time I uploaded a photo, getting a quick serotonin high with the more likes I got. After the feature was removed and I got used to it, I started to post pictures and videos purely because I wanted to and not because I was concerned with the number of likes. I posted more freely, more naturally, and with less concern about what others thought, and this lessened the constant craving to feel loved. While it was a small fix for Instagram, I believe the move helped a lot of people focus less on seeking attention and validation and allowed people to focus more on uploading things that were important to them—not things that they thought other people would want to see, or what would get a lot of likes.

It's up to parents to decide and monitor what their child has access to online, to safeguard them from particular content, and to make sure their child doesn't spend all of their time online rather than pursuing real-world interests like reading books, playing sports, exploring the great outdoors, learning languages, and studying and enjoying themselves through real-world interactions. But social media platforms like TikTok also have a great responsibility in making sure that young people are protected online with safeguards. TikTok introduced a thirteen-plus age confirmation sign-up to stop children under thirteen using the app. However, there is no way to check a person's age using the app, and anyone, even a four-year-old, could technically sign up and just lie about their birth date. While it is important for people to post freely online, it's also up to social media apps to make sure harmful information is not presented to kids and vulnerable people who could be impacted in the real world. Having constant viral trending videos of influencers like Dylan Mulvaney mocking women, calling themselves a "girl," and using targeted language and videos to appeal to young audiences is harmful to the impressionable minds of young users. As we can see with the growing number of teens identifying as the opposite gender, the rise in clinical diagnosis of gender dysphoria, and a huge uptick in teens undergoing gender-affirming care, social media is without a doubt playing a major role in influencing the decisions of these vulnerable groups.

Chapter 36

TikTok Trans Trend

In September 2016, in China, a new app was launched that promised to change the way people consumed videos online: short-form, fifteen-second videos and a homepage where users could scroll endlessly through a diverse range of addictive videos and never get bored. Dance videos, lip syncing, cooking, educational, and comedy videos quickly drew users to the app in droves. This app was named Douyin, the brainchild of tech company ByteDance. After launching the app to the Chinese market, millions of Chinese users downloaded it, spending hours per day scrolling through videos. Many popular users suddenly became instant Internet celebrities themselves by making their own short-form videos—which drew far higher viewers and like numbers than competitive social media apps in China like Weibo, WeChat, and Tencent QQ. After seeing such success and user growth in such a short amount of time, ByteDance decided to roll out an international version of its popular app and named it TikTok. One of the primary reasons for Douyin's instant success was the app's ability to keep users on the app for long periods of time. Just like an addiction, the app knew how to get people hooked. Using AI technology to learn about each user, their viewing habits, their interests, their thought process, Douyin was able to quickly get users addicted by showing them content that would instantly appeal to them.

After the wildly successful launch to the Chinese market, ByteDance was ready to expand to the rest of the world. In 2017, TikTok was launched on iOS and Android in many markets across the world. However, it wasn't until 2018 that TikTok suddenly became mainstream with the acquisition by ByteDance of hugely popular Musical.ly. The app was then merged with TikTok, giving TikTok 80 million mostly US users. Musical.ly was also a Chinese company that launched in 2014, but the main difference was that almost every video was dancing or lip syncing. With TikTok's purchase of the app, all of this changed. TikTok undertook a policy to actively shift the way its predominantly young users think, feel, and behave. As we have seen since the pandemic, the behavior of teens and Generation Z during and after the pandemic completely changed. This was also the exact same time that TikTok really rose to prominence. In 2019, the app was downloaded 693 million times and 850 million times in 2020, during the height of the pandemic.[1] By the end of 2021, the app has reached over 1.2 billion active monthly users—nearly 20 percent of all people on Earth.

Was the rise of TikTok during the pandemic a coincidence or a carefully executed plan by Chinese authorities to weaken the West economically, culturally, and politically? Instead of the dance and lip-sync videos that first dominated TikTok, during the pandemic we saw the rise of influencers talking about pronouns, teens transitioning and sharing their medical and social transition journeys, TikTokers sharing their day-to- day journey of living as the opposite sex, and even adult male influencers directing their videos to young,

---

1 Iqbal, Mansoor. "Home App Data TikTok Revenue and Usage Statistics (2023)." *Business of Apps*, BOA, 9 January 2023, https://www.businessofapps.com/data/tik-tok-statistics/. Accessed 7 March 2023.

impressionable children. Influencers making videos about how fun and easy it is to take puberty blockers, encouraging their young fans to try it, and influencers teaching kids to cut off their parents, to see them as evil and controlling and to escape their clutches so they can go and medically transition. As with any social media app, we know that we can find content from all perspectives, from all viewpoints, and a deeply varied range of videos. But what has been alarming with TikTok is that these harmful videos have been pushed and promoted continuously. Some of these videos get millions of views each time and are promoted on the FYP homepage to millions of young teens who consume these videos. The AI algorithm targets children who have watched videos on gender identity or even pushes them out to children without them even searching for it. If the video keeps their attention span and sparks their interest, the AI learns about their viewing habits and what retains their attention, their interests, and their search terms and forms a complete view of their personality and their thought process. It then targets more of these kinds of videos to the users again and again. We know that teens question themselves during their teenage years and they often question their identity, but the fact that TikTok actively exploits these curiosities to push content on their homepages to make them more confused and to make them fall deeper down the rabbit hole of gender ideology is extremely concerning.

As a TikToker myself, I vividly remember a meeting I had at TikTok's London HQ several years ago when I was advised on best practices for using the app and content creation. Prior to my meeting, most of my videos were lip syncing to popular trending K-pop sounds, but I was told by those high up at TikTok's headquarters that the app wanted to move away from that kind of content and was actively discouraging creators from making these types of videos. While Musical.ly, the app TikTok merged with in 2018, was all about dance and lip-syncing videos, TikTok told me they were now going in a different direction. They wanted content creators to create videos following trends, talking videos, get-to-know-me type videos, and wanted creators to be open about their feelings and emotions and showcase a more intimate look into their life and their identity. As an aspiring TikToker at the time, I only had several hundred thousand followers, and of course I wanted to succeed and I, like any other content creator, would follow the trends that TikTok told me to follow in order to succeed. I stopped doing lip-sync or dance videos and instead tried to share videos of myself being more open with my followers, sharing my life, the ups and downs. Suddenly my videos started getting millions more views each week. From what I was told at TikTok, and from what we see now on the app, long gone are the days it was simply a fun app for people to dance and lip sync to. It has now become a place where young users' minds are being inextricably molded by influencers, the content that is pushed in trends, and the algorithms. The simple, fun, and harmless nature of the app has shifted to one where personal identities, struggles, and new ideologies have become the new promoted trend. Gender ideology videos, videos of people making up new pronouns like xe/xer or fae/faer, make up the homepages of millions and millions of teens—a big contrast to the content the algorithm promotes on Douyin in China.

In a groundbreaking study published in the Online Media and Global Communication Journal by researchers from Bowling Green State University, Ohio, researchers compared the online behaviors of Chinese users vs US users on TikTok and Douyin. The study found that TikTok had a significant impact on influencing cultural norms and how people express and describe themselves online.[2]

---

2   Yang, Yang. "TikTok/Douyin Use and Its Influencer Video Use: A Cross-Cultural Comparison Between Chinese and US Users." *De Gruyter*, 3rd June 2022, https://www.degruyter.com/document/doi/10.1515/omgc-2022–0016/html. Accessed 7 March 2023.

The key difference between the United States. vs China was that TikTok in the United States promotes individualism, whereas China promotes collectivism. In the United States we are seeing a cultural push on TikTok for young users to have individual, unique, and different identities—to be nonbinary, trans, genderqueer, and agender to name but a few of the hundreds of individual gender identities that have been popping up. Contrastingly, in China they promote groups of people as a collective having the same values, sharing the same ideas, the collective family unit, and groups of people having the same identities—male or female. Between the two countries we also know TikTok/ Douyin promotes entirely different content based on geographical location and cultural norms and trends. The US version pushes values and ideals based on current cultural trends, like gender ideology, whereas China's version pushes skill sharing, patriotic videos about loving one's country, strong male and female roles, and educational videos. We also know that TikTok is having a drastic impact on the habits and behaviors of so many impressionable young people, and incredibly, all of this has happened in just five years since TikTok's acquisition of Muscial.ly and thanks to its huge explosion of user numbers during the pandemic.

I joined TikTok when it first started, when the content was innocent, fun, and entertaining. I remember seeing fun dance trends with easy-to-replicate moves and exciting lip-sync challenges. Then, during the pandemic, when I really started to use TikTok a lot more and created content on a regular daily basis, like many people, I saw a complete shift in the style of content being promoted. The crazier a person behaved, the more individual they were, and the more far-fetched their identity, the more they were promoted by the app. I became consumed each day spending hours making content and many hours scrolling through other people's videos. All the while, I, like every other user, was being tracked by the app's powerful AI, which studied and examined every search term, every video that was able to retain our attention for more than five seconds, every trend that we engaged with, and every person we interacted with and followed. This was also the same time when TikTok experienced its biggest growth, with over 1.2 billion active monthly users by the end of 2021—everyone was hooked on the app, everyone was trying to go viral and become a star, and every young kid was being heavily influenced each time they used the app.

Throughout my life, I have been easily influenced, always in search of finding solutions to my problems and a quick fix for the unhappiness, depression, and mental health struggles I experienced since my teenage years. While TikTok helped me escape these past problems, it also consumed the person I was. Like a raw material entering a conveyor belt in a factory, each time I spent on the app, I was molded, new ideas were inserted into my mind, and my thoughts and own identity became manufactured and molded based on the trends I had seen and the content I consumed. My mind became a manufactured product, brainwashed and molded into new belief systems and new ideologies.

While I had always questioned my identity, struggled for years with accepting who I was, and tried to change every aspect of my identity, TikTok quickly accelerated my body dysmorphia and gender dysphoria; it made me question myself, and it made me want to change even more. I would see videos each day with millions of views of a trans person being celebrated and praised with comments, being promoted by the algorithm, and popular trans creators being adored by millions. They were celebrated for being different. I knew I was different; I knew I had always questioned whether I should have been born as a girl, and I knew I was more feminine than the average guy. But all these feelings and questions I had throughout my life suddenly came back to me, thanks to the constant daily reminders while using the app—the app I was completely addicted to and would spend six to eight hours a day on. Seeing endless videos over a three-year period encouraging people to change their gender and identity made me question myself even more. Maybe I could be loved and adored like these trans people, maybe people would stop sending me hate, maybe I would finally feel comfortable in my own skin if I was a woman, maybe I was born in the wrong body?

I would argue that it was a variety of factors that influenced me to transition—from my childhood when I played with girls' toys and tried dressing up as a girl, to my teen years when I was told I was more like a girl, to my adult years when my relentless quest to change myself did not fulfill me and to where ultimately I thought my identity struggles were misplaced and I was actually transgender. These factors certainly led me to want to change, but ultimately all of this combined with my mind being molded on TikTok, an app I had been addicted to, telling me and others to change gender, encouraging it, and giving trans influencers positive reinforcement. I decided that everything TikTok had shown me must have been a sign. A sign that I was born in the wrong body, that I had been living my whole life as a man when really I should have been a woman. I was an adult, yet I had still become indoctrinated by the propaganda-esque videos I had consumed, I was influenced, and I fell victim to it all. I cannot even begin to imagine how hard it must be for a young impressionable teenager going through a time in which they question themselves on a daily basis, being led far astray by TikTok and wanting to medically transition because it has become a TikTok trend. All kids want to be loved, validated, and accepted; TikTok, like a digital fentanyl, has been doing this, giving them a quick fix and giving them attention that they have been craving in the age of social media during a time when 17 percent of all teens aspire to become influencers. These kids would try anything to fit in, to be seen as cool, to be popular, and to become famous—even if it meant changing their gender, whether they believed in it or not, would give them what they thought would be a lifetime of happiness, success, and validation when in reality it is just a quick burst of serotonin that is over all too quickly and leaves a person with far-reaching, long-term consequences.

Through all of this, we must acknowledge the detrimental impact TikTok has had in just a five-year period—its meteoric rise to the top and how the app has been radically shifting society, culture, and beliefs and is shaping the way teenagers now choose to identify. When we correlate TikTok's rise to the high increase in teens wanting to transition and look at the medical figures of teens being put into the gender-affirming care system, we cannot ignore that this increase correlates with the trends seen by teens on TikTok and the app's push to promote content that pushes gender ideology. There is a massive correlation, and we need to look at that as a society and question the inextricable harm TikTok is doing to its billions of global users.

In 2023, TikTok US announced a new policy to limit the screen time of those under eighteen using the app on a daily basis, but this does not stop or solve what kind of content these kids are consuming. Coincidentally, or perhaps not so coincidentally, this policy change came about after US lawmakers in the House of Representatives proposed bills to ban TikTok or impose new laws limiting its use due to the harmful effects it had been causing on young generations and due to national security implications.

While parents know and understand that kids love to be on social media to connect with their friends, and many under the age of eighteen now have TikTok accounts, it is important for parents to be aware of what their children are watching and what they are being exposed to and consider ways to protect their children, such as limiting their time on TikTok each day, not allowing them onto the app until they are a certain age, or having parental controls on their accounts so they can monitor what videos are being pushed to their children. We know TikTok can make kids happy, we know it can be fun for kids to sometimes escape the real world and watch videos online, but we also know that what they are watching and what TikTok is actively pushing to them through its powerful AI system can be incredibly harmful and can ultimately be the catalyst for a child to want to change their gender identity.

Chapter 37

Turning the Tide

For the past few years, we have seen a sharp increase in the number of teens transitioning, people self-identifying and becoming gender fluid. Over 1.6 million people in the United States now identify as transgender, which equates to 0.5 percent of the population.[1] This figure from a 2022 study includes a staggering three hundred thousand people aged just thirteen to seventeen identifying as transgender. Compare this figure to 2016, where only 1 million US citizens identified as transgender and said they identified as a different sex to that assigned at birth.[2] So based on comparing the results between these two studies from 2017 to 2022, we see an increase of six hundred thousand in just five years. Additionally, a Gallup Poll found the percentage of the US

1   Allen, Jonathan. "New study estimates 1.6 million in U.S. identify as transgender." *Reuters*, Williams Institute UCLA, 10 June 2022, https://www.reuters.com/world/us/new-study-estimates-16-million-us-identify-transgender-2022-06-10/. Accessed 26 February 2023.
2   Meerwijk, PhD, Esther L., and Jae M. Sevelius, PhD. "Transgender Population Size in the United States: a Meta-Regression of Population-Based Probability Samples." *American Public Health Association*, 16th November 216, https://ajph.aphapublications.org/doi/full/10.2105/AJPH.2016.303578. Accessed 26th February 2023.

population identifying as a member of the LGBT community in 2022 was 7.2 percent, more than double compared with a Gallup Poll conducted a decade earlier.[3] In the 2012 survey, only 3.5 percent of the US population identified as LGBT. Of the 7.2 percent of adults identifying as LGBT in 2022, Generation Z or those born between 1997 and 2004 were much more likely to identify as LGBT compared to older generations. So, what do these data tell us and how do they correlate with the number of young people being medically transitioned? As we are seeing, over the last decade an increasing number of young people are identifying as LGBT and an additional six hundred thousand now identify as trans compared with just a few years ago. While we have seen examples of trans people throughout history, discussed earlier in this book, such as the GI Joe-to-GI Jane story of Christine Jorgensen, who underwent sex reassignment surgery and a course of hormones to go from male to female, we know that what we have seen in the past decade is not a natural phenomenon. It is undeniable, however, that in recent years, with the advent of social media and a society where children are confused from a young age about their gender, we are seeing a never-before-seen growing rate of people transitioning and numbers never seen in history. From 2017 to 2021, 121,882 children between age six and seventeen received a medical diagnosis of gender dysphoria, and over 14,726 minors were put on hormone treatment over the same period of time.[4] In 2017, according to research by Komodo Health, 1,905 minors received hormone therapy, compared with a staggering 4,231 in

3   Jones, Jeffrey M. "U.S. LGBT Identification Steady at 7.2%." *Gallup News*, 22 February 2023, https://news.gallup.com/poll/470708/lgbt-identification-steady .aspx. Accessed 26 February 2023.

4   Respaut, Robin, and Chad Terhune. "Number of transgender children seeking treatment surges in U.S." *Reuters*, 6 October 2022, https://www.reuters.com /investigates/special-report/usa-transyouth-data/. Accessed 26 February 2023.

2021. Similarly, with puberty blockers in 2017, 633 minors were put on treatments compared with a rise of 1,390 in 2021. These data only include those with a medical diagnosis of gender dysphoria and only include figures from patients who paid using Medicaid or Medicare, so we must consider the number will be far greater.

Clearly, we are seeing a growing trend of people identifying as transgender and a growing rate of minors being put on puberty blockers and hormone treatments. While the trend grows and while we see more young people develop gender dysphoria and become confused with their identity, we are finally seeing a societal shift and a turning tide when it comes to laws to prevent children being harmed, laws to protect children being exposed to harmful ideology and to sexual ideologies, and finally we are seeing a loud and vocal pushback from parents and concerned adults who have been alarmed to witness what has been happening.

Like a phoenix rising from the ashes, 2023 has seen multiple states pass laws or propose bills to ban gender-affirming care, ban children being exposed to gender ideology in the classrooms, a new Tennessee state law classifying drag shows as adult entertainment and banning children from attending, and additional laws designed to protect women's rights like the Kansas Women's Bill of Rights law protecting the sex-based protections of women. We have seen over a dozen states either propose bills or indeed pass bills and sign them into laws, and we will likely see many more join the trend in due course. A total of sixteen states have now passed laws banning gender-affirming care for minors with others set to follow. The tide is changing because people are finally talking, parents are finally finding their voices, people are no longer afraid to speak out and fear being labeled as "transphobic," "bigoted," or "hateful," and doing so has taken the power away from woke mobs and trans activists who have for years been scaring everyone into silence for fear of being canceled.

Across the US in 2023, lawmakers across twenty-four states have introduced legislation to restrict or ban gender-affirming care in minors and more are set to follow. The Governors of Alabama, Arkansas, Arizona, South Dakota, Tennessee, and Utah have already signed bills to stop children being medically transitioned. However, as with other states that try to pass similar laws, they face opposition from federal and state judges, as in the case with Alabama and Arkansas, where federal judges blocked the laws from being enacted.

Florida, under the leadership of Governor Ron DeSantis, has been one of the strongest states in terms of taking action against gender ideology being pushed on children. The widely debated "Parental Rights in Education Bill," infamously and incorrectly dubbed "Don't Say Gay," and its subsequent passing became a pivotal moment in the gender ideology culture war that had been, until recently, unchallenged across much of America. On March 2, 2022, the Florida Senate passed the bill with a 22–17 vote, and Governor DeSantis signed the bill on March 28, 2022. The bill regulates public schools across the state and prohibits these schools from teaching children from kindergarten through to third grade about gender ideology, sexual education, and sexual orientation. The law simply stops teachers pushing these ideas on five- to nine-year-olds and should hardly be something considered controversial, yet the bill's passing sparked intense public scrutiny and backlash from LGBT organizations, mainstream media, Hollywood celebrities, and trans activists who unfairly tried to claim the bill was homophobic or transphobic. LGBT organizations like Human Rights Campaign and Equality Florida labeled the new law "vile" and "dangerous" and claimed that DeSantis had "placed Florida squarely on the wrong side of history and placed his own young constituents in harm's way."[5] Both organizations peddled the claim that the bill was designed to target LGBT people, to silence them and make their existence much more difficult. However, when you actually examine the bill itself, you can see it is simply about keeping certain harmful topics out of the classrooms and giving parents more transparency and more of a voice when it comes to their child's education.

The bill's main focus is to protect parental rights and ensure that parents are able to have a say in their children's education and not have to worry about their children being indoctrinated with woke ideologies. In addition, the bill prohibits schools from hiding the new gender identities of children from their parents. This is an important step, as a child's identity struggles should be a conversation between parents and their own children and not via teachers who may be putting ideas into the mind of an impressionable, easily molded child.

Florida has also been at the forefront of passing legislation to ban gender-affirming care. In April 2022, Governor DeSantis and Florida's Surgeon General Joseph Lapado issued guidance to the Florida Health Department urging for a ban on medical and social transitions on minors.[6] Following this, in October 2022, the Florida Board of Medicine backed a move to ban any gender-affirming care for minors. In an investigation by Florida's Agency for Health

---

5   Luneau, Delphine. "BREAKING: Human Rights Campaign, Equality Florida Vow to Fight for Full Repeal of Vile, Dangerous New Law Signed by Florida Governor DeSantis." *Human Rights Campaign*, 28 March 2022, https://www.hrc .org/press-releases/breaking-human-rights-campaign-equality-florida-vow-to -fight-for-full-repeal-of-vile-dangerous-new-law-signed-by-florida-governor -desantis. Accessed 1 March 2023.

6   Yurcaba, Jo. "Florida medical board votes to ban gender-affirming care for transgender minors." NBC News, 29 October 2022, https://www.nbcnews.com /nbc-out/out-news/florida-medical-board-votes-ban-gender-affirming-care -transgender-mino-rcna54632. Accessed 1 March 2023.

Care Administration, they found that "several services for the treatment of gender dysphoria—i.e., sex reassignment surgery, cross-sex hormones and puberty blockers—are not consistent with widely accepted professional medical standards and are experimental and investigational with the potential for harmful long-term effects."[7] The terms "experimental" and "harmful" are the main focus points here and sum up exactly what transitioning minors is–a harmful experiment. As we have seen throughout this book, and indeed through the many horror stories we are seeing across the news and social media, these are simply experiments on children with no long-term follow-up studies and with extremely limited data and research into long-term consequences to a child's health.

Tennessee has also been a leading state in protecting children. The state's lawmakers moved to protect children from harmful sexual ideology exposure in 2023, by banning "all ages" drag shows and moving to classify drag performances as adult entertainment, in a move that was hailed by parents and attacked by LGBT organizations. Despite the consistent criticism and attacks by LGBT activists against Republican lawmakers, including Republican Tennessee Senate Majority Leader Jack Johnson, who was behind the bill, the bill did not specifically target only drag performers and was simply a law to stop children being exposed to any kind of adult-only entertainment. In actuality, the bill was about banning "adult cabaret performances" which includes drag from either male or female performers. This includes topless performers, go-go dancers, strippers, exotic dancers, and even burlesque dancers, who would be classified as "adult entertainment" under the law and prohibited from performing in front of minors or performing within a thousand feet

---

7   The Agency For Health Care Administration. "Report Overview." *The Agency For Health Care Administration*, https://ahca.myflorida.com/LetKidsBeKids/index.shtml. Accessed 1 March 2023.

of schools, places of worship, and public parks.[8] A common-sense law, to ensure that children are not exposed to sexualized performances and not—as LGBT organizations tried to claim—in any way a specific target on the LGBT community or drag performers. As we have seen in the many viral videos from "all ages" drag shows, many of these shows are indeed only suitable for adults, as they feature sexually explicit dance performances, vulgar language, and sexual activity—completely unsuitable for children. In addition to the bill banning these performances to minors, it goes further by punishing first-time offenders with a Class A Misdemeanor, fines up to $2500, and up to a year of jail time. Repeat offenders would be classed as Class E Felonies and receive a prison sentence of one to six years.

An additional bill, which passed the Tennessee legislature and was signed by Governor Lee, will ban hospitals and clinics from performing gender transitions on minors. The bill requires current medical patients under the age of eighteen to have their gender transition treatments ended by March 2024. Meaning that after that cutoff date, no doctor or medical facility will be allowed to perform gender transitions on teens. Adding to this ban, the bill will allow people who received gender-affirming care as minors to sue physicians, parents, and guardians who coerced them into transitioning and authorized hormones, puberty blockers, or gender-reassignment surgeries.[9]

---

8   Migdon, Brooke. "Tennessee bans on drag shows, gender-affirming care head to governor." *The Hill*, 23 February 2023, https://thehill.com/homenews/3871517 -tennessee-bans-on-drag-shows-gender-affirming-care-head-to-governor/. Accessed 1 March 2023.

9   Brown, Melissa. "Tennessee legislature passes ban on gender-transition health care for minors." *The Tennessean*, 23 February 2023, https://eu.tennessean.com /story/news/politics/2023/02/23/tennessee-legislature-passes-ban-on-gender -affirming-care-for-minors/69935900007/. Accessed 1 March 2023.

In neighboring Missouri, Republican lawmakers proposed Senate Bill SB 49, which passed a Senate vote. The Missouri Save Adolescents from Experimentations (SAFE) Act seeks to take action against medical institutions that perform GAC on children, with the option to have their license removed and legal action to be taken against the health-care provider.[10]

Mississippi also introduced a bill in early 2023, House Bill HB 1125, proposed by twelve Republican lawmakers to "Regulate Experimental Adolescent Procedures Act." The bill passed the Republican-controlled senate, 33–15, and previously in the Mississippi House with a 78–30 vote. It has now been signed into law by the state's governor, Tate Reeves. In a February 2023 announcement, Governor Reeves announced, "Sterilizing and castrating children in the name of new gender ideology is wrong," and upon signing the bill into law stated, "far too many people are fearful of the online woke mob which demands complete and total acquiescence on this issue. It attempts to tell parents they are not allowed to question their children or the origins of these feelings." The governor also spoke up for detransitioners: "They needed somebody to listen to them. They needed help to sort through their problems not to blindly affirm their beliefs."

Arkansas has gone a step further by approving a groundbreaking new law that would allow minors who had received gender-affirming care to seek compensation and file malpractice claims against hospitals that medically transitioned them. Teens who were coerced or pushed into transitioning and who later express regret will now be able to file suit up to fifteen years after the medical transition occurred.

---

10 Missouri Senate. "SB49—Establishes the 'Missouri Save Adolescents from Experimentation (SAFE) Act.'" *Missouri Senate*, 3rd January 2023, https://senate.mo.gov/23info/BTS_Web/Bill.aspx?SessionType=R&BillID=44407. Accessed 1 March 2023.

Alabama, Oklahoma, and Tennessee have banned students from using restrooms that they feel represent their gender identity, meaning they must use restrooms based on their biological sex. As we have seen, this is to protect children from harm and prevent cases like the Loudoun County, Virginia, school bathroom sexual assault that occurred when a boy in a dress entered the girls' restrooms and committed a violent assault on a girl.[11] These laws are designed to protect children and prevent assault. Some trans activists will argue that the majority of transgender people don't assault women, and that may be true. But it's the fact that assault does occur at all, and we see hundreds of cases each year. Even if these laws protect just one girl or one woman from being assaulted and having their life destroyed, then it's worth having the law. Even in cases of transgender people using women's restrooms, it can be very triggering and traumatic to women who feel vulnerable and can trigger those who have experienced prior sexual assault. Other states are also considering similar laws for restrooms and women-only spaces, including Tennessee.

South Dakota became the sixth state to pass legislation restricting gender-affirming care in minors, and a bill was signed into law by Governor Kristi Noem. The "Help Not Harm" bill bans health-care professionals from offering puberty blockers, hormone-replacement therapy, and surgery to minors, anyone under the age of eighteen.[12] Minors currently undergoing hormone treatment or puberty

11 Downey, Caroline, et al. "'They Failed at Every Juncture': Loudoun County Mishandled Bathroom Sex Assault, Grand Jury Finds." *National Review*, 6 December 2022, https://www.nationalreview.com/news/they-failed-at-every-juncture-loudoun-county-mishandled-bathroom-sex-assault-grand-jury-finds/. Accessed 26 February 2023.

12 Yurcaba, Jo. "South Dakota becomes the 6th state to restrict gender-affirming care for minors." *NBC News*, 15 February 2023, https://www.nbcnews.com/nbc-out/out-politics-and-policy/south-dakota-becomes-6th-state-restrict-gender-affirming-care-minors-rcna70592. Accessed 26 February 2023.

blockers must be taken off medication by the end of 2023 and, like other states with similar laws, make exceptions for infants born as intersex, with male and female genitalia. In these rare cases, doctors are still able to perform reassignment surgery to fix the birth defects.

Kansas became the first state to pass a Women's Bill of Rights, enshrining the rights of women and putting the definition of women into law as someone who is born biologically female.[13] The law, which passed through the Kansas senate in a 26–10 vote, received zero support from Democratic senators and was vetoed by Democratic Governor Laura Kelly, but later the governor's veto was overridden to pass the law. The bill defines a woman as someone with a biological reproductive system that is developed to produce ova, while male refers to anyone whose reproductive system is developed to fertilize the ova of a female. A simple, scientific explanation and common sense, to say the least. Yet this is the world we live in today, that we actually have to pass a law to define a woman and a man. It seems like a virtual reality world, one that makes no sense and where simple explanations and definitions are disputed and anyone who uses common sense is seen as being crazy. A dystopia not dissimilar to what George Orwell describes in his novel *1984*. Or even akin to the science fiction film, *Equilibrium,* starring Christian Bale, which features a modern society where no one is allowed to display free thinking, common sense, and emotion, and no one is allowed to even dare to question the status quo, despite the status quo being absurd and delusional. The Kansas bill also lays the groundwork for future legislation that Republicans are planning to pass in the state including banning biological men from female spaces such as restrooms and locker rooms. It also

13 Kansas Senate. "SB 180 | Bills and Resolutions | Kansas State Legislature." *Kansas Legislature*, 23rd February 2023, http://kslegislature.org/li/b2023_24/measures/sb180/. Accessed 26 February 2023.

lays the groundwork for banning males from competing in women's sports, something based on simple fairness in that biological males have an innate biological advantage when competing against women.

With legislation being passed or considered now across almost half of US states and sixteen states banning gender-affirming care for minors, society is making great progress toward a future where young people are protected from harm. Yet we still have much further to go to shift the narrative completely and highlight the general harm transitioning children, exposing them to gender ideology in schools, and pushing sexualization on them is doing. Seven states have now passed laws, others are in the process of following suit, and the conversation is finally shifting, but there is still so much more groundwork to lay. Educating people, particularly the LGBT community, and informing them of the truth about what is happening with teens and getting them to speak out will help advance the cause considerably. If liberal-leaning media like the *New York Times*, which in 2023, to the surprise of many, finally started to question the harm gender affirming is causing, and other mainstream media start to finally expose what is really going on, then this is how we could finally convince the majority to wake up to what is going on. With the *New York Times* publishing several articles critical of gender ideology and despite the subsequent and expected backlash from trans activists and over a thousand of the paper's own journalists and contributors, the fact that they choose to speak out shows the narrative is finally changing. The more we can highlight the harms of GAC and convince, with evidence, the mainstream media and LGBT activists on these harms, the sooner we can end it once and for all and finally get back to a society that protects children, and not one that actively puts them in harm's way, exploits them, experiments on them, and discards them in the process.

Chapter 38

Positive Affirmation

You have seen me at my worst, and you have seen me go from one extreme to another. From a normal British boy to a self-identifying Korean K-pop idol clone, then to a trans woman and back again. You have seen it all; an extreme example, no doubt, but the message here is a microcosm for the world. No matter how extreme, difficult, or challenging your life may be and no matter what circumstances you are in—you have the power to change. There are many people who CAN and WILL support you along the way and help you get through the difficult times and the good times, but only YOU have the true power to make a difference to your own life and way of thinking.

I went through times when I had no beliefs, no sense of being, no internal happiness, and no contentment, yet I was able to turn that around drastically and become the person I am today. For better or for worse, I have finally accepted who I am. We should all follow this message and add it to our daily lives. Whether that's daily prayers, whatever your beliefs, positive affirmations each morning to say aloud what you are grateful for, or making simple steps to change our lifestyles, we can all change. Change is good. But changing too quickly to another extreme is not always the best path to take, as you have no doubt seen with my story. We have seen the irreparable harm social media is having on influencing the decisions of young people, and we have seen thousands of teens being indoctrinated into the belief system that they must change their gender identity in order to be happy. We have also seen that the vast majority of these people grow out of these feelings and grow up to be happy and healthy adults filled with confidence.

The future is bright for you and me. The future is bright for all of us if we believe in ourselves, find self-acceptance, and learn to love who we are—our faults and our blemishes are all part of being a human. We grow with age and experience and gain wisdom through good and bad. Despite my mistakes in the past, I do not live to regret them, I simply live to learn from them. Good or bad, these mistakes are an important part of cognitive development that help shape our futures. If I had not gone through an identity crisis and all of my issues, I wouldn't be where I am today, so despite the hardships I am grateful and thankful for each experience. Each day I wake up and say aloud what I am grateful for, making daily positive affirmations. I express gratitude to the world, gratitude to God for allowing me to have had the opportunity to change, and I'm grateful I am able to share my experiences in order to help others. The future is bright if we learn to believe in ourselves, let go of the past, and have a desire to change and improve ourselves.

I will use all my experience going forward to advocate for others, to help heal the world, to help give a voice to all those who need to be heard, to fight for children and teens being sold an unrealistic dream, and to spread love and compassion for all. The future is now and we are in control of our own destinies; we have the power to make a difference and we all have the power to help fix what is broken—the flawed gender-affirming care system that all too often takes advantage of those with vulnerabilities and pushes them into doing something they don't even understand or truly need. We need to approach every person struggling with kindness and compassion, offer them a helping hand, and a listening ear to help them navigate through the stormy seas and come out on the other side, healthy, happy, and with the ability to accept themselves. Our modern society has far too much focus and pressure to look a certain way, often unattainable for many, advocating an enhanced, unnatural look or a different gender from the way we are born.

We see the pressures young people feel from a variety of factors, from social media and the education system, to the media they consume and their social surroundings. We understand and recognize that many people, especially teens, go through rough patches when they are unclear about their identity, unsure of who they really are. We must recognize that each person in life has to undergo their own personal journey, they have to go through these difficulties in order to develop as a human being, and it is a natural process. We all want answers, we all seek temporary fixes and quick solutions to far bigger problems. But in order to accept ourselves we need to change our way of thinking and how society thinks as a whole and move away from this constant need to change our bodies, our faces, or the way we look in order to fit into modern society, and instead shift these focuses away and toward having healthy minds, nourished souls, and improving our inner confidence. Only then can we conquer these demons and go on to live our lives in the best possible way. Free of worry, free from outside pressures, and free to learn to love ourselves the way we were born.

Chapter 39

Hope around the Corner

My personal story of how I conquered my demons and overcame adversity to become enlightened and become an activist for others is a story that all of us can identify with. We are all antiheroes in some way, though we may not wear cloaks like a traditional super-hero, but we all have the chance to change the world and use our superpowers. I believe most people in the world are good people and they want what's best for others. I believe that a lot of the upsets caused by the issues discussed in this book and the issues of gen-der ideology and self-identity can be resolved through better com-munication and a willingness to hear both sides of the argument. Those who advocate for and those who advocate against—common ground must be found.

Taking back power from these people and finding your own inner power helps to switch up the narrative, to remove the power from bullies, and take away the little satisfaction they have at put-ting down another human being. With the sale of Twitter to Elon Musk, this became a huge victory for free speech with thousands of previously banned accounts from children's activists, women's rights advocates, and conservative voices being allowed back on the platform. Cancel culture has finally been canceled, and a return to free speech has been restored. By staying strong despite the odds being stacked against you, you can make an impact in the world. This is my message for every person reading this book and chapter. You will weather any storm, just keep on telling your truth and fighting for your voice to be heard. Never let others bring you down, no matter how low they try to pull you to the ground. Always get up, dust yourself off, and try again. Giving up means letting the bullies and cancel culture win. They don't deserve to win, and allowing them to do so only emboldens them to continue. You are the one who deserves to win, to triumph against adversity, to stand up for yourself and find your voice, and to fight for others being silenced. Just like many women and feminists are silenced today either online or in the real world, we all have a duty to stand up for them, to voice their concerns, to protect them from being stripped of their rights by biological males identifying as women, and to be a champion for them when they are being pushed to the ground. Lift them up, raise their voices, and you will find yourself winning. Always be on the winning team, for your own self-confidence and for that of others. Winning is believing in oneself, and winning is victory against evil, the negative, and the bad.

There is hope, with more people now wanting a return to normality and free expression being back for good on platforms like Twitter; now is the time to have this open discussion while being sensitive to the voices of all, and work to find a solution that benefits all of society, especially children. I hope to offer a space where we can express our honest opinions without fear of retribution to allow us all to better understand one another. My struggle has taught me that despite the barriers each individual may face, we can overcome all of this, and with the help and support of others and society as a whole, so that we can make the world a better place. A place filled with hope. Hope can heal wounds and bring others together. We all need hope in our lives. Together we can change the world.